DEVIANT BEHAVIOR
IN DEFENSE OF SELF

DEVIANT BEHAVIOR IN DEFENSE OF SELF

Howard B. Kaplan

Department of Psychiatry
Baylor College of Medicine
Texas Medical Center
Houston, Texas

1980

ACADEMIC PRESS
A Subsidiary of Harcourt Brace Jovanovich, Publishers
New York London Toronto Sydney San Francisco

ACADEMIC PRESS, INC.
111 Fifth Avenue, New York, New York 10003

United Kingdom Edition published by
ACADEMIC PRESS, INC. (LONDON) LTD.
24/28 Oval Road, London NW1 7DX

57033

Library of Congress Cataloging in Publication Data

Kaplan, Howard B.
    Deviant behavior in defense of self.

    Bibliography: p.
    Includes index.
    1. Deviant behavior. 2. Self. I. Title.
[DNLM: 1. Self concept. 2. Social behavior
disorders. WM600 K17d]
RC554.K36   157   79–6795
ISBN 0–12–396850–X

PRINTED IN THE UNITED STATES OF AMERICA

80 81 82 83   9 8 7 6 5 4 3 2 1

In the order of the recency in which they came into my life to Rachel Esther, Samuel Charles, Diane Susan

Contents

Contents

Chapter 4

Antecedents of Self-derogation

Chapter 5

Self-attitudes and Deviant Behavior

Chapter 6

Self-attitudes and Deviant Behavior Intervening Variables

Chapter 7

Deviant Behavior and Self-enhancement

Chapter 8

Retrospect and Prospect

References   231

Preface

This volume is a report of a study designed to test a number of hypotheses derived from a previously formulated general theory of deviant behavior. The theory centers on the reciprocal relationship between self-attitudes and deviant behavior. It deals with the variables intervening between self-attitudes and deviant behavior, as well as with the variables that condition the relationship. The theory is a general one in this sense: It considers a broad range of deviant patterns as *responses* to characteristic self-attitudes, and as *antecedents* of changes in self-attitudes, given theoretically specified intervening and conditional circumstances. The theory does not preclude the development of specific theories of delinquency, violence, drug abuse, alcoholism, suicidal behavior, or other more specified modes of deviance. Indeed, it asserts the common preconditions for the adoption of any of these modes, and upon these preconditions circumstances facilitating the adoption of particular patterns of deviant behavior can be specified. Some of these facilitating circumstances will be considered in the volume, but the thrust of the research is the test of hypotheses dealing with factors that have more general relevance, related as they are to multiple modes of deviance.

In Part I of the volume, the study's underlying theory (Chapter 1) and method (Chapter 2) are presented.

Chapter 1 considers the origin of the self-esteem motive, the determinants of positive and negative self-attitudes, the consequences of negative self-attitudes that predispose an individual to adopt any of a range of deviant response patterns, and the conditional consequences of deviant response patterns for change in self-attitudes and continuity of the deviant patterns.

Chapter 2 describes the study itself, a longitudinal survey study designed to test a number of the hypotheses comprising the general theory. This chapter considers the selection of the sample, sample characteristics, the issue of sample attrition, data collection procedures, operational definitions, and modes of analysis.

Part II describes the results of the analysis. Chapter 3 offers evidence in support of the postulated prevalence of the self-esteem motive in response to this question: Is there reason to believe that, universally, individuals characteristically need to maintain or improve their level of self-acceptance? Chapter 4 considers the factors that influence the development of more or less positive/negative self-attitudes. Are individuals who subsequently develop negative self-attitudes more likely to be characterized by antecedent deficits in self-protective mechanisms, experiences of rejection by significant others, and characterization in terms of self-devaluing qualities and performances? Chapter 5 considers the relationship between self-attitudes and deviant responses. Hypotheses are tested regarding the relationship between antecedent levels of self-attitudes and antecedent change in self-attitudes, on the one hand, and subsequent adoption of any of a range of deviant response patterns, on the other hand. Chapter 6 considers the variables that intervene between the genesis of negative self-attitudes and the subsequent adoption of deviant response patterns. Does antecedent self-rejection lead to an increasingly greater perception of the association between negative self-attitudes and membership group experiences? Does it lead to the loss of motivation to conform to normative structure, and the acquisition of motivation to deviate from it? And does it also lead to an increased pressure upon self-protective mechanisms and a concomitant increased vulnerability to self-devaluing membership group experiences, as well as an increased tendency to seek and become aware of alternative deviant response patterns? And does each of these factors influence the adoption of each of a broad range of deviant response patterns?

In Chapter 7 are reported data relevant to the general hypothesis that deviant responses have self-enhancing consequences that presumably confirm the person in the deviant pattern. The conditions under which the general hypothesis is supported will be considered.

Finally, Chapter 8 sums up the preceding chapters, evaluates the empirical support observed for the general theory of deviant behavior, and outlines the implications for further development of the theory.

Many of the findings reported (H. B. Kaplan, 1975a, 1975c, 1975d, 1976a, 1976b, 1977a, 1977c, 1978c) are integrated with more recent, unpublished findings, permitting for the first time an evaluation of the utility of the revised theoretical orientation that guided the analysis of the results. The empirical findings of the longitudinal survey study lend a good deal of support to the general theory. Where support was equivocal, there were clear indications with regard to what further conditions might be stipulated or to further theoretical specifications. Thus, the theory, even in this primitive stage of development, shows evidence of having value for both integrating current empirical findings and stimulating further research in the quest for an explanation of deviant behavior.

Acknowledgments

Where I know the origins of my ideas, I have acknowledged them through appropriate citations in the text. Unfortunately I am unable to trace the beginnings of many of the central ideas expressed in these pages. To some extent (as in the final chapter) I have relied on others to place in historical perspective the general theory of deviant behavior that guided this research, trusting that their observations were veridical.

In the later stages of writing this volume, the description of the theoretical framework, the discussion of certain of the results, and a consideration of indications for future research were greatly enriched by the research then being done in connection with the preparation of the successful research grant application, "Drug Abuse and Other Deviant Adaptations to Stress." This grant (DA 02497), awarded by the National Institute on Drug Abuse, will permit further refinement of the general theory of deviant behavior particularly with regard to those features relating to continuity–discontinuity of deviant adaptations to stress between adolescence and young adulthood.

Finally, I happily acknowledge the successful efforts of Robert L. Williams and Alex D. Pokorny of the Baylor College of Medicine in providing a stimulating and facilitative work environment without which my ability to complete this project as well as earlier undertakings would likely have been seriously hindered.

Part I

Theory and Method

Chapter 1

Toward a General Theory of
Deviant Behavior

This volume reports the results of a study designed to test selected hypotheses among those comprising a general theory of deviant behavior. This previously published theoretical statement (H. B. Kaplan, 1975b) centers about the reciprocal relationship between self-attitudes and deviant behavior. This chapter will discuss the meaning of the terms *self-attitude* and *deviant behavior* and will summarize the theoretical structure that guided the empirical reports to be presented in subsequent chapters.

Basic Concepts: Self-attitudes and Deviant Behavior

Although all sociological concepts have various meanings to different investigators, none can lay claim to more numerous definitions than the concepts of self-attitude and deviant behavior. At the outset, the reader is reminded that concepts in themselves may not be judged true or false. Only the statements of relationships alleged to exist among concepts are amenable to such judgments. What is arguable is whether or not one mode of conceptualization is more useful than another. For discourse to be meaningful, the participants must understand the conceptual definitions employed. To facilitate such consensus, the meanings of the concepts in the present context are discussed at some length.

Self-attitudes

I define *self-attitudes* or *self-feelings* as the affective or emotional responses of individuals to themselves upon perceiving and evaluating their own attributes and behaviors.

3

These emotional responses to self vary in intensity and range from positive (pleasurable) to negative (distressful). The precise manner in which individuals display and characterize their various self-attitudes is in part a function of their sociocultural circumstances.

In describing a person's self-attitudes, one must simultaneously deal with two independent dimensions. The first dimension relates to the generality of the object of the self-attitudes. Is the person said to be emotionally responding to particular aspects of himself or to himself in general? In the latter case, the polarity (positive versus negative) and intensity of the "global" self-attitude presumably will be affected differentially by the person's attitudes (of variable polarity and intensity) toward different aspects of himself at the time the self-attitudinal response is made. The second dimension is temporal. Does the self-attitude in question refer to a momentary emotional response or to a characteristic self-attitude over a period of time? Over a specified time span, a person might express a number of self-attitudes. If it were possible to draw a representative sample of instants within that time span and then describe the polarity and intensity of the self-attitudes (if any) expressed at those points in time, the person's characteristic self-attitude would be said to be a function of the frequency with which the observed self-attitudes of variable polarity and intensity were expressed. Generally, the term *self-attitude* will refer to a person's characteristic global affective response to self-perception and self-evaluation. Where the term is otherwise used, the meaning should be apparent from the context.

Feelings or attitudes represent only one of the dimensions along which subjective responses to self vary. People perceive (and conceive) themselves, evaluate themselves (that is, judge themselves regarding the degree to which they, or particular aspects of themselves, approximate desirable qualities), present themselves to others in ways calculated to evoke particular responses, and otherwise respond to themselves as objects. These responses are mutually influential. For present purposes, the most significant effects are the influences of self-perceptions and self-evaluations upon self-feelings.

To be distinguished from these behavioral responses is the objectified self— that which is perceived, judged, and presented, and evokes feelings. The content of the objectified self as it is perceived and, thereby, otherwise responded to may include perceptions of physical aspects (big-boned, hook-nosed, weight 150 pounds), behavioral predisposition (aggressive, task-oriented, happy, logical), ascribed or achieved social positions (male, father, Roman Catholic, friend, businessman, motorist, middle class), characteristic role behaviors (as a father who takes an interest in his children, an active member of the church, someone willing to do anything for a friend), specific behaviors in specific situations (as someone who just told a "white" lie to his mother), personal values (loyalty, honesty, bodily pleasures, economic success), and other forms of reflexive meaning. The responses of the person to himself, in turn, may become part of the objectified self. Thus, an individual's specific self-evaluations may be incorporated into the his self-image so that he perceives himself as an individual who devalues his athletic ability or as a self-depreciating person in general. These self-perceptions may in turn become the object of self-evaluation processes. For example, a person may positively evaluate himself because of his ability to depreciate himself insofar as this self-evaluative behavior approximates other personally held values, such as the ability to be "realistic" about personal limitations. Self-feelings may also be incorporated into the self-image, and as such may stimulate further self-evaluation and self-feeling. A person who perceives himself as filled with self-hate may devalue himself and respond to this negative evaluation with negative self-feelings.

Although the objectified self and various self-referent behaviors will continue to be discussed both in the theoretical statement and in the report of the empirical study, their relevance will be mediated by their relationship to self-attitudes.

Deviant Behavior

A person generally holds membership in a number of groups—family, voluntary associations, work groups, peer groups, a community, a more inclusive society, and so on. Each of these groups has shared normative expectations regarding how people with specified social characteristics will (or will not) and should (or should not) behave in specified circumstances. A normative expectation may be applicable to the subject by virtue of his group membership (that is, it might be applicable to any member of the group) or by virtue of his particular position in the group (that is, all group members apply the normative expectation only to people occupying the particular position in the group). If the individual changes his position in the group, different normative expectations may be applicable to him.

Over time the normative expectations applicable (according to group consensus) to all group members or to occupants of particular positions in the group may change. However, at any given time, there tends to be group consensus with regard to which normative expectations apply to all group members or to those differentiated according to the positions they occupy in the group. Failure to conform to these shared normative expectations is greeted with surprise, negative evaluation, and more or less severe negative sanctions from the members of the group or their surrogates.

Deviant behavior is said to have occurred when a person (by his own judgment and the judgment of other group members a member of a specified group) fails to conform to the applicable normative expectations of the group. This

5

failure may be due to the person's loss of preexisting motivation to conform to normative expectations, or to his acquisition of motivation to deviate from normative expectations.

This definition excludes behaviors that might be seen as deviant by other traditional definitions. Such behaviors are excluded either because (*a*) they occur in the absence of consensus among the subject and group members that the subject is a member of the group and therefore subject to applicable normative expectations, or (*b*) the behaviors derive neither from a loss of motivation to conform to normative expectations nor from the motivation to deviate from normative expectations.

SELF–OTHER DEFINITIONS OF GROUP MEMBERSHIP

Membership in a group is evidenced both by the person's prior (predeviance) acceptance of (conformity to) normative expectations and by the application of normative expectations to the person by other group members. Behavior that is *only* a self-defined or *only* an other-defined violation of a particular group's normative expectations would not be regarded here as deviant behavior; it would therefore not be explicable by the emerging general theory of deviant behavior. If the person had *never* viewed the group's normative expectations as applicable to him, their application to him by members of the group would not establish his group membership; therefore, his failure to conform would not be deviant behavior. For example, a lifelong member of a criminal subgroup might be sufficiently insulated from the more inclusive society so that he would perceive the normative expectations of the larger society as inappropriate guides for the behavior of the members of his criminal subgroup.

Nor would group membership be established and deviant behavior be judged to have occurred if the person judged himself to have violated group norms that the group members did not recognize as applicable to him. Under this condition it would be more appropriate to speak of the person's *reference* (rather than membership) group. This situation is illustrated by the case of a person identified with the lower class (by representatives of both this class and more prestigious classes) who is motivated but fails to conform to the leisure patterns characteristic of the more prestigious strata.

MOTIVATED DEVIANCE

Deviant behavior must also arise from a loss of motivation to conform to or the acquisition of motivation to deviate from normative expectations. Frequently, the person shares and therefore accepts as applicable to himself the normative expectations that the group applies to him at the time he deviates from them. He is motivated to conform to the normative expectations regarding the desirable qualities he should possess and the goals he should achieve (and, of course, the undesirable qualities and goals he should not possess or achieve).

Perhaps according to both group and personal standards he should be brave, industrious, wellborn, physically healthy, occupationally successful, good-looking, successful as a thief, and so on. For one reason or another, against his will, he has been unable to display these hypothetically highly valued behaviors or traits. The occasions for the failure to conform in the face of motivation to do so might have been the result of socially ascribed or constitutionally given deficits, the inability to conform to multiple sets of applicable but conflicting expectations, ignorance of which normative expectations were situationally applicable (due either to the absence of visual cues or to inadequate socialization), or other circumstances.

Such instances of failure to conform to expectations of self and others evoke negative evaluations and sanctions by the person and by others in his group (as he would be the object of positive evaluations and sanctions from himself and others in his group to the degree that he approximated the desirable qualities and achievements in question). However, because the "deviant" act was un-motivated (that is, against the person's will), it is excluded from the present concept of deviant behavior. It is recognized, nevertheless, that such instances of involuntary deviation from applicable normative expectations may lead to other instances of motivated deviance. For example, the possession of stig-matized attributes may influence the person actively to reject the group stan-dards by which he is stigmatized, and to emphasize the "virtue" of the stigma.

Given these exclusions from the category of deviant behavior as it is here defined, what remains is the not inconsiderable category of instances in which the following occurs: A person who is motivated to conform to those normative expectations that he and the group view as applicable to him comes to lose motivation to conform to these expectations, and/or acquires motivation to deviate from them, and in fact does violate them.

One further point should be made. Deviant behavior is viewed as a change in the state of person–group relationships. Deviant behavior (as the term is used here) arises from a loss of motivation to conform to and the acquisition of a motivation to deviate from applicable normative expectations of a membership group. However, once the deviant behavior has occurred, its consequences in terms of changing self–other definitions of the subject's membership groups may change the character of the subject's behavior with regard to deviance.

If a person violates the norms of a specified *membership* group, his behavior is deviant even if it should (by chance or intent) conform to the normative expec-tations of some other group. However, if he then no longer considers the normative expectations of the first group as applicable to him but accepts those of another group and comes to be recognized by members of that group as one to whom the group expectations should apply, then a change in both his group membership and the deviant (or conforming) character of his behavior occurs. He ceases to be considered a member of the first group and comes to be viewed

7

as a member of the second. The behavior that violated the standards of the first group is no longer characterized as deviant; rather, it is perceived as conforming to the standards of his new membership group. Indeed, any instances of subsequent conformity to the standards of the first group would be regarded as deviant behavior by virtue of the failure of such instances to conform to the normative expectations of the new membership group.

Theoretical Overview

The theory guiding the research reported in subsequent chapters stipulates general processes thought to influence the initial adoption and continuity of any of a broad range of deviant response processes. These processes more or less directly relate to the genesis of and change in self-attitudes. Since the theoretical statement and supporting empirical citations have been presented elsewhere (H. B. Kaplan, 1975b) only a brief overview will be given now.

The Self-esteem Motive

The theoretical model is based on the premise that, universally, the self-esteem motive is a characteristic feature of human personality development. The *self-esteem motive* is defined as the personal need to maximize the experience of positive self-attitudes and to minimize the experience of negative self-attitudes.

The self-esteem motive is said to be the normal outcome of processes traceable to the infant's early dependence on adults for physical need satisfaction. The infant makes a subjective association between the presence of adults and the satisfaction of his physical needs. This association influences the acquisition of a need for the presence of adults (independent of their physical need-satisfying function) and a sensitivity to the range of adult behaviors. The infant's perception of an association between satisfaction or frustration of his physical needs and specific adult behavior leads to the acquisition of a need to behave in a way that will evoke the kinds of adult responses earlier associated with need-satisfaction and avoid the kinds of adult responses earlier associated with need-frustration. These adult behaviors are conceptualized as the expression of positive or negative attitudes toward the subject. In order to maximize the satisfaction of the acquired need to evoke expressions of positive attitudes (and to avoid expressions of negative attitudes) from others, the child adopts the role of others. He perceives, evaluates, and expresses attitudes toward himself from their point of view in order to provide guides for his own behaviors; on the basis of past experience he imagines that such behavior will evoke positive attitudes from others. The child then responds, *with positive or negative affect,* to his own *imagined* expressions of attitudes toward himself as if they were *in fact* the expressed attitudes of others. In this way, through the symbolic association between the imagined responses of others and his own attitudinal responses to himself, the child acquires the need to behave in a way that will maximize the experience of positive self-attitudes, and minimize the experience of negative self-attitudes. The child has thus acquired the self-esteem motive.

Determinants of Self-attitudes

The extent to which a person fails to satisfy the self-esteem motive—that is, develops characteristically negative, as opposed to positive, self-attitudes—is a function of three sets of mutually influential factors:

1. Self-perceptions of failure to possess personally valued attributes or to perform personally valued behaviors (and self-perceptions of the possession of personally disvalued attributes or the performance of disvalued behaviors)
2. Self-perceptions of failure to be the object of positive attitudes by personally valued others (and self-perceptions of being the object of negative attitudes by personally valued others)
3. The failure to possess and employ normatively defined self-protective response patterns that might preclude the occurrence or mitigate the self-devaluing effects, of such experiences

The probability of these outcomes, in turn, is influenced by such variables as placement in the social structure (which influences such outcomes as disjunctions between socially defined goals and access to the goals and/or the probability of other stigmatizing experiences) as well as family socialization patterns, including those relating to level of aspiration, and those influencing the nature of symbolically transmitted self-protective patterns.

SUBJECT ATTRIBUTES AND BEHAVIORS

The first class of determinants of an individual's self-attitudes relates to his history of self-perceptions and self-evaluations of his own attributes and behaviors. An individual will tend to develop negative self-attitudes or feelings to the extent that he has, in balance, a history of perceiving himself as possessing attributes and performing behaviors that, according to the criteria of *high-priority values* in his personal system of values, he evaluates negatively. Likewise, an individual will tend to develop positive self-attitudes to the extent that, in balance, he has a history of perceiving himself as possessing attributes and performing behaviors that he evaluates positively.

Ordinarily, the group or individual will subscribe to many different values. Certain values will be employed to judge particular attributes or behaviors in given situations, and other values will be used for judging other attributes and behaviors in other situations. Values of strength and beauty might be appropriate for judgments about physical characteristics; values of honesty and efficiency might be relevant for judging the performance of one who holds political office; and values of leadership potential and courage might be relevant to the evaluation of an army officer in the field. Very often, however, a person is placed in a situation in which he can behave in accordance with one value only if he deviates from another value. In part to avoid such conflict situations, groups and individuals will order their values hierarchically, so in choice situations one value is judged to take priority over another. For example, it might be more important to act for the public good and be disloyal to a friend than to be loyal to a friend at the cost of the public good. Similarly, it might be more important to have a job that is creative but pays little rather than to have one that pays well but does not permit creativity. The totality of the values of a group or an individual organized in terms of such principles as situational specificity and hierarchical priority will be referred to as a *value system*.

The desirable qualities or values in question may be conceptualized as continuous dimensions, such that they may be approximated in varying degrees. For example, a person may be more or less industrious, or more or less beautiful. Alternatively, they may be conceptualized as discrete and mutually exclusive categories. For example, a person is either good or bad, either beautiful or not beautiful. The poles of the continuous dimensions or the discrete and mutually exclusive categories may be thought of in terms of opposite qualities, one of which is defined as desirable, the other, as undesirable (for example, beautiful versus ugly, healthy versus diseased, moral versus immoral). Or, they may be thought of in terms of the presence or absence of a desirable or undesirable quality (for example, beautiful versus nonbeautiful, healthy versus nonhealthy, moral versus nonmoral).

The qualities or values are "desirable" (or, in the instances of opposite poles or categories, "undesirable") in the sense that approximation to the value tends to evoke positive sanctions (rewards), and deviation from the value (or approximation of the opposite quality) tends to evoke negative sanctions (punishment). Thus, an individual who is judged to be honest, industrious, efficient, or good-looking compared to a person who is judged to be dishonest, less than industrious, inefficient, or not as good-looking is more likely to receive expressions of approval. He is less likely to be shunned, more likely to be offered positions of responsibility, more likely to be invited into the company of others, and, in general, more likely to evoke behaviors defined as rewarding by his social group (and less likely to be the object of behaviors defined by his social group as punitive).

In the course of the socialization process, by virtue of the association between attitudinal responses by others and the subject's behaviors or attributes, the child becomes aware of this system of standards by which he is judged by others—that is, that certain behaviors and attributes are "good" things since they evoke positive attitudinal responses and that other behaviors and attributes are "bad" things since they evoke negative attitudinal responses.

Given the association between the subject's attributes and responses by the motivationally significant others, and given the need for self-approval stemming from the need for the approval of others, the child tends to adopt the value system of the significant others. Particular attributes or behaviors come to have intrinsic motivational significance and, via self-perception processes, evoke self-attitudes appropriate to the valuation of the perceived traits and behaviors.

OTHERS' ATTITUDES TOWARD THE SUBJECT

The second set of determinants of an individual's self-attitudes or self-feelings relates to his history of perceiving and interpreting how more or less highly valued other people in his environment behave toward him. He may see their behavior as expressing more or less positive attitudes about himself or aspects of himself. An individual will tend to develop negative self-attitudes if he has, in balance, a history of perceiving and interpreting the behavior of highly valued others as expressing negative attitudes toward him in general or toward personally valued aspects of him. Similarly, the individual will tend to develop positive self-attitudes if he has, in balance, a history of perceiving and interpreting the behavior of highly valued others as expressing positive attitudes toward him in general or toward personally valued aspects of him.

The expressed attitudes of significant others toward the subject have a two-fold significance. First, in the course of socialization experiences in membership groups, the person learns that to be the object of positive attitudes by significant others (to be loved by one's parents, to be well liked) is in itself the basis for approving responses from others and self. He learns that to be hated by others is a basis for rejection by others and self-rejection. Second, and more indirectly, the perceived attitudes of others may provide cognitive cues that in turn influence self-evaluation. Particularly when the subject lacks personal standards for self-evaluation, the perceived attitudes of others toward him are interpreted as providing information about the value of his attributes or the level of his performance. Such information influences self-evaluation and, thereby, self-attitudes.

The attitudes of others toward the subject are influenced by the first set of factors, since others will express more or less positive attitudes toward the person depending on their perception of how closely his actual behaviors and attributes conform to their values.

SELF-PROTECTIVE RESPONSE PATTERNS

The likelihood that a person will perceive himself as characterized by disvalued attributes and behaviors and as the object of rejection by valued others, and that having these experiences he will be able to forestall or assuage distressful self-rejecting feelings, will be a function of his self-protective response patterns. The likelihood that the person will experience events with self-devaluing implications is, in part, a function of his ability to adapt to normatively defined and personally subscribed environmental demands. It is also a function of his ability (within personally and socially defined bounds of acceptability) to change the environment to make it more congruent with his personal need/value system.

Such abilities are frequently termed *adaptive* and *coping mechanisms* (Coelho, Hamburg, & Adams, 1974). Sometimes a person is unable to forestall such experiences because of deficient adaptive and coping mechanisms relative to environmental demands. In such cases the capacity to forestall or diminish the intensity of negative self-attitudes that would otherwise follow upon (mediated by self-perceptions and evaluations) these adverse life experiences is a function of the effectiveness and acceptability of response dispositions variously labeled "protective attitudes" which are defined as "a constellation of related ideas by means of which the individual maintains, enhances, and defends the self [Washburn, 1962, p. 85]," or "controls and defenses," which "refer to the individual's capacity to define an event filled with negative implications and consequences in such a way that it does not detract from his sense of worthiness, ability, or power [Coopersmith, 1967, p. 37]."

Self-protective patterns may exercise their influence upon self-attitudes more or less directly. Their direct influence might diminish the experience of negative self-feeling by removing it from consciousness or by evoking a counterbalancing affect. They may more indirectly influence self-attitudes by permitting the subject to distort his perceptions of, and reevaluate, his own attributes and behaviors and/or the expressed attitudes toward him by others in his environment. Thus, an individual, through the use of protective mechanisms, might not perceive that he possesses disvalued attributes or has performed disvalued behaviors or that valued others have expressed negative attitudes toward him. Alternatively, rather than distorting his perception of reality, the subject's protective attitudes might permit him to effect changes in his evaluations such that he (*a*) gives higher priority to, or adopts, values that permit him to evaluate his existing attributes and behaviors positively (for example, the subject happens to be a good athlete so he defines athletic ability as a more highly valued trait, although he had not previously considered this ability to be quite so valuable); (*b*) gives lower priority to, or rejects, values by which he would necessarily evaluate himself negatively (for example, the subject happens to be receiving poor grades at school so he comes to value good grades less than he had previously valued them); (*c*) comes to value, more positively than previously, groups or individuals who are perceived by the subject as positively evaluating him (for example, the individual comes to seek out the company of a particular clique of students whose company he did not previously value, because he now perceives that they admire him or probably would admire him if they became acquainted with him); and/or (d) comes to more negatively value than previously individuals or groups who are perceived as negatively evaluating him (for example, an individual may come to reject a group of students at school to whom he had previously been attracted because he perceives himself as being rejected by them). Any of these actions would be expected to function to enhance the subject's self-attitudes. In one sense, all protective attitudes or defenses in their more indirect influences on self-attitudes are viewed here as mediated by their influence upon perception (whether of a subject's own attributes and behaviors or of the attitudes toward the subject expressed by others) or evaluation (whether of a subject's own attributes and behaviors or of the other people who are perceived as expressing attitudes toward the subject).

Self-attitudes and Deviant Behavior

Individuals whose past experiences in membership groups were such that they were unable to forestall the experience of perceiving themselves as possessing negatively valued attributes, performing negatively valued behaviors, or being the object of negative attitudes by valued others, and were unable to employ self-protective patterns to mitigate the adverse effects of these experiences, tend to develop characteristic negative self-attitudes. Insofar as their experiences in membership groups *in fact* were associated with the genesis of negative self-attitudes, the probability is increased that they will *subjectively* associate the membership group with the genesis of highly distressing negative self-attitudes.

Such experiences (and any other future experiences that are apparently related to these experiences), because of their subjective association with the development of emotionally distressing (negative) self-attitudes, would come to be experienced as highly distressing in their own right. The individual would thus be unlikely to behave voluntarily in ways that were likely to foster these experiences. To continue (a) to perceive himself as possessing personally and socially disvalued attributes, performing disvalued behaviors, and being an object of negative attitudes by valued others, (b) to endorse values that he cannot approximate and to value people who express negative attitudes toward him, (c) to behave in ways that in the past were ineffective in facilitating the achievement of valued attributes and the performance of valued behaviors, and (d) to behave in ways that were ineffective in the past in forestalling or reducing the effects of expressions of negative self-attitudes would be to continue to engage in intrinsically distressing activities. The individual would thus be not only unmotivated to continue these intrinsically distressful normative activities but also positively motivated to deviate from them in ways that would facilitate the avoidance, destruction, or displacement of the normative experience.

Those elements of the normative structure that in the past were subjectively associated with the genesis of negative self-attitudes would be generalized to other aspects of the normative structure that were not specifically associated with past experiences of negative self-attitudes, but were subjectively associated with the general normative structure. Thus, an individual who has developed characteristically negative self-attitudes in the course of his membership group experiences would not be motivated to adopt new behavior patterns (endorsed by the group) of which he has recently become aware because of the subjective association of these patterns with a group, past experiences in which were highly distressing. In short, the person would lack motivation to conform to the group's normative expectations *in general,* and would be positively motivated to deviate from them, whether or not the expectations were originally associated in the subject's mind with experience of highly distressing negative self-attitudes.

Continuing exposure to the very normative experiences that resulted in the loss of motivation to conform to and the genesis of the motivation to deviate from the normative structures of his membership groups exerts increasing pressure upon the person's capacity to forestall or mitigate life experiences that have self-devaluing implications. The person's incapacity to use effective mechanisms, his tendency to employ maladaptive mechanisms, and his consequent vulnerability to self-devaluing circumstances exacerbate the self-esteem motive—that is, the need to minimize the experience of negative self-attitudes and to maximize the experience of positive self-attitudes.

The intensified experience of the self-esteem motive provides a second impetus toward deviant behavior in addition to the negative hedonic tone now associated with the membership group structure, namely, the need to enhance self-attitudes. Given the negative hedonic tone associated with the normative structure, deviant patterns represent the only motivationally acceptable alternatives that might effectively serve self-enhancing functions.

Against the background of the motivation to deviance, the person would become increasingly sensitive to the existence of deviant alternatives. Upon becoming aware of the alternatives, the person would be likely to adopt a deviant pattern to the extent that he came to anticipate that this action would have, in balance, consequences that would increase positive self-attitudes.

Which of several deviant patterns is adopted then would be a function of the person's history of experiences (including personal and social predisposition) influencing the visibility and subjective evaluation of the self-enhancing potential of the patterns in question. Entering the equation would be such factors as the compatibility of the deviant behavior with internalized roles (e.g., the behavior is appropriately masculine) that are not themselves the basis of one's self-rejection, and the ability to neutralize residual guilt or the promise of negative sanctions with appropriate self-justifications. However, given the initial adoption of the pattern, the further establishment of the individual in the deviant pattern will be a function of his actual experiences with the self-enhancing or self-derogating consequences of the deviant behaviors.

Deviant Behavior and Self-enhancement

Deviant patterns tend to serve any or all of three functions with reference to the experience of self-devaluing or self-enhancing functions. These three functions are termed *avoidance, attack,* and *substitution.*

The avoidance function of the deviant pattern might be served by activities at intrapsychic and/or interpersonal levels. In the former case the person may distort his perception of reality such that he does not correctly perceive his disvalued attributes or performances. He may incorrectly perceive himself as possessing valued attributes and performing valued behaviors, and he may fail to perceive the negative attitudes expressed toward him by valued others. He may incorrectly perceive the positive attitudes expressed toward him by valued others, or incorrectly interpret circumstances in ways that justify his posses-sion of disvalued attributes, his performance of disvalued behaviors, and his being the object of negative attitudes by valued others (or not being the object of positive attitudes by valued others). At the interpersonal level the deviant act may facilitate avoidance of performing in normatively prescribed roles. It may also enable him to avoid other interpersonal interactions in which it appears to be probable that he will fail to manifest valued attributes (or will manifest disvalued attributes); he will fail to perform valued behaviors (or will perform disvalued behaviors); or he will fail to evoke positive attitudes by valued others (or will evoke negative attitudes by valued others) by weakening the relation-ship between himself and the membership group.

Response patterns that function to attack group members or the normative structure (as a whole or in part) may range from drastic reduction of the value placed upon previously valued people or normative standards to more overtly hostile responses by the individual. Such hostile responses may include physical aggression toward both group members and material representations of the normative structure (which originally was subjectively and in fact associated with the genesis of negative self-attitudes).

Both avoidance and attack functions may be facilitated or accompanied by substitutive functions served by such deviant patterns as those involving the adoption of new group memberships and normative standards. For example, an individual may avoid participating in a group (membership in which was as-sociated with failure to achieve value standards, negative attitudinal responses by valued others, and so on) by (or at the same time as) substituting participa-tion in a different (deviant) group that seems to offer more easily attainable standards and greater promise of positive attitudinal responses from other group

15

members. An individual may also devalue previously valued group members who respond to him with negative attitudes, or he may devalue previously valued standards that he had been unable to approximate. He may do this through (or at the same time as) placing a higher value on other standards that he already approximates or on other people who express positive attitudes toward him.

Insofar as the deviant act facilitates intrapsychic or interpersonal avoidance of self-devaluing experiences associated with the predeviance membership group, serves to attack (symbolically or otherwise) what is perceived as the basis of the person's self-rejecting attitudes (that is, representations of the normative group structure), and/or offers substitute patterns with self-enhancing potential for behavior patterns that were associated with the genesis of self-rejecting attitudes, the person to that extent will experience enhancement of self-attitudes.

However, although the probability is high that adoption of deviant patterns will have self-enhancing consequences, the adoption of a deviant pattern will not necessarily have *exclusively* positive consequences for a person's self-attitudes. Some of the effects of the deviant pattern might exacerbate the experience of negative self-attitudes. For example, the rejection of the standards of one's social group in favor of membership in a deviant group may result in failure to approximate the deviant standards or rejection by the deviant group membership. Such experiences may obviate any self-enhancing consequences of the avoidance or destruction of those aspects of the former membership group structure that were associated with the development and maintenance of negative self-attitudes. Thus, in discussing the likelihood that a person will become confirmed in his use of the initially adopted deviant response patterns, we must consider the *net* positive effects with regard to experiences of self-attitudes.

To the extent that self-devaluing consequences outweigh self-enhancing outcomes, it is likely that the person will search for and experiment with alternative modes of deviance, since normative patterns will continue to be motivationally unacceptable. However, to the extent that the person, having adopted a deviant response pattern, is able to defend against any (anticipated or unanticipated) intervening adverse consequences of the behavior, and does not perceive alternative responses with greater self-enhancing potential, he is likely to be confirmed in the pattern.

Whether or not the net outcome of the deviant response pattern is positive will be a function of such mutually influencing variables as the nature of the deviant act, societal response to the act, and the person's need/value and adaptive/coping/defensive patterns. For example, a highly visible and highly disvalued act might lead to apprehension and adjudication with consequences of stigmatization, enforced deviant role enactment, exacerbation of a need to justify the act by its continued performance, isolation from social control, isolation from legitimate opportunities, and exposure to self-enhancing illegitimate patterns. At the same time, such an act may be congruent with personal need disposition (e.g., power) and adaptive/coping/defensive mechanisms (e.g., attack). The deviant pattern might become part of the subject's personal and (new) social life-style, with gratification coming from conformance with the life-style. Insofar as the new life-style precludes the experience of the self-devaluing life events characteristic of former membership group experiences, *a fortiori* the deviant pattern should have self-enhancing consequences.

Alternatively, the deviant pattern may have a low probability of severe (or any) sanctions from membership groups (perhaps because of low visibility), but still may have self-enhancing consequences, in which case the subject may be expected to perform the pattern in response to discrete life events with self-devaluing implications. The frequency of the deviant pattern becomes a function of the frequency of self-devaluing life events and the continuity of a net aggregate of gratifying over punishing consequences of the deviant adaptation.

If the currently preferred deviant pattern offers a good deal of self-devaluing potential (for example, peer rejection) but is still preferable to normative patterns with their self-devaluing implications, then continuity of the pattern will persist only until the person becomes aware of alternative deviant patterns with self-enhancing potential, or becomes aware of the self-enhancing potential of aspects of normative response patterns. With regard to the latter, the person is likely to adopt normative response patterns only where they are so discontinuous with the remainder of the normative context to preclude their subjective association with the same normative context that was, in fact and subjectively, associated with the genesis of self-rejecting attitudes. Such discontinuity might occur for the adolescent when he matures sufficiently to be exposed to the potential gratifications to be derived from new occupational and familial roles.

The theoretical statement clearly incorporates a number of concepts other than those of self-attitudes and deviant behavior. Nevertheless, all of the factors are plausibly, but more or less directly, related to self-attitudes. It is around the central explanatory significance of self-rejecting attitudes that an outline for a general theory of deviant behavior has emerged.

In the following section of this volume, the results of the empirical study designed to test selected hypotheses from those comprising the general theory of deviant behavior are reported.

Chapter 2

Method

The selected hypotheses derived from the general theory of deviant behavior were tested by data collected for this purpose in the course of a longitudinal survey research project.

Sample

The target sample was made up of all of the seventh-grade students in 18 of the 36 junior high schools in the Houston Independent School District as of March 1971. The schools were selected by use of a table of random numbers. The registered seventh-grade students in the selected schools comprised 49.77% of the seventh-grade students in all 36 schools. This method of selecting a 50% sample of seventh-grade students was chosen in order to minimize disruption of school functioning during data collection.

The selected schools appeared to be representative along a number of parameters. Included were 10 of the 20 schools in the district having above 1500 total enrollment and 8 of the 17 schools in which at least 25% of the total student enrollment was black.

The seventh grade was selected to minimize instances of prior involvement in deviant activities (since certain of the hypotheses assume an initial deviance-free state) and permit the observation of an adequate (for purposes of hypothesis testing) number of instances of adoption of deviant responses over the next 2 years. In addition, the period between age 11 and age 13, during which most students begin junior high school, seems to be the developmental period (relative to 5–7, 8–10, and 14–16) that is most predictive of adult status. Thus, Livson and Peskin (1967) reported that only the 11–13 period yielded significant prediction to adult psychological health from personality trait evaluations.

Of the eligible seventh-grade students in the selected schools 7618 (81.6%) returned usable questionnaires at the time of the first administration: 49% were male and 51% were female; 61% were white Anglo, 28% were black, and 11% were Mexican American; with regard to the mother's education, 4% had mothers who did not graduate from elementary school, 13% had mothers who graduated from elementary school, 54% had mothers who graduated from high school, and 30% had mothers who graduated from college; 4% were 11-years-old or younger at the time of the first test administration, 33% were 12-years-old, 48% were 13-years-old, and 16% were 14-years-old or older; 59% were Protestant, 25% were Catholic, 3% were Jewish, 4% indicated other non-Christian denominations, and 9% indicated they were unaffiliated with any organized religion. It was not possible to determine how the composition of this grouping corresponded to the total seventh-grade population, since demographic data for each grade were not available from the school system. Nor did we collect data on whether the failures to obtain usable questionnaires were due to absences from the test sessions, refusal of permission by parents, unwillingness of the student to participate in the study, or invalid (mutilated, blank, same answer throughout, and the like) questionnaires.

Those students who provided usable questionnaires at the first testing were not uniformly willing or able to continue participation in the study over the next 2 years. In addition to the possible reasons specified regarding nonparticipation in the study, the sample attrition might also be accounted for in part by movement to nonsample schools in the school district or movement out of the district.

Of the students who returned usable questionnaires, 30% did not continue in the study. The remaining 70% responded to either or both of the T_2 (second year) and T_3 (third year) questionnaires. Table 2.1 shows how the completed questionnaires were distributed with regard to subsequent test administration at annual intervals.

Thus, for analyses considering more than one point in time, as many as

TABLE 2.1
Follow-up of Completed Baseline Questionnaires over 3-Year Period

Tests taken	Percentage of usable first administration tests ($N = 7618$)	Percentage of eligible respondents ($N = 9335$)
First test only	30.0	24.5
First two tests only	20.3	16.6
First and third tests only	8.4	6.8
All three tests	41.3	33.7

61.6% of those subjects providing usable first administration questionnaires and 50.3% of all eligible respondents were available—those providing questionnaire data at both T_1 and T_2; and as few as 41.3% of those subjects providing usable first administration questionnaires and 33.7% of all eligible respondents were available for analyses considering all three points in time.

Although data are not available that would permit us to describe the characteristics of the student grouping that did not respond to the first test administration, it was possible to determine the characteristics of those who did not respond to either or both of the subsequent (second and third) test administrations after having responded to the first test. This analysis was carried out for a 5% sample of the population. For purposes of this analysis the small grouping of those who responded only at the first and third testings was excluded.

Sample attrition was associated with ethnicity, mother's education, subject's age, religious affiliation, mobility patterns, deviant behavior of freindship groups, attitudinal predispositions to leave school, and self-reports of early deviant behavior.

Mexican Americans constituted 17% of those present only for the first test administration, but only 8 and 6%, respectively, of subjects present for the first two tests or for all three tests. Subjects whose mothers did not graduate from elementary school constituted 8% of those present only for the first test, but less than 2% of those present for subsequent tests. Subjects aged 14 or older constituted 24% of those present only for the first test, but only 17% of those present for the first two tests and 9% of those present for all three tests.

Those indicating that they were unaffiliated with any organized religion constituted over 16% of the students present only for the first test administration compared with less than 10% of those present for the first two testings and 4% of those present for all three tests.

A linear relationship was observed between sample attrition and mobility patterns. Thus, subjects who reported that their family had moved to a different house or apartment within the past year constituted 30% of those taking the first test only, 24% of those taking the first two tests, and 18% of those taking all three tests. Consistent with this, those reporting that they had lived in Houston more than 5 years constituted only 76% of those taking only the first test compared with 84% of those taking the first two tests and 92% of those taking all three tests.

Subjects who did not continue in the study tended to report that their close friends displayed deviant patterns. Thus, those students who affirmed that many of their good friends took narcotic drugs to get high constituted 24% of those responding to the first test only, but only 12% of those responding to the first two tests only and 10% of those responding to all three tests.

Not surprisingly, students who indicated that they were predisposed to leave

TABLE 2.2

Percentage of Students Reporting Deviant Behavior during the Specified Period[a]
Prior to the First Administration, by Number of Test Administrations

Test item[b,c,d]	T_1 only[e]	T_1 and T_2 only[e]	T_1, T_2, and T_3[e]
3. Took things worth between $2 and $50* ($df = 1$)	9.2 (109)	2.6 (76)	4.5 (154)
5. Was suspended or expelled from school* ($df = 1$)	14.8 (108)	10.7 (75)	5.8 (154)
7. Took things worth less than $2	19.3 (109)	14.7 (75)	13.0 (154)
10. Thought about or threatened to take own life	19.1 (110)	8.0 (75)	13.7 (153)
11. Came in contact with police, sheriff, or juvenile officers**	22.7 (110)	9.2 (76)	8.4 (154)
14. Became angry and broke things* ($df = 1$)	28.4 (109)	14.7 (75)	20.1 (154)
17. Carried a razor, switchblade, or gun as a weapon*	12.0 (108)	2.6 (76)	6.5 (153)
24. Sold narcotic drugs (dope, heroin)	3.7 (107)	0 (74)	.6 (154)
26. Received a failing grade in one or more subjects***	48.2 (110)	30.3 (76)	26.0 (154)
28. Used wine, beer, or liquor more than two times***	24.5 (106)	5.3 (75)	12.5 (152)
29. Cheated on exams	17.3 (110)	14.5 (76)	13.7 (153)
31. Attempted to take own life	12.0 (108)	2.6 (76)	8.4 (154)
33. Started a fistfight**	20.9 (110)	9.5 (74)	7.8 (154)
38. Took narcotic drugs*	8.3 (109)	2.7 (75)	2.0 (153)
44. Skipped school without an excuse***	17.4 (109)	5.3 (75)	3.9 (153)
48. Took part in social protest	14.5 (110)	10.8 (74)	7.9 (152)
50. Took part in a gang fight*	12.7 (110)	2.6 (76)	5.8 (154)
56. Was sent to a psychiatrist, psychologist, or social worker*	10.1 (109)	4.0 (75)	2.6 (153)
57. Used force to get money or valuables	9.2 (109)	3.9 (76)	5.2 (153)

(*Continued*)

school were significantly less likely to be present for subsequent test administrations than those who did not so indicate. Those students who reported that they would like to quit school as soon as possible constituted 29% of those present for the first test administration only compared to as few as 18% of those present for the first two testings only and 17% of those present for all three tests. This finding, in addition to its implication with reference to subject characteristics associated with sample attrition, provides validation of attitudinal items as predictors of behavior. In this case the reported predisposition to leave school was associated with de facto absence from school (insofar as this can be inferred from the failure to respond at the second and/or third test administrations).

TABLE 2.2—*Continued*

Test item[b,c,d]	T_1 only[e]	T_1 and T_2 only[e]	T_1, T_2, and T_3[e]
61. Broke into and entered a home, store, or building**	6.5 (107)	0 (76)	0.6 (154)
64. Damaged or destroyed public or private property on purpose* ($df = 1$)	10.1 (109)	2.6 (76)	4.6 (153)
68. Was taken to the office for punishment*	38.2 (110)	28.9 (76)	22.9 (153)
69. Took things from someone else's desk or locker	13.9 (108)	6.6 (76)	9.1 (154)
72. Took a car for a ride without the owner's permission* ($df = 1$)	7.3 (109)	1.3 (76)	3.2 (154)
75. Beat up someone for no reason at all* ($df = 1$)	9.2 (109)	5.3 (76)	2.6 (153)
78. Stole things worth $50 or more	4.6 (108)	2.6 (76)	1.3 (154)
82. Smoked marijuana**	13.8 (109)	6.7 (75)	3.2 (154)
84. Took part in strike, riot, or demonstration	5.5 (109)	2.6 (76)	1.3 (154)

[a] The time period was "within the last month" for all items except the following, where the time period was an indicated: 5 (ever); 11 (ever); 26 (during the last 9 weeks); 28 (within the last week); 29 (during the last exam period); 56 (ever); 68 (within the last year).

[b] Numbers refer to student questionnaire items.

[c] Asterisks indicate significant χ^2 comparison: $*p < .05$; $**p < .01$; $***p < .001$.

[d] Where degree of freedom is not indicated, the significant comparison is for all three administration groupings ($df = 2$). Where $df = 1$, the comparison is significant for the T_1 only category versus all others.

[e] Parenthetical entries indicate N. This table is based on a 5% sample ($N = 386$) of all students present for the first test administration. Students taking the first and third tests only were excluded.

From the point of view of the general theory of deviant behavior under consideration, the most significant correlate of sample attrition was self-report of early deviant behavior. The attrition rate in the sample is disproportionately accounted for by subjects who had already been involved in deviant patterns by the time of the first test administration. Reference to Table 2.2 will indicate that with regard to each of 28 deviant acts students who returned usable questionnaires only at the first administration were appreciably more likely to have reported early deviant activity (referring to the period prior to the first testing) than students who were present for the second and/or third testings. The relationship was significant ($p < .05$) for 18 of the 28 acts.

Equally interesting are the factors not associated with sample attrition. No significant relationship was observed between sample attrition on the one hand and gender, self-derogation level, psychophysiological indicators of subjective distress, birth order, broken family, reports of deviant activity on the part of "many of the kids at school," or stability of self-attitudes on the other hand.

The observation that sample attrition was related to the subjects' reports of their own deviant behavior and the deviant behavior of their friendship groups but not to indices of subjective distress, self-derogation level, and the prevalence of the deviant activity in the more inclusive environment (the school) suggests that those students who were least likely to continue in the study were those engaged in peer-supported activity that reflected neither adaptive attempts to assuage subjective distress or self-derogating feelings nor more inclusive subcultural definitions of deviant/conforming responses. In addition, the patterns of characteristics associated with, as well as those unassociated with, sample attrition suggest that those who dropped out of the study tended to be those who were least well integrated into the social system. This is indicated by their higher rates of mobility, absence of affiliation with any organized religion, predisposition to leave school, and adoption of deviant patterns (along with their close friends) that were apparently not endorsed by the more inclusive peer group (the kids at school).

These observations are offered tentatively. In any case, the implications of the sample attrition patterns for interpretation of the findings are highly variable, depending as they do upon the particular plan of analysis. For example, the disproportionate attrition of students who admitted to deviant acts at the first test administration was not as significant for testing hypotheses regarding the relationship between antecedent self-derogation and subsequent adoption of deviant response patterns as it was for other analyses. The logic of the former analysis (to be described in a subsequent chapter) required those students reporting the performance of the deviant act during the month prior to the first testing to be excluded from the analysis in any event. Therefore, the lesser representation of these students did not constitute as serious a bias in the sample as would have been the case if they had been included in the analysis.

In view of the variable significance of the patterns of sample attrition, the implications of these patterns will be considered with reference to each set of findings separately.

Data Collection

The seventh-grade students who were to take the test at a particular school generally were convened during the morning of a school day at one or two common locations (lunchroom or auditorium) where they responded to a 209-item structured self-administered questionnaire.

The test was administered three times, at annual intervals, during March or April of 1971 (T_1), 1972 (T_2), and 1973 (T_3). The questionnaires were identical each year with the exception of the time reference in items dealing with self-reports of deviant behavior. For the second and third years the time reference with one exception was "within the last year," whereas for the first test the time reference was variable (see subsequent discussion) but generally "within the last month."

For the first 2 years, the test was administered on a Friday at the same time of day. A second test administration was arranged a week later under the same conditions for those students who were absent the week before but who were willing and were not refused parental permission to take the test. For the third year, scheduling problems and considerations of absenteeism suggested the advisability of administering the test on a Thursday. A second testing session was not provided that year. During the third year we also permitted, in those schools where the school counselor found it necessary due to absence of adequate common facilities, the tests to be administered in the classroom under teacher supervision.

Each year, more than 1 week prior to the scheduled testing, forms were distributed to parents through their children. These forms gave the parent the opportunity to refuse permission for the child to participate. In addition, students were advised that they need not participate if they did not wish to.

The questionnaires were provided with a face sheet that requested identifying information. The students were promised that the data would be treated confidentially. Following the testing, students were permitted to remove the face sheets and hand them in separately, to prevent the supervising school personnel from finding out what a particular student's answers might be. However, the questionnaires were clearly marked with identification numbers. The students were told that this number, in conjunction with the identifying face sheet data, would be the means for collating a student's responses from one year to the next. In practice, separate computer tapes were prepared each year. On one tape appeared the identifying data and the randomly distributed questionnaire number. On the other tape were the reponses to the 209 items as well as the questionnaire number. The identification tapes permitted the collation of questionnaire numbers with common identifying data.

The content of the questionnaire will become apparent with the presentation of the results.

Operational Definitions

Of the several variables operationalized in the analyses to be reported, the two most meaningful variables are self-attitudes and deviant behavior.

SELF-ATTITUDES

Self-attitudes were measured by scores on a self-derogation scale. The seven constituent items of this scale were derived in an earlier study (H. B. Kaplan &

Pokorny, 1969) from a factor analysis of responses to 10 items. These 10 items were employed by Rosenberg (1965) in a Guttman scale to measure self-esteem. This scale appeared to have good predictive validity (Rosenberg, 1965) and convergent validity (Silber & Tippett, 1965). The factorial refinement was undertaken on the assumption, which subsequently proved to be warranted (H. B. Kaplan & Pokorny, 1969), that the scale contained both affective and nonaffective components. The factor analysis permitted derivation of what was taken to be a measure of affective response (self-derogation in its negative polar extreme). This measure showed strong relationships as predicted with measures of depressive affect and psychophysiological indicators of anxiety, and otherwise showed good construct validity in a study of correlates of self-derogation among a representative sample of adults in Houston, Texas (H. B. Kaplan, 1970a, 1970b, 1971a, 1971b, 1973; H. B. Kaplan & Pokorny, 1969, 1970a, 1970b, 1971, 1972).

The component items of the self-derogation measure, the inter-item correlations, and the test-item correlations are presented in Table 2.3. The self-derogation score was computed by assigning a weight of 2 to self-derogating responses to items 109, 180, and 184 and a weight of 1 to self-derogating responses to the remaining items. The weights were added (a maximum of 10), the sum was divided by the number of units for which data were available (a maximum of 10), and the result was multiplied by 100. The scores varied between 0 and 100. Scores were not computed if data were missing for three or more *units*. (Because of the differential weighting, one item might constitute two units.)

The inter-item correlations generally were low but statistically significant. The test-item correlations were moderate to high with the greatest magnitudes, as would be expected, manifested for the double-weighted items.

The weighting of the items as described resulted in a pattern of test-item correlations that was strikingly similar to the item loadings on the self-derogation factor derived in the earlier study (H. B. Kaplan & Pokorny, 1969, p. 424). The two patterns are presented in Table 2.3.

Theoretical considerations pose particular problems regarding the evaluation of the stability of the self-derogation measure. The self-esteem motive leads us to expect that subjects with more positive self-attitudes would be motivated to retain this self-image, whereas individuals with more negative self-attitudes would be motivated to behave in ways permitting the attainment of more positive self-attitudes. Indeed, other investigators have reported that measures of self-concept stability are related to more positive self-attitudes and that change in self-attitudes tends to be associated with initially negative self-concepts (Brownfain, 1952; Engel, 1959; French, 1968; Rosenberg, 1965). Given this situation, correlations between self-derogation scores over time should be at best moderate. In any case, for students present at all three yearly test adminis-

TABLE 2.3

Self-derogation Score: Inter-item and Test-item Correlations[a,b]

Test item[c]	Inter-item correlations[d]							X̄ Inter-item correlation	Test-item correlations	Item loading on self-derogation factor[e]
	109	113	118	142	152	180	184			
109. I wish I could have more respect for myself. (true)	—	-16	21	18	-06	20	21	17	62	61
113. On the whole, I am satisfied with myself. (false)		—	-15	-18	17	-20	-16	17	42	44
118. I feel I do not have much to be proud of. (true)			—	28	-12	17	17	18	44	37
142. I'm inclined to feel I'm a failure. (true)				—	-14	19	15	19	41	46
152. I take a positive attitude toward myself. (false)					—	-11	-07	11	31	41
180. At times I think I'm no good at all. (true)						—	45	22	72	76
184. I certainly feel useless at times. (true)							—	20	70	76

[a] This table, first printed as Table 1 of "Self-attitudes and Deviant Response," by Howard B. Kaplan, is reprinted with stylistic changes from Social Forces, 1976, 54 (4), pp. 788–801, by permission of the publisher, the University of North Carolina Press.
[b] Signs are corrected to give the high value to the self-derogating response.
[c] Numbers refer to student questionnaire items; parentheses give the self-derogating response.
[d] All correlations were significant at the p < .001 level. The correlations were observed for students tested on all three occasions. These correlations refer to the score on the first test. The smallest N for any correlation from this study presented here is 3056. Decimal points are omitted.
[e] From the Houston Adult Study (H. B. Kaplan & Pokorny, 1969).

trations, the correlations between self-derogation scores (all significant at p < .001) were as follows: between T_1 and T_2, $r = .46$; between T_2 and T_3, $r = .55$; and between T_1 and T_3 (a 2-year interval), $r = .40$.

Although space limitations do not permit its detailed specification here, the measure of self-derogation demonstrated good predictive validity in the present study, as in earlier studies. Based upon theories of the genesis of negative or positive self-attitudes (Coopersmith, 1967; Kaplan, 1972b, 1975b; Rosenberg, 1965), self-derogation was predicted and observed to be significantly associated with student reports of the following: self-devaluing experiences among peers (.42), in the family (.41), and at school (.36); an inability to redefine events in ways that would permit mitigation of self-devaluing effects (.18); a subjectively distressful vulnerability to the expression of negative attitudes toward the subject by apparently positively valued others (.48); and a number of other theoretically relevant variables.

DEVIANT BEHAVIOR

Deviant behavior was measured by self-reports of presumably deviant acts investigated in a number of studies of undetected crime and delinquency. Many of these studies are cited by Clark and Tifft (1966) and Gold (1970). The items that are of concern here were presented in Table 2.2. At the first test administration, the students were asked to indicate whether or not they performed the deviant behavior in question during a specified period prior to the test. The specified period was "within 1 month" for all of the items except the following, where the time period was as indicated parenthetically: 5 (ever); 11 (ever); 26 (during the last 9-week period); 28 (within the last week); 29 (during the last exam period); 56 (ever); and 68 (within the last year). At the second and third testings the time reference was "within the last year," except for item 28, which retained the same time reference (within the last week). The relatively brief time period reference at the first administration was used in an attempt to differentiate between students who had already adopted deviant response patterns and those who had not. This differentiation facilitated analyses of the relationship between antecedent self-derogation and subsequent *initial* adoption of motivationally relevant deviant responses. It was assumed that students indicating nonperformance of the act were less likely to have already adopted a motivationally relevant deviant response pattern, in contrast to those who did indicate recent performance of the act. To have used a more extended time period would have increased the probability of excluding subjects who only occasionally performed the deviant act (by way of experimentation or special circumstances) as well as those who had already adopted the deviant act as a motivationally relevant response pattern.

The decision was made to use the 28 self-report items of deviant behavior as separate variables rather than combining them into a composite index of deviant behavior, primarily on the basis of theoretical considerations. In the general theory of deviant behavior being tested, self-attitudes were viewed as common antecedents and consequences of multiple modes of deviance. Therefore, it was necessary to choose indicators of a broad range of deviant responses, which were essentially uncorrelated among themselves. The choice of the 28 indicators of deviant responses for this purpose seems justified in terms of the low order of correlations (Pearson r's) observed among them. The correlation matrix is present in Table 2.4. The mean correlation (disregarding sign) was only .11. For only 2 of the 378 pairs (3, 7; 10,31) did one of the variables account for as much as 10% of the variance in the other variable. At the same time the low magnitudes of correlations suggest that no general predisposition to affirm or deny deviant responses was operating.

The prevalence of each deviant act for the indicated period prior to T_1 may be estimated from the data provided in Table 2.2. The prevalence of each deviant act for the period between the first and second test administrations may be derived from the data reported in Table 2.5. The incidence (new reports per unit of population) is reflected (roughly) in the second column of this table, which indicates the percentage of the subjects reporting each deviant act at T_2 after having denied performance of the act at T_1.

With four exceptions, the self-report items of deviant behavior reflect behavior *by the subject*. In the case of the four items, however, the deviant behavior is reflected not in the behavior of the subject but in the responses by others to the presumed behavior of the subject. These items cover suspension or expulsion from school, contact with police, sheriff, or juvenile officers, being sent to a psychiatrist, psychologist, or social worker, and being taken to the office for punishment. In analysis of the data it is recognized that these four items, whether or not they reflect voluntary deviant behavior on the part of the subject, may reflect such factors as the visibility of the subject's deviant behavior and the nature of available social control mechanisms.

It may be questioned whether other items, such as "received a failing grade in one or more subjects," represent *voluntary* deviant behavior. This particular response would be in part a function of ability, as well as or instead of motivation to fail. An attempt was made to take this factor into account by controlling on earlier self-reports of receiving failing grades. That is, if the question under consideration was whether or not self-attitudes anticipated a presumably voluntary deviant response of failing examinations, only those students who had affirmed that they had not received failing grades during the earlier period (and therefore presumably had the ability to pass) were considered in the analyses. However, the rationale would fail if, with advancing grades, more difficult material posed increasingly greater challenges to the students' ability.

It might be objected that an item such as "took an active part in social protest either in school or outside of school" or "took part in a strike, riot, or demon-

TABLE 2.4

Correlation Matrix for Self-reports of Deviant Behavior (N = 387)[a,b]

Item number

Item number	3	5	7	10	11	14	17	24	26	28	29	31	33	38	44	48	50	56	57	61	64	68	69	72	75	78	82	84
3		13	34	00	16	08	04	06	10	18	28	12	08	19	11	07	00	07	08	12	20	09	14	17	08	24	17	01
5			18	09	23	15	12	13	23	07	18	10	12	17	16	08	13	13	15	13	03	25	04	24	08	12	23	07
7				19	14	10	15	03	10	13	24	12	13	11	19	04	-06	12	09	12	08	08	17	02	-01	07	06	-02
10					08	18	10	-06	07	15	10	52	05	07	19	18	15	10	15	08	06	02	02	13	06	03	06	13
11						14	22	07	14	14	10	18	17	11	11	10	11	14	17	12	10	23	14	08	10	02	14	07
14							12	01	14	21	10	15	15	05	02	07	14	11	18	10	13	17	05	07	04	05	12	07
17								03	04	21	02	15	23	07	08	05	15	-01	17	07	08	19	10	11	18	03	10	07
24									11	06	09	12	04	08	-05	02	12	-04	05	08	25	-03	13	07	03	23	05	05
26										15	07	03	08	01	23	10	17	04	15	18	15	22	13	18	10	14	14	05
28											17	17	24	06	13	06	10	01	13	25	23	17	14	09	05	01	13	08
29												23	-03	14	09	17	-01	03	11	15	14	07	05	15	09	25	15	17
31													04	10	08	32	16	07	06	06	06	04	10	14	01	02	09	21
33														05	08	04	26	12	07	10	09	19	17	06	14	-02	13	09
38															09	05	-04	11	03	06	13	10	04	13	00	18	28	09
44																11	19	09	06	05	12	10	18	13	08	01	11	08
48																	20	07	06	05	06	02	07	23	01	02	16	29
50																		05	16	-04	02	12	14	14	14	04	04	24
56																			06	12	10	15	11	22	12	08	17	06
57																				11	13	13	09	30	07	05	16	00
61																					20	08	24	06	08	08	09	03
64																						08	02	14	04	25	24	07
68																							08	16	22	01	17	07
69																								16	16	13	02	11
72																									16	17	03	08
75																										09	31	02
78																											09	05
82																												15
84																												

TABLE 2.5

Percentage of Subjects Affirming Deviant Pattern at T_2, by Affirmation or Denial at T_1

Test item[a]	Affirmed at T_1[b]	Denied at T_1[b]
3. Took things worth between $2 and $50 (.77***)	48.0 (202)	10.6 (4389)
5. Was suspended or expelled from school (.81***)	39.8 (274)	6.6 (4270)
7. Took things worth less than $2 (.71***)	61.5 (722)	21.5 (3853)
10. Thought about or threatened to take own life (.74***)	53.3 (615)	14.4 (3955)
11. Came in contact with police, sheriff, or juvenile officers (.69***)	33.4 (533)	8.6 (4062)
14. Became angry and broke things (.60***)	58.2 (992)	25.6 (3564)
17. Carried a razor, switchblade, or gun as a weapon (.79***)	47.4 (304)	9.8 (4240)
24. Sold narcotic drugs (dope, heroin) (.78***)	26.5 (83)	4.2 (4401)
26. Received a failing grade in one or more subjects (.68***)	56.9 (1259)	19.9 (3286)
28. Used, wine, beer, or liquor more than two times (.68***)	58.7 (482)	21.4 (4035)
29. Cheated on exams (.59***)	69.0 (655)	36.6 (3854)
31. Attempted to take own life (.78***)	39.6 (318)	7.6 (4241)
33. Started a fistfight (.72***)	48.4 (546)	13.0 (3956)
38. Took narcotic drugs (.82***)	54.2 (142)	10.7 (4343)
44. Skipped school without an excuse (.73***)	57.9 (247)	17.6 (3524)
48. Took part in social protest (.63***)	36.1 (490)	11.4 (4016)
50. Took part in a gang fight (.79***)	42.0 (276)	7.6 (4289)
56. Was sent to a psychiatrist, psychologist, or social worker (.74***)	21.7 (254)	4.0 (4203)
57. Used force to get money or valuables (.68***)	21.0 (200)	4.9 (4321)
61. Broke into and entered a home, store, or building (.71***)	22.3 (94)	4.6 (4415)
64. Damaged or destroyed public or private property on purpose (.79***)	42.9 (210)	3.0 (4279)
68. Was taken to the office for punishment (.74***)	64.4 (1044)	21.5 (3414)
69. Took things from someone else's desk or locker (.68***)	43.0 (398)	12.5 (4137)
72. Took a car for a ride without the owner's permission (.57***)	18.5 (108)	5.9 (4402)
75. Beat up someone for no reason at all (.74***)	32.8 (262)	6.7 (4224)
78. Stole things worth $50 or more (.73***)	19.5 (77)	3.7 (4445)
82. Smoked marijuana (.82***)	61.7 (193)	13.8 (4269)
84. Took part in strike, riot, or demonstration (.78***)	32.1 (140)	5.5 (4286)

[a] Number in parentheses is gamma for association between T_1 and T_2 responses. All gamma significant at *$p < .05$; **$p < .01$; ***$p < .001$.

[b] Number in parentheses is response N at T_1.

stration" should be considered not deviant behavior but rather behavior oriented toward pursuit of socially valued norms. Nevertheless, it is argued that the means to achieve the valued norms contravene accepted standards, as was indicated by the theoretically derived relationships based on the assumption that such behaviors contravene previously accepted norms.

The deviant meaning of other acts is less in question in popular understanding of the term. Fewer people would disagree that suicidal behavior, theft, drug abuse, gang fights, breaking and entering, and vandalism were truly deviant responses. Of course, within the definition of the term used here, it is still possible that some of these behaviors in the objectively defined subcultures of the students might represent socialized deviance, which is to say (in the terms used here) no deviance at all. However, again, the data presented throughout this volume suggest that generally the behavior does indeed represent a contravention of the subjects' membership groups.

A discussion of the validity of the measure of deviant behavior must deal with two issues: (a) the question of whether the item content truly reflects instances of failure to conform to the normative expectations of a membership group because of the loss of motivation to conform or the acquisition of motivation to deviate and (b) the question of whether or not self-reports of behavior are adequate indices of the actual performance of the behaviors.

The first issue appears to be resolved by virtue of the observation of theoretical relationships based on the assumption that the self-report items are indeed deviant as defined earlier. If the items do reflect deviant behavior, then affirmative responses should be less in evidence for people who find satisfaction in and lack motivation to leave their membership groups (family, school) than for people who have had adverse experiences in and desire to leave these groups. Affirmative responses also should be less in evidence for those who do not anticipate greater gratification from contranormative than normative patterns. Finally, affirmative responses should be less in evidence among those who do not experience these items as standard responses in their environment. These relationships were in fact observed, as will become apparent in Chapter 6.

The second issue, regarding the relationship between self-reports of behavior and actual behavior, was addressed by considering the relationship between self-reports and reports made by others. For a variety of practical reasons, the only available external validating criterion was provided by reports made by vice-principals or school counselors about the students' behavior. Either the vice-principal or the appropriate grade school counselor in each school— whichever in the judgment of these personnel was best informed about the students—was asked to fill out a form that included the following instruction: "Based on available records or any other knowledge you may have of the student please indicate whether or not the student has done any of the following things during the preceding 12 months." The items referred to 24 of the 28 student self-report items. Excluded were "became angry and broke things," "used wine, beer, or liquor more than two times during the preceding week," "received a failing grade in one or more subjects," and "took part in social protest."

The forms were administered following the second student testing and referred to student behavior during the preceding 12 months—that is, the year between the first and second student testings. Three response categories were presented for each of the deviant behavior items: "Reasonably certain he (she) has done so"; "Suspect he (she) had done so"; "No reason to believe he (she) has done so."

The school personnel, with school administration permission, filled out the forms on their own time and received a fee based on the number of hours they spent. Each form carried a precoded identification number and was attached to a card that gave the name of the student. The form was filled out, and then the name card was removed.

These reports constitute a less than ideal validating criterion for a number of reasons, not the least significant of which is the general lack of familiarity with student behavior admitted to by those who made the reports. Data derivable from Table 2.6 indicate that appreciably fewer instances of student deviant responses were reported by the school personnel than were reported by the students. In addition, there was evidence that the care with which the forms were filled out was somewhat uneven. These limitations should be kept in mind in evaluating the findings that follow.

Table 2.6 summarizes the findings resulting from the comparison of student self-reports and school personnel reports of student deviant behavior. The following conclusions appear warranted. First, substantial portions of known instances of student deviant behavior reported by school personnel were also reported by the students. For 10 of the 24 items, at least 50% of the "known" instances were also self-reported. For an additional 10 items, between 30 and 50% of the known instances were self-reported. For the remaining four items, only 21 to 27% of the known instances were also reported by the students. Second, substantial portions of "known" instances of deviant behavior were unreported by students. Third, students were significantly and appreciably more likely to report deviant behavior in instances where the act was known to have occurred than in instances where no external knowledge of the act was said to have occurred (with the exception of cheating on exams). Conversely, student self-reports of deviant behavior were appreciable, and statistically more likely to be validated externally than were student denials of deviant behavior.

Using gamma as a measure of association, the association between student self-reports of deviant behavior and school personnel reports of student deviant behavior ranged from $-.02$ (cheated on exams) to .87 (was suspended or expelled from school). For 14 of the items, gamma was .50 or above.

Finally, most student self-reports of deviance were unsubstantiated, by virtue of the general lack of familiarity of the school personnel with student behavior. Thus, the extent of student overreporting cannot be evaluated.

On the basis of these observations, student self-reports were accepted as a rough and variable indicator of deviant behavior. The agreement for "other" and "self" reports was greatest for items referring to responses by the au-

TABLE 2.6

Proportion of Students Reporting Deviant Acts^{a,b} between T_1 and T_2, by Vice-Principal/Counselor Reports

Test item^c	All students^d		
	Has	May have	No knowledge
3. Took things worth between $2 and $50 (.40***)	.35 (51)	.20 (138)	.12 (4243)***
5. Was suspended or expelled from school (.87***)	.47 (314)	.22 (32)	.05 (4050)***
7. Took things worth less than $2 (.27***)	.45 (88)	.36 (248)	.27 (4059)***
10. Thought about or threatened to take own life (.57***)	1.00 (2)	.40 (15)	.18 (4388)**
11. Came in contact with police, sheriff, or juvenile officers (.55***)	.55 (31)	.23 (118)	.11 (4272)***
17. Carried a razor, switchblade, or gun as a weapon (.57***)	.50 (14)	.29 (58)	.12 (4310)***
24. Sold narcotic drugs (dope, heroin) (.69***)	.33 (12)	.15 (33)	.04 (4297)***
29. Cheated on exams (−.02)	.42 (106)	.40 (308)	.41 (3943)
31. Attempted suicide (.23)	1.00 (2)	.09 (32)	.10 (4365)***
33. Started a fistfight (.23**)	.25 (95)	.24 (139)	.17 (4124)*
38. Took narcotic drugs (.69***)	.60 (30)	.35 (110)	.11 (4189)***
44. Skipped school without an excuse (.59***)	.53 (324)	.28 (210)	.16 (3837)***
50. Took part in gang fights (.35**)	.21 (24)	.17 (81)	.10 (4287)*
56. Saw a psychiatrist, psychologist, or social worker (.62***)	.44 (25)	.10 (84)	.05 (4204)***
57. Used force to get money or valuables (.54***)	.30 (10)	.14 (72)	.05 (4284)***
61. Broke into and entered a home, store, or building (.55***)	.60 (10)	.07 (60)	.05 (4287)***
64. Damaged or destroyed public or private property on purpose (.37***)	.27 (26)	.15 (181)	.09 (4130)***

(*Continued*)

thorities (suspension or expulsion from school; contact with police, sheriff, or juvenile officers; being sent to a psychiatrist, psychologist, or social worker; being taken to the office for punishment), for items referring to drug abuse and traffic (selling narcotic drugs, using narcotic drugs, smoking marijuana), for selected items generally accepted as instances of delinquent behavior (carrying a razor, switchblade, or gun as a weapon; using force to get money or valuables; breaking and entering; and stealing things worth $50 or more), and for other items that may be less widely accepted as instances of deviant responses (suicidal ideation or gestures; skipping school without an excuse; participating in a strike, riot, or demonstration). The variable degrees of agreement should be considered in interpreting the findings to be presented in subsequent chapters.

Test item[c]	All students[d]		
	Has	May have	No knowledge
68. Was taken to the office for punishment (.69***)	.62 (1020)	.37 (60)	.22 (3241)***
69. Stole things from someone else's desk or locker (.20*)	.23 (43)	.20 (194)	.15 (4138)*
72. Used a car without the owner's permission (.47***)	.50 (4)	.12 (48)	.06 (4297)***
75. Beat up someone who did nothing to them (.29*)	.32 (19)	.10 (90)	.08 (4249)***
78. Took things worth $50 or more (.57***)	.30 (10)	.09 (44)	.04 (4305)***
82. Smoked marijuana (.76***)	.74 (39)	.50 (153)	.14 (4127)***
84. Participated in strike, riot, or demonstration (.73***)	.43 (7)	.25 (48)	.06 (4235)***

[a] Part of this table, drawn from Table 2 of "Self-attitudes and Deviant Response," by Howard B. Kaplan, is reprinted with stylistic changes from *Social Forces*, 1976, 54 (4), pp. 788–801, by permission of the publisher, the University of North Carolina Press.

[b] Data were not collected from vice-principals or student counselors regarding four modes of deviant response for which student self-report data are available: getting angry and breaking things, using alcohol, getting failing grades, and participating in social protest.

[c] Number in parentheses is gamma for association between school personnel and student reports of deviant behavior. Asterisks indicate significance levels of gamma: $^*p < .05$; $^{**}p < .01$; $^{***}p < .001$.

[d] Categories refer to reports from vice-principals or student counselors of deviant behavior. First number indicates proportion of students in the cell admitting to the behavior. Number in parentheses indicates cell N. Asterisks indicate significant χ^2 relationship between vice-principal/counselor and student reports of deviant behaviors: $^*p < .05$; $^{**}p < .01$; $^{***}p < .001$.

The results of the foregoing analysis generally were consistent with the observations of others. Farrington (1973, p. 102) has observed that "whatever combination or variety, frequency, and seriousness of deviant behavior has been used constructing self-report scores, they have usually been significantly associated with appearances in official records." This is in accordance with the assertion that self-reports and official records are both measures of deviant behavior, although they are subject to different biases. In this connection Farrington cites the work of Erickson and Empey (1963), Gibson, Morrison, and West (1970), Gold (1966), and Hirschi (1969). Concurrent validity has also been estimated by Clark and Tifft (1966), who used a polygraph criterion to estimate the honesty represented in self-reports. They concluded that 92% of self-reports were given honestly and that concealment was three times as common as exaggeration among the remainder. As Farrington (1973) notes, however, honest responses may still be objectively incorrect as a result of such factors as forgetfulness. Furthermore, the validity of the polygraph is itself problematic. Concurrent validity has been tested using reports of others. Gold (1966), using data given by informants about offenses committed by others and self-reports, classified 72% of these others as truth tellers, 11% as questionables, and 17% as concealers. Jessor and co-workers reported self-reports of deviant behavior to be correlated significantly with reports by teachers and peers (Jessor, Graves, Hanson, & Jessor, 1968). In general, then, self-reports by a variety of methods appear to be concurrently valid. Farrington (1973), using data from the Cambridge Study in Delinquent Development (a long-term follow-up study of a sample of 411 normal schoolboys first contacted at ages 8–9), reported both predictive and concurrent validity (by a criterion of official delinquency) for a self-report delinquency scale. The relationship between self-report scores and prediction of official delinquency could not be accounted for by their common relationship to some other predictive factor. At virtually all levels of low income, large families, separation, criminal parents, poor supervision, low attainment, and lower intelligence, self-reports of delinquency were predictive of official delinquency. However, though these tests showed good test-retest reliability over a few weeks, retesting after a 2-year period showed that a quarter of all initial admissions turned into denials (Farrington, 1973).

This last finding is corroborated by certain of the data presented in Table 2.5. For three of the items (5, 11, 56) the time reference was "ever" at each test administration. Therefore, for these items it could be determined the extent to which initial affirmations turned into subsequent denials of the items, and at least 60% of those who initially affirmed the item (at T_1) subsequently denied it (at T_2). It is noteworthy, however, that these items all refer to coming to the attention of others in ways in which "offenses" would become part of the record—a circumstance that might increase the disposition to deny the offense as the subject matured. Whether or not responses to the other items would be similarly unreliable is problematic.

OTHER SCALES

In addition to the strategic measures of self-attitudes and deviant behaviors, a number of other variables were considered as antecedents and/or consequences of these factors, and as conditions for the mutual interaction among these variables. With the exceptions noted, these measures were derived by Principal Components factor analyses with the factors rotated to the normalized varimax criterion of orthogonal simple structure. Where applicable, the orthogonally rotated factor loadings for each item are presented parenthetically. These scales will be described in detail at the point in the volume where they first appear in the analysis.

Analysis

For the most part the tests of hypotheses comprising the general theory of deviant behavior tested in this volume employ contingency analysis and comparison of subgroup means with significance of difference between means generally determined by a t test (one-tailed) assuming unequal variances (Welch, 1947).

Since statistical and (frequently) substantively stated theory leads to the expectation that initial values influence the magnitude of observed change over time, with few exceptions change in a given variable was measured by a residual change score. A gain is residualized "by expressing the posttest score as a deviation from the posttest-on-pretest regression line [Cronbach & Furby, 1970, p. 68]." The raw residual change in a variable between the first and second testing (Rch 1–2) scores is defined as

$$Rch\ 1\text{--}2 = Y - \overline{Y} - (\beta y \cdot x\ [X - \overline{X}])$$

where

Y = time = 2 score;
$\overline{Y}$ = mean time = 2 score;
X = times = 1 score;
$\overline{X}$ = mean time = 1 score;
$\beta y \cdot x$ = the regression coefficient, $r_{yx}\ (\sigma y / \sigma x)$.

The effect of residualizing is to remove "from the posttest score, and hence from the gain, the portion that could have been predicted linearly from pretest status. . . . The residualized score is primarily a way of singling out individuals who changed more or less than expected [Cronbach & Furby, 1970, p. 74]." The use of residual gain measure thus makes less tenable any argument that would account for observed differential rates of change in terms of variable baseline measures.

The details of the analyses will be described immediately preceding the tests of the various hypotheses, the results of which now follow.

Part II

Results

Chapter 3

Prevalence of the Self-esteem Motive

The postulated prevalence of the self-esteem motive is a basic premise of the general theory under consideration as well as of a number of other theories. Surprisingly, however, there have been few systematic attempts to provide empirical justification for the postulate. To be sure, a good deal of data have been reported that are interpretable as providing support for the prevalence of the self-esteem motive. Unfortunately such findings have tended to be derived from studies of uneven methodological merit and/or have tended to be reported as the by-product of the tests of other hypotheses rather than as the result of conscious intent to consider support for the postulate. In any case, any one study contributed no more than a few results which were interpretable as support for the prevalence of the self-esteem motive, and these admitted of alternative explanations. Within the context of the same study, a broader range of independent findings, each of which implied the prevalence of the self-esteem motive, would have provided firmer support even if each finding considered separately were interpretable as permitting alternative explanations.

The assertion that the need to avoid self-rejecting attitudes and to achieve self-acceptance is universally a characteristically human motive implies (*a*) that a low level of self-esteem is a subjectively distressful state, and increasingly higher levels of self-acceptance are associated with states having less stress; (*b*) that people will tend to behave in ways that increase the subjective probability of experiencing self-accepting attitudes and decrease the subjective probability of experiencing self-rejecting attitudes; (*c*) that more self-rejecting subjects, being further removed from the goal of self-acceptance, will be more highly motivated than more self-accepting individuals to behave in ways calculated to increase experiences of self-acceptance and reduce experiences of self-rejection; (*d*) that persons who behave in ways calculated to increase experiences of self-accepting attitudes and to reduce the experience of self-rejection will be more likely to reduce their level of self-rejection and increase their level of self-acceptance than persons who do not so behave; and (e) that persons characterized by self-accepting attitudes will be relatively common whereas those characterized by self-rejection will be relatively rare.

Since these implications were translatable into testable hypotheses, consistent empirical support for the broad range of implications were expected to provide a firm empirical foundation for the postulate that persons characteristically need to avoid the experience of negative self-attitudes and to maintain or restore the experience of positive self-attitudes. Furthermore, the credibility of these findings as empirical support for the postulate would be appreciably greater than that of previously existing data, since (a) many of the methodological deficits of earlier studies would have been avoided, (b) the hypotheses were formulated and tested for the expressed purpose (among others) of considering the tenability of the postulated prevalence of the self-esteem motive, and (c) several implications of the postulate were considered in the context of the same research project.

Each of the hypotheses translating one or more of the implications of the postulated prevalence of the self-esteem motive into testable form will be considered in turn.

Change in Self-rejection

The first hypothesis implied by the postulated prevalence of the self-esteem motive asserts that the subjects who were present for all three testings would manifest a significant decrease in mean level of self-derogation from the first to the second testing, and from the second to the third testing. It was reasoned that if a self-esteem motive was prevalent people would be motivated to behave in ways that would be expected to enhance self-attitudes. It was further expected that individuals who (stimulated by the self-esteem motive) in fact behaved in ways calculated to raise their levels of self-esteem (or lower their levels of self-rejection) would be more likely to experience a decrease in self-rejection than people who were not so stimulated and did not in fact behave in such ways. (The "ways of behaving" calculated to enhance self-attitudes will be considered later in greater detail.)

The tendency for the self-attitudes of specified groupings to change over time has been noted in a number of studies. Engel (1959) tested and retested 2 years later 172 public-school students, of whom 104 were in the eighth grade and 68 were in the tenth grade at the time of the first testing. She observed that for both sexes and grade levels students increased in mean positiveness on a self-concept, Q-sort paper-and-pencil form. However, with the sexes combined, the shift in a positive direction was significant only for the older group. Nickols (1963), 3 years following the first testing, retested 22 high-school freshmen and observed that self-ratings were significantly higher for the senior year. In a third study, Clifford and Clifford (1967) reported a significant change in self-ratings in a positive direction over a 1-month period for 36 adolescent boys enrolled in an Outward Bound School summer camp. Finally, data from the Youth in Transition study (Bachman, 1970; Bachman *et al.*, 1967, 1971) for 1374 boys who stayed in the same public high schools through their sophomore to senior years indicated increasing mean self-esteem scores over three points in time: time 1; time 2, 18 months later; and time 3, 12 months after time 2 (T. N. Davidson, 1972, p. 28).

Thus, several studies dealing with samples of variable size and representativeness apparently agree in the observation that over variable intervals (ranging from 1 month to 3 years) self-attitudes, variably measured, on the average become increasingly positive. The results of the present study, based on data collected from a large sample at three points in time over a 3-year period, provide further support for the postulated prevalence of the self-esteem motive.

An examination of the first row of Table 3.1 reveals that students present for all three test administrations showed a decrease in self-rejecting attitudes over time. The mean self-derogation score declined from 37.18 at the first testing to 32.63 and 29.38 at the second and third testings respectively. The t-test comparisons between correlated means for adjacent administrations (T_1, T_2 and T_2, T_3) were significant ($p < .001$).

These findings, as well as those just reviewed, are interpreted as support for the self-esteem motive only on the assumption that the decreases in self-rejection (or the increases in positive self-attitudes) over time can be accounted for in terms of the individual's own behaviors stimulated by the self-esteem motive. It was reasoned that if a self-esteem motive was prevalent, then people would behave in ways calculated to increase levels of self-esteem and decrease levels of self-rejection, and so behaving would have some degree of success in achieving their goals. Nevertheless, a decrease in self-derogation could conceivably occur for reasons other than the motivated behavior of the subjects. The most noteworthy of these reasons are those relating to the possible increasingly benign effects of the environment on self-attitudes during the periods in question. Does the environment have such benign outcomes, perhaps by decreasing the levels of expectations and other potential threats to self-esteem, increasing the number of possible routes to self-esteem, or increasing the range of interpersonal supports that might function to assuage the impact of self-devaluing circumstances? If so, the observation of increasingly positive (decreasingly negative) self-attitudes over time could not properly be interpreted as necessarily indicative of a prevalent self-esteem motive. Another possibility is that increasingly positive self-attitudes over time are a consequence of maturational changes rather than effective behavioral responses in the services of the self-esteem motive.

TABLE 3.1

Mean Self-derogation Scores for the First (T_1), Second (T_2), and Third (T_3) Test Administrations, by Self-derogation Level at T_1 for Students Present at All Three Test Administrations[a,b,c]

Category	T_1	T_2	T_3
All students			
$\bar{X}$	37.18	32.63	29.38
SD	26.59	27.90	27.57
N	3127	3011	3090
Students with low (0–20) self-derogation scores			
$\bar{X}$	10.00	20.24	19.19
SD	9.17	23.13	23.20
N	1213	1178	1200
Students with medium (21–50) self-derogation scores			
$\bar{X}$	39.95	33.42	29.21
SD	7.64	25.53	25.46
N	1030	990	1013
Students with high (above 50) self-derogation scores			
$\bar{X}$	71.28	49.03	43.50
SD	11.51	27.98	29.17
N	884	843	877

[a] This table, drawn from "The Self-esteem Motive and Change in Self-attitudes," by Howard B. Kaplan, is reprinted with stylistic changes from *The Journal of Nervous and Mental Disease*, 1975, *161* (4), pp. 265–275, by permission of the publisher, Williams & Wilkins.

[b] All *t*-test comparisons between correlated means for adjacent administrations are significant at $p < .001$ with one exception: the comparison between T_2 and T_3 mean self-derogation scores for students with low initial self-derogation scores.

[c] N varies across time intervals because of occasional missing self-derogation data.

These alternative explanations were considered by examining characteristic levels of and changes in self-evaluation associated with particular ages or grade levels in cross-sectional studies. Since the same subjects were not followed over time, any observed associations between grade or age on the one hand and self-attitudes on the other could be attributed to environmental or age-related maturational changes or perhaps, unfortunately, to biases resulting from the underrepresentation of certain types of students (such as dropouts) in the older age groups.

A consideration of these studies, however, leads to the conclusion that any observed changes in self-evaluation that might be attributed to these causes were not compatible with the observed tendency (in this as well as studies previously reviewed) for adolescents observed at different points in time to have, on the average, increasingly positive self-attitudes. Such grade- or age-related changes in self-attitudes, therefore, must be (at least partly) independent of this tendency. For example, observations of a stabilization of self-ideal congruence from age 13 through age 18 following a decrease in self-ideal congruence between age 8 and age 12 (Jorgensen & Howell, 1969), and a downward trend in self-ratings on a merit factor from the sixth through eighth grades with a recovery in the ninth grade (Yamamoto, Thomas, & Karns, 1969), are not congruent with the increasingly positive attitudes from grades 8 through 10, 10 through 12, and 7 through 9 that were observed in the present study or in the other studies reviewed. Such compatibility would have been noted if the increasingly positive attitudes were to be accounted for in terms of age- or grade-related factors. That is, a trend toward increased positiveness of self-attitudes with increasing grade or age should have been noted if correlates of age and grade are to account for all of the observed improvements in self-attitudes. Rather, the relationships between age or grade and self-derogation noted, as well as the results of studies to be mentioned later in conjunction with the noted tendencies for the same individuals to improve in self-attitudes over time, suggest that a generalized need for self-acceptance is indeed operative; however, the extent to which the self-esteem motive is satisfied will be a function of other factors, including environmental and maturational concomitants of particular times of life. In any case, the observed decrease in self-rejection over three points in time covering a 3-year interval is compatible with the postulated prevalence of a self-esteem motive.

Initial Self-attitudes and Subsequent Change

The second hypothesis implied by the postulated prevalence of the self-esteem motive asserts that persons with initially more negative self-attitudes subsequently would manifest significantly greater decreases in self-rejecting attitudes than subjects with initially less negative self-attitudes. It was reasoned that, if the self-esteem motive was indeed prevalent, those individuals with more negative self-attitudes would be more highly motivated than those with less negative self-attitudes to behave in ways calculated to decrease the experience of self-rejecting attitudes, since the former were further removed from their goal of experiencing self-accepting attitudes. Insofar as the initially more self-rejecting persons were more motivated to so behave, they indeed would be more likely to behave in ways expected to have self-enhancing outcomes and, thereby, would be more likely to display such outcomes.

This hypothesis was consistent with certain of the findings from studies cited earlier. Clifford and Clifford (1967), in addition to noting the significant change in self-ratings over a 1-month period in a positive direction, also noted that most of the change was accounted for by those adolescent boys with the initially poorer self-ratings. Engel (1959), reporting on change in self-concept of eighth- and tenth-graders over a 2-year period, reported that the students who were said to have negative self-concepts at the initial measurement more closely approached the mean 2 years later; the subjects whose self-concepts were originally positive showed no such shifting toward the mean. The greater tendency of self-rejecting subjects to change in a positive direction is even more clearly demonstrated by these results: Although 55% of those whose self-concepts were initially negative shifted to a positive self-concept by more than 20 points, only 16% of those in the initially positive group shifted to a negative self-concept by more than 20 points.

In the present study the hypothesis was tested by comparing initially (at T_1) low, medium, and high self-derogation groupings with regard to mean change in self-derogation over the 1-year intervals T_1-T_2 and T_2-T_3, and the 2-year interval T_1-T_3. The initial self-derogation groupings were composed by arbitrary division of the self-derogation scores into three intervals: 0–20 (low), 21–50 (medium), and above 50 (high). Change in self-attitudes was measured as the arithmetic difference between self-derogation scores at the later and earlier points in time, with negative scores indicating a decrease in self-derogation and positive scores indicating an increase.

The results are summarized in Table 3.2, where the mean change scores (along with standard deviations and Ns) of the low, medium, and high self-derogation groupings for each of the time intervals under consideration are presented. As expected, for each of the time intervals the high self-derogation grouping showed the greatest decrease in self-derogation, followed in order by the medium and low self-derogation groupings. For each time interval the paired comparisons between the three groupings (high versus medium, high versus low, medium versus low), with regard to mean change in self-derogation, were both appreciable and significant ($p < .001$), with one exception. For the T_2-T_3 period, the initially high self-derogation grouping, although consistent with the hypothesis in showing a greater decrease in self-derogation, did not differ *significantly* in this regard from the initially medium self-derogation grouping.

Over the 2-year period T_1-T_3, the initially high self-derogation group showed a decrease in self-derogation of 27.70; the medium self-derogation grouping showed a decrease of 10.67; and the low self-derogation grouping showed an *increase* of 9.16. The bulk of the change occurred during the first period (T_1-T_2), with the high group showing a decrease of 22.30, the medium grouping showing a decrease of 6.44, and the low group showing an increase of 10.27—although, as has been noted, the same ordering was observed for the T_2-T_3 period with the initially most self-derogating grouping showing the greatest decrease and the least self-derogating grouping showing the lowest decrease.

Thus, the data were consistent with the hypothesis insofar as for all time periods (T_1-T_2, T_2-T_3, T_1-T_3) the most self-rejecting group showed the greatest subsequent decrease in self-rejecting attitudes.

46

TABLE 3.2

Mean Change in Self-derogation between First (T_1), Second (T_2), and Third (T_3) Test Administrations, by Self-derogation Grouping at T_1[a]

	Self-derogation change[b,c]		
	T_1-T_2	T_2-T_3	T_1-T_3
Total			
$\bar{X}$	−4.35	−3.24	−7.80
SD	28.40	26.34	29.80
N	3011	2979	3090
Low self-derogation (0–20)			
$\bar{X}$	10.27[d]	−1.04	9.16
SD	22.92	24.31	23.20
N	1178	1167	1200
Medium self-derogation (21–50)			
$\bar{X}$	−6.44	−4.34	−10.67
SD	25.58	26.64	25.33
N	990	975	1013
High self-derogation (above 50)			
$\bar{X}$	−22.30	−5.04	−27.70
SD	27.30	28.39	29.19
N	843	837	877

[a] This table, drawn from "The Self-esteem Motive and Change in Self-attitudes," by Howard B. Kaplan, is reprinted with stylistic changes from *The Journal of Nervous and Mental Disease*, 1975, *161* (4), pp. 265–275, by permission of the publisher, William & Wilkins.

[b] Negative sign indicates *decrease* in self-derogation.

[c] N varies across change intervals because of occasional missing self-derogation data.

[d] All paired comparisons, t test assuming unequal variances (Welch, 1947), between self-derogation groupings for each change interval are significant at the $p < .001$ level with one exception: medium and high self-derogation subjects do not differ significantly in self-derogation change T_2-T_3.

However, some troublesome issues remain that cause the interpretation of these data as support for the postulated prevalence of the self-esteem motive to be equivocal. The first issue relates to the question of whether or not the observed increase in self-derogation from T_1 to T_2 by the initially low self-derogation grouping is consistent with the postulated self-esteem motive. The second question (possibly related to the first, insofar as the increase might be accounted for in terms of regression effects) concerns whether or not the observed changes were "real" ones rather than consequences of the measurement process. This question is considered in analyses involving the use of residual gain scores and stability coefficients over variable time intervals. A third question concerns the implication of the hypothesis for ultimate parity in level of self-acceptance between the initially different self-derogation groupings. Each of these issues will be considered in turn.

INCREASED SELF-DEROGATION BY SUBJECTS LOW IN SELF-REJECTION

Assuming that the increase in self-rejection from T_1 to T_2 is not the consequence of regression effects (this will be considered subsequently), does the observed change speak against the existence of the self-esteem motive? Should not individuals low in self-rejection manifest some decrease in self-rejection over time (or at worst no change) on the postulate of the self-esteem motive, although the change would be less than that shown by initially more self-rejecting individuals? The position taken here is that this observation is indeed consistent with the operation of the self-esteem motive if certain other factors are taken into account. The increase in self-derogation on the part of the initially less self-rejecting persons could be accounted for by the occurrence of life experiences with self-devaluing implications that accompany the age and/or grade during which the increased self-rejection was noted.

That such life experiences do accompany entry into seventh grade and/or the age of 13 (the modal age of our seventh-grade students) is suggested by data from a number of studies, some of which have already been cited. Yamamoto and associates (1969), it will be recalled, noted a decrease in evaluation of "myself" on a merit factor from the seventh grade through the eighth (and an increase from the eighth through ninth grades). Although Jorgensen and Howell (1969) noted a stabilization of self-ideal congruence from age 13 through age 18 (following a decrease in self-ideal congruence between ages 8 and 12), it is possible to discern in their data a slight decrease in self-ideal congruence between ages 13 and 14, and a slight increase from age 14 to age 15. These two studies reveal a pattern that is similar to that observed for the initially low self-derogation grouping in the present study, characterized as it was by an increase in self-derogation from the seventh to eighth grades and a slight decrease in self-derogation between the eighth and ninth grades. Also consistent with this pattern was the report by Simmons and her associates that subjects aged 12 to 14 show somewhat lower global self-esteem than subjects aged 15 and older. (Simmons, Rosenberg, & Rosenberg, 1973). These authors also cite findings by Offer (1969) that older adolescents and their parents perceive ages 12–14 as the period of greatest turmoil in their lives.

These findings are compatible with the conclusion that factors associated with this period in life are threatening to the adolescent's self-image. These factors may include the onset of puberty, entry into junior high school with its attendant impersonality, shifting social relationships, expectations that the adolescent behave more responsibly and independently, and the need to make initial career decisions (Simmons *et al.*, 1973). Simmons and her associates suggest that environmental changes (entry into junior high school) may have greater impact on the self-image than age maturation, since the 12-year-old subjects in junior high school tended to have lower global self-esteem than children of the same age in elementary school. No comparable changes were observed between 11- and 12-year-olds in the sixth grade or between 12- and 13-year-olds in the seventh grade. Similar adverse effects of environmental changes upon self-attitudes might account for the observation that high-school upperclassmen showed greater self-ideal congruence than did college under-classmen (Hess & Bradshaw, 1970). Whether environmental factors and/or age maturation play a part, life circumstances associated with the period following entry into the seventh grade appear to affect self-attitudes adversely.

These studies then suggest that the failure to observe a slight enhancement of, or no change in, self-attitudes during the seventh grade for the initially most accepting subjects (as might have been expected otherwise on the assumption of the self-esteem motive) is accounted for by the occurrence of circumstances with self-devaluing implications that are associated with the period in life under consideration. Why, then, did the most self-rejecting segment of the population not succumb to these same self-devaluing implications? Again, based on the postulated prevalence of the self-esteem motive, it is argued that this segment of the population is more highly motivated to behave in ways that decrease the experience of self-rejecting attitudes (including behavior that serves to defend against any threats to self-attitudes associated with puberty and/or entry into junior high school). Indeed, were it not for the countervailing effects of these events, the decrease in self-rejection noted for this group might have been even greater. The initially more self-accepting adolescents, on the other hand, being therefore less strongly motivated to behave in ways that would reduce the experience of self-rejecting feelings, were more likely to be adversely affected by the self-devaluing implications of the events associated with this time of life. In effect, the greater degree of self-acceptance of these subjects made it less pressing for them to defend against the adverse consequences of these events for self-attitudes.

Consistent with this conclusion are findings reported by Tippett and Silber (1966). In this study, college students were exposed to fictitious research staff evaluations involving the alteration of subject self-ratings on selected items in a "less favorable but plausible direction." Those students who were evaluated as having *high self-esteem*, less psychopathology, and more autonomous behavior with parents tended to change in the direction of the fictitious unfavorable ratings *more* than the subjects assessed as having *low* self-esteem, more psychopathology, and oppositional behavior with parents. The latter subjects were said to be less open to influence—a resistance apparently "based more on negativism than on considered reflection [Tippett & Silber, 1966, p. 384]." Also, these authors, observing that the low self-esteem subjects tended to change in a negative direction *more* than the high self-esteem subjects *on the unaltered items,* speculated: "It is as though being challenged in one area leads to a more generalized disturbance in their function of self-evaluation [Tippett & Silber, 1966, p. 384]." These observations may adumbrate the vulnerability of initially low self-esteem subjects to long-term self-rejection following initial decreases in self-rejection attributable to activation of the self-esteem motive. This issue will be considered subsequently in greater detail.

In any case, the considerations introduced here suggest plausible reasons for observing a unique increase in self-derogation between the seventh and eighth grades on the part of the initially most self-accepting grouping of subjects, and these reasons do not necessarily speak against the prevalence of the self-esteem motive. The data are consistent with the view that these subjects, by virtue of their greater initial self-acceptance, were less motivated to employ self-protective strategies and thus were to a degree adversely influenced by the self-threatening changes associated with environmental changes and/or the onset of puberty. The initially more self-rejecting subjects, on the other hand, were more highly motivated (assuming the self-esteem motive) to employ self-enhancing strategies and were able (by virtue of the more intensely felt self-esteem motive) to employ self-enhancing strategies that functioned not only to resist the self-devaluing influences associated with the seventh-grade period but also to *decrease* their level of self-rejection over the same period.

"REAL" CHANGE VERSUS MEASUREMENT ARTIFACT

The question of whether the differential changes in self-derogation noted for the initially high, medium, and low self-derogation groupings represent "real" changes or are artifacts of the measurement process will be considered with reference to adjustment for regression effects and examination of stability coefficients over variable time intervals.

In the analyses presented in Table 3.2, subjects whose initial self-derogation scores were high were observed to manifest substantially greater subsequent decreases in self-derogation than did initially less self-rejecting subjects. The same relationship might have been expressed in terms of correlations between earlier self-derogation scores and the raw changes (arithmetic differences between later and earlier scores) in self-derogation. Thus, considering all subjects providing data at both T_1 and T_2 ($N = 4489$), the correlation between T_1 self-derogation and change in self-derogation T_1-T_2 was $-.49$. Considering all subjects providing data at both T_2 and T_3 ($N = 3045$), the correlation between T_2 self-derogation and change in self-derogation T_2-T_3 was $-.48$. Considering all subjects providing data at both T_1 and T_3 ($N = 3737$), the correlation between T_1 self-derogation and change in self-derogation T_1-T_3 was $-.53$.

These observations are what would be expected from proceeding on the premise that the self-esteem motive is prevalent. The individuals who are more highly motivated to increase self-esteem (that is, the initially most self-rejecting) display the greatest subsequent decrease. Unfortunately these results are also congruent with the generally noted negative correlation between a score at a given point in time and subsequent change in the score so that the higher the initial score the greater the negative change observed over a subsequent period (Bohrnstedt, 1969; T. N. Davidson, 1972). Whenever a variable is less than perfectly correlated with itself at two points in time, regression toward the mean may be expected. That is, extreme scores based on the arithmetic difference between T_2 and T_1 scores then imply that a person with a higher initial score will have a greater probability of having a lower subsequent score and, therefore, a negative raw gain. Davidson (1972, pp. 97–98) presents calculations showing that in the usual case where T_1 and T_2 scores have approximately equal variances change from T_1 to T_2 on a given variable will be negatively correlated with initial scores.

The question then is whether the observed tendency of initially more self-derogating subjects to show greater subsequent decreases in self-derogation than initially less self-derogating subjects (and, for that matter, for initially less self-derogating subjects to show greater subsequent increases in self-derogation than initially more self-derogating subjects) may be accounted for wholly in terms of regression effects or at least partly in terms of some other factor, independent of regression effects—presumably the differential strength of the self-esteem motive. The "regression effects" explanation may not be ruled out completely. Reference to Table 3.1 will reveal that the mean self-derogation scores of the initially low, medium, and high self-derogation subgroupings more closely approximate the population mean with the passage of time. That is, as one proceeds from T_1 to T_2 to T_3 the arithmetic difference between each subgroup and the total population with regard to mean self-derogation score at the same point in time decreases.

One approach to determining whether the initial level of self-derogation as an indicator of the strength of the self-esteem motive influences subsequent decreases in self-rejection uses residualized gain scores. Residualizing, it will be recalled from Chapter 2, removes from the change that portion of the change that might have been predicted from the score at the earlier point in time. If a comparison of the three initial self-derogation groupings revealed the same ordering with regard to subsequent residualized gain scores as it did with regard to raw gain scores—with the initially most self-derogating grouping manifesting the greatest subsequent decrease in self-derogation—then some support would be gained for the position that initial level of self-derogation (implying differential strength of the self-esteem motive) exercises an influence upon subsequent change in self-attitudes independent of regression effects.

Such an analysis was in fact carried out using a raw residual gain score computed in the fashion described in Chapter 2. The decision was made, however, to exclude from this analysis those subjects who were under relatively severe situational stress. It was reasoned that under conditions of such severe stress the influence of the self-esteem motive upon subsequent decreases in self-rejection would be obscured. Regardless of initial self-derogation level, uniformly greater than expected increases in self-derogation would be likely to occur because the experience of stress implies a *uniform* absence of self-protective devices. On the other hand, in the absence of severe stress, the greater motivation of the more self-rejecting subjects to employ whatever self-enhancing strategies were available to them would be expected to result in greater subsequent decreases in self-derogation relative to that experienced by initially less self-rejecting subjects.

For the purpose of this analysis severe situational stress was said to be absent if subjects denied thinking about or threatening to take their own lives during the month preceding the first testing and during the year intervening between the first and second testings. Among such "nonsuicidal subjects" it was expected that, for either the 1-year interval between T_1 and T_2 or the 2-year interval between T_1 and T_3, the initially high self-derogation grouping would show the greatest residualized decreases in self-derogation followed in order by the initially medium and low self-derogation groupings. The results of this analysis are summarized in Table 3.3.

Referring to the first and third columns in Table 3.3, it will be observed that, as expected for both T_1-T_2 and T_1-T_3 (the T_2-T_3 period will be considered later in another connection), the initially high self-derogation subjects showed the greatest residualized decreases (or the smallest residualized increases) in self-derogation followed in order by the medium and low self-derogation groupings. For the T_1-T_2 period the difference between the high grouping on the one hand and the low and medium groupings on the other was significant ($p <$ .001). The difference between the low and medium groupings was not significant but was in the hypothesized order. For the T_1-T_3 period the high ($p < .01$) and medium ($p < .05$) groupings manifested significantly greater decreases than the low grouping. Although the difference between the high and medium groupings was not significant, again, they were ordered as hypothesized.

In summary, then, these data support the position that initially higher self-rejection is related to subsequent decrease in self-rejection independently of regression effects, a relationship that is consistent with the postulate of the self-esteem motive.

A related approach to the question of whether or not "real" changes in self-derogation have occurred uses stability coefficients—correlations between self-derogation scores at earlier and later points in time—covering variable time intervals. To the extent that the correlations are less than perfect, some reordering of the subjects on self-derogation must have occurred. The question is whether or not such reordering (less than perfect stability) reflects unreliability in the measuring instrument and/or real changes along the dimension under

TABLE 3.3

Mean Residualized Changes in Self-derogation, T_1-T_2, T_2-T_3, T_1-T_3, by T_1 Level of Self-derogation for Subjects Denying Suicidal Ideation and Threats at T_1 and T_2

| | Residualized change in self-derogation[a] | | | | | | | | |
| | T_1-T_2 | | | T_2-T_3 | | | T_1-T_3 | | |
T_1 self-derogation level	Low	Medium	High	Low	Medium	High	Low	Medium	High
$\bar{X}^b$	-1.76	-2.39	-6.41	-3.74	-1.21	4.36	-0.36	-2.67	-4.07
SD	20.82	23.90	25.87	20.03	22.73	25.55	21.97	24.56	27.97
N	1428[c]	1085	761	1005	734	517	1034	757	540

[a] One-tailed test assuming unequal variances (Welch, 1947) indicated the following significant comparisons: For T_1-T_2: low versus high, $p < .001$; medium versus high, $p < .001$. For T_2-T_3: low versus medium, $p < .01$; low versus high, $p < .001$; medium versus high, $p < .001$. For T_1-T_3: low versus medium, $p < .05$; low versus high, $p < .01$.

[b] Negative signs indicate greater than expected decreases (or less than expected increases) in self-derogation over the period indicated. Positive signs indicate greater than expected increases (or less than expected decreases) in self-derogation over the period indicated.

[c] Analyses were conducted for all nonsuicidal subjects present for the two points of time indicated.

consideration. T. N. Davidson (1972, pp. 32–34) observes that having data from three points in time helps make the distinction.

Thinking of an observed score as consisting of a true score and random measurement error, Davidson (1972) assumed a normal distribution of the error components around a zero mean, and the absence of correlation between the error components and the true score. He also assumed that the error components are uncorrelated across time. He then reasoned that if no true changes were occurring over time the observed correlations would vary from unity as a result of variation in the error component, *but* since the error components are said to be uncorrelated across time the score correlations *should not vary with the length of the interval.* However, if real change were occurring, lower stability coefficients for longer intervals and higher stability coefficients for shorter periods would be expected, because when real change occurs more changing is expected over longer periods of time. In effect, there would be more opportunity for change over longer periods. Davidson (1972, p. 33) examined the stability coefficients for 18 criteria over three intervals of varying length for 1374 boys who stayed in the same public high schools from their sophomore to senior years. One of these criteria was a self-esteem measure. The data were consistent with the conclusion that some real change (independent of a less than perfect reliability in the measure) in self-esteem was occurring over time: The highest stability coefficient (.66) was observed for the shortest period of time (T_2–T_3, 12 months) and the lowest stability coefficient (.49) was observed over the longest period of time (T_1–T_3, 30 months). The third stability coefficient (.54), for the time interval T_1–T_2 (18 months, falling between the other two in length) fell between the other two stability coefficients.

Similar results were observed in this study. For subjects present at all testings, the stability coefficients for the self-derogation measure were higher for the two 1-year intervals (.46 for T_1–T_2, .55 for T_2–T_3) than for the 2-year interval T_1–T_3 (.40), again consistent with the conclusion that real change was occurring independent of that resulting from unreliability in the measuring instrument. The difference in magnitude of stability coefficients observed for the two 1-year intervals will be considered later.

Together, the results presented in this section should lend further credibility to the conclusion that the differential decreases in self-derogation over time experienced by subjects in the initially low, medium, and high self-derogation groups reflect, in part, consequences of differential strength of the self-esteem motive and are not solely artifacts of the measurement process.

IMPLICATIONS FOR PARITY IN SELF-ATTITUDES

We have the hypothesis that over a given period of time subjects having initially high self-derogation show greater decreases in self-derogation. Does this hypothesis necessarily imply that during subsequent periods these subjects will continue to manifest greater decreases in self-derogation until ultimate parity in self-attitudes with initially less self-derogating subjects is achieved? If so, does the observation in the present study that, relative to the T_1-T_2 changes, the T_2-T_3 changes appear to be approximately parallel slopes necessarily fail to support the hypothesis and, thus, the postulated prevalence of the self-esteem motive? The answer is no to both questions. The postulate of the self-esteem motive implies that the more self-rejecting individuals at a given point in time, relative to less self-rejecting persons, will be more highly motivated to behave in ways calculated to reduce self-rejecting feelings, and will be more likely to so behave with some degree of effectiveness. What benign effects on self-attitudes these behaviors have are likely to be observed during the period following high motivation to produce such effects—that is, following high levels of self-rejection. However, such effects will necessarily be limited. With the passage of time, the initial reduction of self-rejecting feelings through the use of whatever personal and external resources are available to the individual will be accompanied by a reduction of the *need* for self-enhancing outcomes as well as the reduction of the *capability* of further self-enhancement, insofar as the subject will already have expended the resources available to him. Thus with the passage of time the initially self-rejecting person will cease to close the gap in self-acceptance between himself and initially more self-accepting individuals.

Indeed, over time the gap may widen once more. Individuals who have developed highly self-rejecting feelings in the past have proven themselves less than able to adapt to, cope with, or defend against circumstances having self-devaluing implications. Thus, even if life events with self-devaluing implications were randomly distributed among the population, such circumstances would disproportionately exacerbate the self-rejecting feelings of those less able to contain the self-relevant consequences of those circumstances. Of course, as shall be emphasized in the next chapter, those events are not randomly distributed. Rather, they are more likely to accrue to those individuals who are not able to defend against their experience and who were destined to develop self-rejecting feelings. In short, the same adverse experiences and personal deficits that influenced the development of negative self-attitudes in the first place may exacerbate the experience of negative self-feelings at a point in time *following a period of decrease in level of self-rejection that is attributable to the functioning of the self-esteem motive up to the person's maximum capacity to reduce self-rejecting attitudes.*

This formulation is compatible with a number of observations from the present study as well as from other investigations. First, as has been noted, the decrease in self-derogation from T_2 to T_3 was markedly less than that from T_1 to T_2 on the part of the initially most self-rejecting subjects. Indeed the mean decrease in self-derogation from T_2 to T_3 on the part of this group was not significantly different from the decrease experienced by the initially medium self-derogation grouping. An examination of the T_1-T_2 and T_2-T_3 slopes indicated that the latter slopes were approaching parallel lines for the three initial self-derogation groupings. The general picture suggests that initially more self-derogating groups experience relatively swift reductions in self-derogation but soon tax their capacity for further reduction.

Second, at both T_2 and T_3 the initially more self-derogating subjects continued to display higher self-derogation scores than the less self-derogating subjects, as reference to Table 3.1 will confirm. All paired comparisons between initial self-derogation groupings with regard to self-derogation scores at T_2 and T_3 were significant ($p < .001$). In another study cited earlier, Clifford and Clifford (1967) also noted that although the bulk of overall positive change in adolescents' self-ratings over a 1-month period was accounted for by the boys with the initially poorer self-ratings, these boys retained their relative position to boys with initially more favorable self-concepts with regard to the later self-concept ratings. These observations suggest that the same adverse life experiences and personal inability to adapt to, defend against, or cope with such experiences that influenced the genesis of self-rejecting attitudes to begin with continue to hinder the acquisition of self-attitudes that are as self-accepting as those of initially less self-rejecting individuals.

Third, even though over the 1-year period T_1-T_2 and the 2-year period T_1-T_3, as has been noted, the initially more self-derogating subjects manifested greater decreases (or lower increases) in self-derogation than did initially less self-derogating subjects—even after removing from the change the portion of the change that could have been predicted linearly from the earlier score (that is, using residualized scores)—over the period T_2-T_3 the pattern was reversed. Reference to Table 3.3 once more will reveal that for the T_2-T_3 period the initially high self-derogation subjects manifested the greatest residualized *increases* (or smallest residualized decreases) in self-derogation, followed in order by the initially medium and low self-derogation subjects. The differences in residualized change scores in the paired comparisons between the three initial self-derogation groupings were all statistically significant ($p < .001$). This suggests that following a period of relatively great decrease in self-derogation (attributable to more intense stimulation of the self-esteem motive) the initially high self-derogation subjects remain particularly vulnerable to exacerbation of negative self-attitudes, presumably because of continued greater exposure to life circumstances having self-devaluing implications and personal inability to defend against, adapt to, or cope with any actual self-devaluing consequences of such circumstances.

Fourth, considering only subjects present for all three test administrations ($N = 2950$), the stability coefficient for self-derogation scores (that is, the correlation between earlier and later scores) was higher for the T_2-T_3 period (r

$= .55$) than for the T_1-T_2 period ($r = .46$). It is interesting to note that a similar situation was observed for the Youth in Transition study data considered earlier (T. N. Davidson, 1972, p. 33). In that study a coefficient of .54 was reported between self-esteem scores at T_1 and T_2 and a coefficient of .66 was reported for the self-esteem scores at T_2 and T_3. However, interpretation of these data is complicated by the fact that the T_2-T_3 period was shorter (a 12-month interval) than the T_1-T_2 interval (18 months). Nevertheless these data, as well as those from the present study, are consistent with the view that change in self-derogation attributable to the intensity of the self-esteem motive (manifested in relatively low stability in self-derogation scores from T_1 to T_2) is likely to occur over the period following the initially high self-derogation. With the passage of time and the initial decrease in self-rejection, the initially high self-derogation subjects will be less motivated to behave so as to maximize the experience of self-accepting attitudes. They will be less able to do so as they approach the limits of their ability to reduce the experiences of self-rejecting feelings (a situation that will be manifested in an increased stability in self-attitudes over time).

In sum, the observation of a decreasing tendency to reduce self-rejecting feelings with the passage of time on the part of initially self-rejecting persons does not rule against the prevalence of the self-esteem motive. Such an observation does suggest, however, that early success in reducing self-rejecting feelings will both weaken the intensity of the self-esteem motive and signal approximation to the limits of the self-rejecting person's ability to continue to reduce the experience of negative self-attitudes. Nor do the other two issues raised gainsay the conclusion that the observed greater tendency of initially more self-derogating subjects to manifest subsequent decreases in self-derogation is attributable (at least in part) to consequences of a more intensely experienced self-esteem motive.

Stability of Self-attitudes

The third hypothesis implied by the self-esteem motive asserts that persons with more negative self-attitudes will tend to have more unstable self-attitudes—that is, self-attitudes that would change from one point in time to another—than individuals with more positive self-attitudes. This prediction follows from two related considerations. First, the more self-rejecting individuals, insofar as they are said to be more highly motivated to behave in ways that maximize self-accepting attitudes, would be expected to respond more quickly with self-protective responses to self-devaluing circumstances so as to change their self-attitudes in a more positive direction. The more self-accepting individuals would be less highly motivated (by virtue of their initial self-acceptance) to respond similarly in such circumstances. Second, the more self-rejecting individuals (independent of the more frequent self-devaluing experiences in their pasts), would be more likely, by virtue of their greater motivation to avoid self-rejecting attitudes, to be *sensitive* to the self-devaluing implications of life events and thereby to experience ephemeral increases in self-rejection, thus exacerbating the need to respond quickly with self-protective responses aimed at reducing feelings of self-rejection.

The expectation that the more self-rejecting persons would be less stable in self-attitudes than the more self-accepting persons was compatible with earlier findings reported by other investigators. Engel (1959) measured stability in terms of correlations between self-concept Q sorts in 1954 and 1956. She reported that subjects whose self-concepts were negative in 1954 were significantly less stable than those whose self-concepts were positive or defensive–positive (positive self-concept subjects who also obtained a K score greater than 17 on the MMPI). In cross-sectional analyses both Rosenberg (1965, pp. 152–154) and French (1968, p. 149) reported for their adolescent subjects that those having high self-esteem were more stable in the opinions or ideas they had of themselves than were those having relatively low self-esteem.

Unlike the first of these studies, the method employed to test the hypothesis in the present investigation used indicators of stability that were independent of the self-concept measure, and unlike the other two studies, the method employed tested the hypothesis in a way that more easily permitted inferences regarding the temporal relationship between self-attitudes and stability.

The hypothesis was tested by comparing the initially (T_1) high, medium, and low self-derogation subjects with regard to responses on the stability indices at T_3, *considering only subjects who had denied having unstable self-concepts at T_2*. The stability of self-attitudes was measured in terms of responses to two items adapted from the Rosenberg (1965) stability measure: "Do you ever find that on one day you have one opinion of yourself, and, on another day, you'll have a different opinion?" and "Does your opinion of yourself tend to change a good deal?"

This mode of analysis made it possible to determine if antecedent self-derogation was related to subsequent instability of self-attitudes, whether or not antecedent instability was also related to subsequent self-derogation. By considering only subjects with "stable" responses at T_2, two ends were accomplished. First, the hypothesized relationship could not easily be accounted for in terms of a response tendency such as willingness to admit to unfavorable self-responses (that is, instability and self-derogation), since all subjects at one point denied instability. Second, later instability could not be said to be a reflection of earlier instability, which could have been an antecedent to rather than a consequence of self-derogation.

TABLE 3.4
Percentage of Subjects Indicating Instability of Self-attitudes at T_3, by Initial (T_1) Self-derogation among Subjects Denying Unstable Self-attitudes at T_2[a]

Test item	Self-derogation[b]			Gamma
	Low	Medium	High	
19. Do you ever find that on one day you have one opinion of yourself, and on another day, you'll have a different opinion? (yes)[c]	30.1 (505)	42.6 (310)	47.4 (192)	(.26)*
76. Does your opinion of yourself tend to change a good deal? (yes)[c]	18.3 (814)	24.6 (564)	32.1 (396)	(.24)*

*$p < .001$

[a] These items, first published as part of Table 1 drawn from "Self-attitudes and Schizophrenia," by Howard B. Kaplan, are reproduced with stylistic changes from W. E. Fann *et al.* (Eds.), *The Phenomenology and Treatment of Schizophrenia,* 1978, pp. 241–287, by permission of the publisher, Spectrum Publications.

[b] Number in parentheses is cell N.

[c] Response indicative of instability in self-attitudes.

The results of the analyses are summarized in Table 3.4. For each of the two indices of instability, the hypothesis was supported. Subjects having increasingly greater levels of self-derogation at T_1 were increasingly likely to report at T_3 instability of self-attitudes after having denied such instability at an intermediate point in time. Although alternative explanations of the data are possible, these results remain consistent with the reasoning that led to the hypothesis and, therefore, with the postulated prevalence of the self-esteem motive.

Positive Self-descriptions

A fourth hypothesis derived from the postulate of the prevalence of the self-esteem motive asserts that a given population will overwhelmingly tend to endorse socially desirable self-descriptions and deny socially disvalued self-descriptions. This outcome may be arrived at through any of three routes, each of which is consistent with the assertion that the self-esteem motive influences behavior. First, if it is assumed that the subjects are factually reporting that they possess desirable behaviors, it is consistent with the postulate of the self-esteem motive that people would have strived successfully to possess the qualities and perform the behaviors that would earn the approval of others and themselves. Second, if it is assumed that the positive self-descriptions reflected not reality but rather the subjects' perceptual distortion of their own actual disvalued attributes and behaviors, it is compatible with the postulate of the self-esteem motive that persons would need to distort reality in order to perceive themselves in ways that would evoke positive self-attitudes. Third, if it is assumed that the positive self-descriptions reflect the subjects' conscious unwillingness to describe themselves to others in the unfavorable terms they know to be warranted, it is consistent with the postulate of the self-esteem motive that they would need to present themselves to others in ways that would avoid the expression of negative attitudes toward themselves by significant others and consequent exacerbation of self-rejecting feelings.

Numerous studies have been reported in which the tendency of subjects to present themselves in positively valued terms was apparent. French (1968) reviewed several studies in which high correlations were observed between the social desirability values of self-descriptive items and the tendency to endorse the items. Earlier, Crowne and Stephens (1961) had cited a number of investigations that similarly suggested a general tendency to employ positive (and to eschew negative) self-descriptions in the course of their discussion of the possible influence of "defensive behavior," "self-protective responses," and "social desirability" on the endorsement of favorable self-descriptive items.

The data relating to the prevalence of positive self-descriptions generally may be derived from two types of study. In one type the frequencies of positive or negative self-descriptions are offered. From such data it cannot be determined whether the self-descriptions are accurate or whether some conscious or unconscious distortion of reality is taking place. Thus, according to Chamblis (1964), the responses of college freshmen to adjective checklists revealed that the most frequently used adjectives had favorable implications and the least frequently used adjectives were less than flattering. In the other type of study it is possible to infer some degree of distortion in self-evaluative responses. For example, in a study in which 92 members of management evaluated their own performance relative to the other men on the unit doing the same job, it was to be expected that if the evaluations were totally objective they would have been distributed equally above and below the fiftieth percentile of the scale. The fact that only two of the subjects reported their performance as falling below this value strongly suggested that some conscious or unconscious distortion of reality was occurring (French, 1968).

That unconscious as well as conscious distortion of reality occurs (apparently toward the goal of increasingly self-enhancing attitudes) is suggested by Fisher and Mirin (1966). Male college students were asked to rate, for degree of friendliness, tachistoscopically presented shadow pictures of themselves and four other people. The students tended to ascribe significantly more favorable ratings to their own shadow profiles, although the pictures were obtained without the subjects' knowledge and they did not appear to consciously recognize their own pictures.

The rare instances in which subjects apparently *underrated* themselves on socially desirable traits are interpretable in terms of culturally variable values. Such an observation for Chinese college students (Trow & Pu, 1927), the authors speculated, could have been the expression of a trait—humility—that was highly valued in traditional Chinese culture. In this instance the failure to observe prevalently positive self-descriptions did not gainsay the prevalence of the self-esteem motive, since the very act of underrating was an assertion of a quality that justified positive self-attitudes.

The hypothesis was tested in the present study by examining the percentages of subjects endorsing or rejecting each of 17 items selected on a face-valid basis as desirable or undesirable self-descriptions of attributes and behaviors. The data from the second testing were arbitrarily chosen to test the hypothesis. The results are summarized in Table 3.5.

TABLE 3.5

Percentage of Subjects Subscribing to Selected "Socially Desirable" Qualities and Behaviors at T_2 among Subjects Present at All Three Administrations

Test item[a]	Percentage affirming trait or quality[b]
12. Do your parents obey the law? (yes)	95
16. Are you usually kind to others? (yes)	93
25. Do you usually have good manners? (yes)	92
39. Are you a fairly honest person? (yes)	91
42. Are you good at sports? (yes)	77
58. Are you fairly good-looking? (yes)	81
63. Do you usually obey your teachers? (yes)	89
65. Do you tell lies often? (no)	76
75. Within the last year did you beat up someone who had not done anything to you? (no)	93
83. Are you liked by kids of the opposite sex? (yes)	90
85. Do you usually get good grades? (yes)	83
88. Are you patriotic? (yes)	74
97. I do what I think is right even when I'm criticized for it. (true)	85
128. By my teachers' standards I am a failure. (false)	90
175. Most of the kids do not like me very much. (false)	83
178. I don't care much about other people's feelings. (false)	89
201. My parents do not like me very much. (false)	93

[a] Parenthetical entry indicates socially desirable response.
[b] All percentages based on Ns of at least 2824.

As anticipated, the subjects overwhelmingly endorsed the positively valued self-descriptions and rejected those negatively valued. In no instance did fewer than 74% of the subjects provide the expected response. For eight of the items at least 90% of the subjects provided the appropriate response and for six of the items between 80 and 89% did so. For the remaining three items between 74 and 77% endorsed the positively valued items and denied those negatively valued. As will be recalled from Chapter 2, sample attrition was not significantly associated with initial self-derogation, so it is not likely that these resluts can be explained in terms of a disproportionate loss from T_1 to T_2 of the initially more self-rejecting subjects.

Although it cannot be determined which of the three explanations considered are appropriate for these results, again it is noted that any or all of them are consistent with the postulate of the self-esteem motive.

Subjective Distress

The fifth hypothesis implied by the postulate that the self-esteem motive is prevalent asserts that persons characterized by increasingly greater levels of self-rejection are increasingly likely to experience subjective distress. If persons were indeed motivated to maximize the experience of positive self-attitudes and to minimize the experience of negative self-attitudes, then those who were most frustrated in their attempts to attain the desired goal (that is, the initially most self-rejecting individuals) would be expected to experience subjective distress, whereas those who were least likely to be frustrated in this regard (initially more self-accepting subjects) would be less likely to experience subjective distress.

Numerous investigations have consistently reported relationships between low self-esteem and high scores on various indicators of emotional distress, notably including depressive affect and physiological manifestations of anxiety, among preadolescent, adolescent, and adult subjects (Engel, 1959; French, 1968; F. D. Horowitz, 1962; H. B. Kaplan & Pokorny, 1969; Rosenberg, 1965; Rosenberg & Simmons, 1972). However, since the data regarding self-esteem and emotional distress were collected at the same point (or points, in the instance of Engel, 1959) in time it could not be determined whether or not low self-esteem and emotional distress were both reflections of some underlying factor such as general psychopathology or response bias, or whether low self-esteem was an antecedent and/or consequence of emotional distress.

That the temporal relationship between self-esteem and emotional distress is problematic is noted by Rosenberg (1965). He summarizes Horney's (1950) position, which would suggest that anxiety is an antecendent of self-rejecting attitudes. In order to cope with basic anxiety engendered by various adverse circumstances in the family, the child is said to imagine an idealized image that functions to give him a sense of strength and confidence. But when the child compares this highly admirable image with his real self, the latter suffers by comparison and the child, therefore, experiences self-contempt. Rosenberg (1965) argues that it is equally plausible to assert that low self-esteem gives rise to the idealized image and, in any case, offers that low self-esteem may generate anxiety for reasons other than those considered by Horney (1950).

The hypothesis under discussion also implies that self-rejecting attitudes give rise to emotional distress. The hypothesis was tested by comparing subjects who were initially (at T_1) low, medium, or high in self-derogation with regard to self-reports at T_3 on each of 16 items interpreted as reflecting dimensions of emotional distress. As in the analysis of the relationship between self-esteem and stability of self-attitudes (described earlier), only those subjects who had denied the indicator of emotional distress at T_2 were considered. This strategy, again, made it difficult to interpret any observed relationship between earlier (T_1) self-derogation and later (T_3) emotional distress in terms of response bias or, for that matter, any other common factor that might be hypothesized to influence both self-derogation and emotional stress, since all subjects considered in the analysis had denied the symptoms at T_2. (It does, however, remain possible that the hypothetical factor had a simultaneous influence on self-derogation but a delayed influence on symptoms until other elements such as adverse life events had been added to the equation.)

This strategy also permitted demonstration of an antecedent–consequence relationship between self-derogation and emotional distress. By virtue of excluding those who affirmed the indicators of emotional distress at T_2, any observed relationship between earlier self-rejection and subsequent subjective distress could not be accounted for easily by an argument that the later report of distress was an indicator of an earlier distressed condition that *antedated* the measure of self-rejection.

The data relating to the hypothesis are summarized in Table 3.6. Self-derogation was significantly associated with each of the 16 indicators of emotional distress. Subjects having increasingly greater levels of self-derogation at T_1 were increasingly likely to report the indicator of emotional distress at T_3 after having denied the symptom at T_2. The items included self-reports of self-distress, depressive affect, interference with cognitive processes, and, generally, a wide variety of psychophysiological manifestations of anxiety. Subjects who at T_1 were characterized by higher levels of self-derogation were, 2 years later, significantly and appreciably more likely to report being bothered by nervousness; getting angry, annoyed, or upset; having trouble sitting still for a long time; and becoming deeply disturbed when ridiculed or blamed. For exam-

TABLE 3.6

Percentage of Subjects Affirming Indicators of Subjective Distress at T_3, by Initial Level of Self-derogation (T_1), Considering Only Subjects Denying the Indicator at T_2[a]

Test item	Self-derogation (T_1)[b]			Gamma
	Low	Medium	High	
1. Are you often bothered by nervousness?	13.3 (896)	16.9 (668)	21.7 (457)	(.19)***
2. Do you wish you could be as happy as others seem to be?	17.4 (726)	24.4 (491)	35.1 (308)	(.30)***
20. Would you say that most of the time you feel in good spirits?[c]	7.6 (1063)	10.6 (857)	14.6 (643)	(.24)***
27. Are you often bothered by shortness of breath when not exercising or not working hard?	6.7 (1057)	11.3 (842)	12.0 (665)	(.22)***
30. Are you often bothered by bad dreams?	10.8 (772)	15.5 (566)	18.0 (456)	(.20)***
37. Do you often get angry, annoyed, or upset?	24.4 (594)	24.8 (395)	36.8 (228)	(.16)**
46. Do you often feel downcast and dejected?	9.9 (951)	16.1 (696)	23.6 (445)	(.33)***
49. Do you often lose track of what you were thinking?	15.6 (831)	19.7 (544)	21.8 (363)	(.14)**
52. Do you often have difficulty keeping your mind on things?	13.6 (936)	19.1 (639)	24.2 (463)	(.24)***
53. Are you often troubled by your hands sweating so that they feel damp and clammy?	10.2 (915)	12.8 (705)	15.2 (527)	(.15)**
55. Do you get a lot of fun out of life?[c]	6.6 (1078)	8.4 (870)	9.2 (649)	(.12)*
77. On the whole, would you say you are a fairly happy person?[c]	5.9 (1100)	7.9 (888)	11.7 (717)	(.24)***
81. Does your memory seem to be all right (good)?[c]	7.8 (1077)	9.7 (864)	13.1 (697)	(.19)***
86. Are you often bothered by pressures or pains in the head?	10.5 (1046)	12.0 (782)	14.7 (607)	(.12)*
89. Do you often have trouble sitting still for a long time?	23.8 (592)	24.5 (428)	32.9 (307)	(.13)*
91. Do you become deeply disturbed when someone laughs at you or blames you for something you have done wrong?	18.1 (674)	28.5 (460)	29.5 (315)	(.23)***

*$p < .05$
**$p < .01$
***$p < .001$

[a] These items, first published as part of Table 1 drawn from "Self-attitudes and Schizophrenia," by Howard B. Kaplan, are reproduced with stylistic changes from W. E. Fann et al. (Eds.), The Phenomenology and Treatment of Schizophrenia, 1978, pp. 241–287, by permission of the publisher, Spectrum Publications.

[b] Number in parentheses is cell N.

[c] Denial of the symptom is indicated by affirmative response to the item. Percentage figures refer to negative responses to this item at T_3 among subjects who offered affirmative responses at T_2.

ple, among subjects who denied being frequently bothered by nervousness at T_2, 22% of the initially high self-derogation subjects compared with 17% of the medium and 13% of the low self-derogation subjects reported being so bothered at T_3.

In like manner subjects who were relatively more self-derogating at T_1 were more likely at T_3 to report wishing they could be as happy as others seem to be, not feeling in good spirits most of the time, feeling downcast and dejected, not getting a lot of fun out of life, and, on the whole, not being fairly happy. For example, among subjects who denied feeling downcast and dejected at T_2, 24% of the subjects whose self-derogation levels were initially (T_1) high, compared with only 16% of those with medium levels and 10% of those with low levels, reported such feelings at T_3.

Subjects with increasingly greater levels of self-rejecting feelings at T_1 were also more likely to report at a later time that they often lost track of what they were thinking, that they had difficulty keeping their minds on things, and that their memories did not seem to be all right. Thus, among subjects who at T_2 denied that they often had difficulty keeping their minds on things, 24% of the initially high, compared with 19 and 14% of the initially medium and low self-derogation subjects, respectively, reported such difficulty 2 years later.

Finally, those who were more self-derogating at T_1 were more likely later to report being bothered by shortness of breath when not exercising or working hard, bad dreams, hands sweating so they feel damp and clammy, and pressures or pains in the head. For example, among subjects who at T_2 denied being bothered by shortness of breath when not exercising or working hard, 12% of the high, and 11% of the medium self-derogation subjects, compared to 7% of the initially (T_1) low self-derogation subjects, reported being bothered by this at T_3.

Although these findings are interpreted as support for the self-esteem motive insofar as self-rejection is associated with the genesis of emotional distress, it is possible that the relationship is accounted for by consequences of self-derogation that in turn were associated with the genesis of distress. Along this line of reasoning, Rosenberg (1965) argued that low self-esteem influences instability of self-image, the "presenting self," vulnerability, and feelings of isolation, and these conditions in turn influence anxiety. Indeed, Rosenberg (1965) noted that self-esteem was associated with these factors and that, when controlling on these factors, the relationship between self-esteem and psychosomatic symptoms decreased. However, despite the decrease, the relationship remained a strong one, an observation that is consistent with the postulate of the self-esteem motive and, in particular, the derived expectation that those who were more frustrated in their attempts to satisfy the self-esteem motive (that is, the more self-rejecting subjects) would be more likely to develop feelings of emotional distress.

Self-protective Responses

The sixth implication of the self-esteem motive is that people who are more highly motivated to reduce feelings of self-rejection (that is, the initially most self-rejecting subjects) would be most likely to adopt self-protective responses that are apparently calculated to forestall or reduce the distressful effects of self-devaluing experiences. If in the course of membership group experiences subjects have developed relatively intense negative self-attitudes as a result of (*a*) failure to possess positively valued attributes and to perform positively sanctioned behavior, or possession of disvalued attributes and performance of disvalued behaviors and/or (*b*) failure to evoke positive responses from valued others, or the expression of negative responses toward the subjects by valued others, what options are available to them that might forestall or reduce the intensity of self-rejecting feelings? Since they apparently failed to do so up to the point in time at which their self-rejection was measured, it is not likely that they have the personal and social resources that in the future would permit them to possess the desirable attributes and to perform the desirable behaviors that would earn them the positive attitudinal responses of others, and thereby self-acceptance. What else, then, might be expected from subjects who were most frustrated in their attempts to attain self-acceptance?

First, it might be expected that they would lower their levels of aspiration, thus increasing the probability of subjectively defined success and decreasing the probability of self-reproach at failure to attain the earlier (higher) standards. Furthermore, since the subjects now regard the older standards as inappropriate, criticism by others for failure to attain the loftier standards would be regarded as similarly inappropriate and would be less likely to adversely influence self-attitudes. Second, whether or not the subjects revise their self-expectations, they would be expected to attempt to justify their (as they perceive them) disvalued attributes and behaviors, and their felt rejection by significant others, through a denial of personal responsibility for these conditions—that is, by perceiving their outcomes to be the consequences of forces (personal or social) beyond their control. Even if unable to justify their attributes, behaviors, or rejection by others in such terms, they might be able to justify discontinuance of self-rejecting feelings in terms of having atoned in some way for past deficiencies. Third, if self-rejecting individuals have been unable to justify their past deficiencies, and maintain their self-expectations and the justifiability of others' expectations of them, they may still attempt to present themselves to others in ways that disguise their deficiencies and, thereby, avoid compounding the basis of their self-rejection by evoking negative attitudes from valued others.

The self-protective responses to frustration of the self-esteem motive reviewed up to this point presume that self-rejecting subjects remain affectively tied to the interpersonal relationships and value systems of their membership groups. Although they may revise their personal expectations of approximating the values, they do not reject them as standards for the behavior of others. Indeed, if these people cannot revise their personal expectations with regard to attainment of the values, they must justify their failure to do so in ways that would be considered legitimate by themselves and other group members. Nor do they reject the other group members but, rather, feel the need to appear in a favorable light to them as a basis for self-acceptance. However, as was noted in the first chapter, if individuals cannot revise their personal expectations, justify the self-perceived disvalued attributes, behaviors, and personal rejections, and present themselves to others as worthy of positive responses, then they may be expected to respond in ways that increase the emotional distance between themselves and their membership groups (whether by devaluation of group members and values or by avoidance of situations in which they might be influenced by group expectations and responses) and to substitute new interpersonal relationships and values for those of their increasingly distanced membership groups.

Although consistent with other interpretations as well, numerous studies have reported results compatible with these expectations. Thus, congruent with the expectation of revised self-expectations on the part of highly self-derogating subjects are Rosenberg's findings (1965, pp. 232–239). Adolescents with lower self-esteem were more likely to report lower expectations of success in work, getting ahead in life, being as successful as most people seem to be, or going into the business or profession they would most like as a life career. Moreover, compatible with the expectation of denial of personal responsibility for self-devaluing circumstances on the part of highly self-rejecting subjects is Washburn's report (1962, p. 88) that more self-devaluing students had significantly higher scores on the Self-Other Distortion subtest involving "exaggeration of threats in the physical environment and elaboration of symptoms of physical illness to excuse one's own behavior." And congruent with the expectation that more self-rejecting subjects would favorably misrepresent themselves to others than would less self-rejecting subjects is Rosenberg's observation (1965, pp. 154–157) that the former are more likely to agree that they put on an act to impress people and tend to put up a false front to people.

The expected tendency for self-devaluing subjects to reject group members and standards was foreshadowed by a number of studies in which experimentally induced failure or rejection by others was related to the subject's rejection of the group (Goldfried, 1963; Johnson, 1966). That the influence of the experimentally induced success or failure upon rejection of the group was a function of initial level of self-rejection was specifically indicated by Frankel's study (1969) with the influence being greatest among the subjects having low self-esteem. The expectation that the more self-rejecting persons would be more likely to show tendencies to avoid situations having self-devaluing implications was consistent with the observation of Washburn (1962, p. 88) that such subjects received significantly higher scores on the Reality Rejection subtest involving "seeking to detach oneself from potentially threatening situations by refusing to accept and face things as they are." Finally, the expectation that highly self-rejecting subjects would tend to substitute new interpersonal relationships and values for those emotionally distanced was consistent with the observation by Long, Henderson, and Ziller (1967) that subjects with high originality scores manifested significantly less self-esteem. This expectation was also consistent with the observed relationship between experimentally induced approval or disapproval and change in stated behavioral preference (Ludwig & Maehr, 1967).

Unlike the studies reviewed here, the present study permits the simultaneous consideration of the relationship between antecedent level of self-derogation and subsequent adoption of each of several self-protective responses. As in the analysis of the hypothesized relationships between self-derogation on the one hand and stability of self-attitudes and subjective distress on the other, the strategy employed involves the comparison of the initially (T_1) low, medium, and high self-derogation subjects with regard to the percentage reporting each of 42 self-protective responses at T_3, considering only subjects who denied the self-protective response at T_2. Again, this strategy made it difficult to account for any observed relationships between antecedent self-derogation and subsequent adoption of self-protective responses in terms of a third factor, such as response set, that simultaneously influenced self-derogation and self-protective response. Nor could the antecedent–consequence relationship between self-derogation and self-protective responses be explained in terms of the latter items being reflections of self-derogation; moreover, the relationship could not be nullified by the assertion that the self-protective strategy was a reflection of an earlier use of the strategy antedating the self-rejecting responses.

The 42 items were selected on a face-valid basis to reflect the various categories of self-protective responses. In many instances it might be argued that the items are inappropriately categorized and/or that the items reflect multiple self-protective categories. However, for present purposes it is only necessary that they be interpretable as a response that is calculated to forestall or diminish the intensity of the felt distress associated with self-devaluing experiences.

The results of the analysis are summarized in Table 3.7. Consistent with the hypothesis, for each of the 42 items initial self-derogation level was significantly associated with subsequent adoption of the self-protective pattern. With increasingly greater earlier self-derogation, subjects were increasingly likely to report the self-protective response 2 years later, after having denied the response at an intermediate point in time. The results will be considered with reference to each of the categories previously described. The parenthetical numbers identify the relevant items in Table 3.7.

REVISED SELF-EXPECTATIONS

The tendency for more highly self-derogating subjects to revise their expectations of themselves downward (presumably to forestall occasions for self-devaluation) was reflected in the observation that subjects having increasingly greater levels of self-derogation at T_1 were increasingly likely at T_3 to agree that they expected too much of themselves (99), doubt that they would get ahead in life as far as they would like (137), and say that if they could not get what they wanted they tried for something just as good but easier to get (190), after having disagreed with these statements at T_2.

JUSTIFYING DISVALUED ATTRIBUTES AND BEHAVIORS

Increasingly greater levels of self-derogation are apparently related as well to the adoption of responses that appear to justify the postponement or discontinuance of blame (by self or others) in response to disvalued attributes or behaviors, on the grounds that the attributes or behaviors are beyond the personal control of the individual, or that atonement has already been made. Thus, after having denied the relevant statements at T_2, subjects with higher levels of self-derogation at T_1 were more likely at T_3 to assert that it was mostly luck if one succeeded or failed (96), that they would do better if society did not have the cards stacked against them (117), that their families could not give them the chance to succeed that most kids had (141), that when they did something wrong it was almost as if someone else was doing it (143), that the law is always against the ordinary guy (173), that people often talked about them behind their backs (181), that they were often punished unfairly as children (186), that people frequently put them down because their families were poor (192) or because of their religion (200), and that their parents hardly ever trusted them to do something on their own (100). The implication is that their shortcomings were not blameworthy, since they resulted from virtually insurmountable barriers, from rejection by others for attributes that were not the fault of the subjects, from unjustified maleficence by others, and from other circumstances beyond the control of the subject. The predisposition of subjects to justify discontinuance of self-blame by atoning for their shortcomings is suggested by the tendency of initially more self-derogating persons to endorse at T_3 the statement, "I sometimes wish I could be punished for the bad things I have done and start all over" (136), after having disagreed with it at T_2.

PRESENTATION OF SELF

Consistent with the expectation that self-rejecting subjects would tend to present themselves to others in ways that would disguise their self-perceived

TABLE 3.7

Percentage of Subjects Affirming Self-protective Strategies at T_3, by Intial (T_1) Level of Self-deroge among Subjects Denying the Strategy at $T_2{}^a$

Test item	Self-derogation (T_1)[b]			Gan
	Low	Medium	High	
13. Do you sometimes wish you were a little kid again?	20.5 (736)	23.0 (534)	28.1 (381)	(.13)
21. Within the last year, have you refused to do what your parents told you to do?	28.2 (655)	31.5 (520)	37.5 (349)	(.13)
32. Are most of your friends older than you?	16.1 (752)	18.0 (572)	21.1 (479)	(.11)
51. Would you like to quit school as soon as possible?	11.9 (986)	14.9 (756)	18.0 (621)	(.16)
60. Are most of your close friends also friends with each other?[c]	7.4 (1049)	9.1 (877)	10.7 (758)	(.13)
62. Do many of your good friends smoke marijuana (grass)?	21.3 (900)	25.5 (725)	27.2 (585)	(.11)
65. Do you tell lies often?	10.3 (950)	13.3 (746)	16.5 (562)	(.18)
71. Do you try to avoid situations in which you have to compete with others?	18.2 (817)	22.2 (591)	25.4 (503)	(.14)
79. Do many of your good friends take narcotic drugs to get high?	19.8 (929)	22.8 (732)	26.1 (613)	(.12)
80. Do you like to spend a lot of time by yourself?	22.0 (731)	27.9 (581)	33.9 (451)	(.20)
93. It is very important to me what my parents think of me.[c]	6.9 (1068)	7.9 (900)	9.7 (749)	(.12)
94. I have a better chance of doing well if I cut corners than if I play it straight.	8.1 (1010)	12.4 (850)	12.4 (703)	(.16)
96. It's mostly luck if one succeeds or fails.	6.0 (1010)	8.8 (822)	12.4 (645)	(.26)
97. I do what I think is right even when I'm criticized for it.[c]	7.5 (1016)	9.8 (835)	10.5 (694)	(.13)
98. I would like to travel with a circus or carnival.	4.0 (1059)	3.4 (871)	6.5 (727)	(.17)
99. Sometimes I think I expect too much of myself.	22.8 (729)	27.2 (556)	34.7 (421)	(.19)
100. My parents hardly ever trust me to do something on my own.	9.8 (966)	10.7 (740)	17.4 (540)	(.20)

TABLE 3.7—*Continued*

Test item	Self-derogation $(T_1)^b$			Gamma
	Low	Medium	High	
I think it is important to be good at drawing or painting.	9.0 (916)	10.9 (734)	13.7 (598)	$(.16)^{**}$
I would do a lot better in life if society didn't have the cards stacked against me.	9.5 (959)	15.1 (714)	20.9 (545)	$(.30)^{***}$
If someone insulted me, I would probably avoid talking to him in the future.	11.9 (940)	15.3 (745)	20.4 (612)	$(.21)^{***}$
If you want people to like you, you have to tell them what they want to hear, even if it isn't the truth.	10.5 (973)	13.3 (769)	15.9 (615)	$(.16)^{**}$
When I do something wrong, I usually admit it and take my punishment.^{c}	19.8 (820)	22.8 (151)	24.0 (524)	$(.09)^*$
I think it is important to get good grades.	47.6 (103)	60.5 (124)	61.0 (118)	$(.17)^*$
I sometimes wish I could be punished for the bad things I have done and start all over.	26.6 (582)	33.3 (412)	37.9 (346)	$(.18)^{***}$
I doubt if I will get ahead in life as far as I would really like.	12.5 (883)	20.9 (599)	27.9 (430)	$(.33)^{***}$
I think it is important to be good at sports.	25.0 (508)	27.8 (392)	32.2 (320)	$(.12)^*$
My family can't give me the chance to succeed that most kids have.	4.9 (1052)	10.5 (808)	10.9 (640)	$(.28)^{***}$
When I do something wrong, it's almost like it's someone else who is doing it, not me.	13.9 (878)	16.9 (663)	24.8 (529)	$(.23)^{***}$
I would like to leave home.	13.1 (963)	16.6 (765)	20.0 (574)	$(.17)^{***}$
I think it is important to be kind to others.^{c}	4.6 (1090)	6.7 (931)	6.8 (778)	$(.14)^*$
If someone insulted me, I would probably figure, "Who cares what he thinks."	30.2 (590)	34.1 (460)	40.0 (375)	$(.14)^{**}$
My experiences outside my home make me wonder whether my parents' ideas are right or not.	25.5 (635)	38.0 (476)	44.6 (314)	$(.28)^{***}$

(*Continued*)

TABLE 3.7—*Continued*

Test item	Self-derogation $(T_1)^b$			
	Low	Medium	High	Gamma
173. The law is always against the ordinary guy.	9.6 (979)	13.3 (788)	16.1 (634)	$(.20)^{***}$
176. Most of my close friends are the kinds of kids who get into trouble a lot.	9.3 (1003)	12.0 (793)	15.1 (656)	$(.18)^{***}$
178. I don't care much about other people's feelings.	7.1 (1063)	11.3 (8511)	9.7 (720)	$(.12)^{*}$
181. People often talk about me behind my back.	17.1 (768)	25.5 (525)	27.0 (352)	$(.21)^{***}$
182. I get nervous when things aren't just right.	20.1 (742)	25.2 (556)	33.7 (362)	$(.22)^{***}$
186. I was often punished unfairly as a child.	7.2 (1027)	9.1 (824)	11.4 (638)	$(.17)^{**}$
190. If I can't get what I want, I try for something just as good that's easier to get.	32.8 (543)	38.1 (402)	39.2 (344)	$(.10)^{*}$
192. People often put me down because my family is poor.	1.8 (1137)	1.9 (932)	4.8 (805)	$(.34)^{***}$
196. I spend a lot of time daydreaming.	23.4 (741)	24.3 (547)	36.7 (376)	$(.18)^{***}$
200. People often put me down because of my religion.	3.4 (1085)	4.1 (908)	6.6 (747)	$(.23)^{**}$

$^{*}p < .05$
$^{**}p < .01$
$^{***}p < .001$

^{a} Many of these items, first published as part of Table 1 drawn from "Self-attitudes and Schizophrenia," by Howard B. Kaplan, are reproduced with stylistic changes from W. E. Fann *et al.* (Eds.), *The Phenomenology and Treatment of Schizophrenia*, 1978, pp. 241–287, by permission of the publisher, Spectrum Publications.

^{b} Number in parentheses is cell N.

^{c} Denial of the strategy is indicated by affirmative response to the item. Percentage figures refer to negative responses to this item at T_3 among subjects who offered affirmative responses at T_2.

shortcomings were several observations. Subjects with increasingly greater levels of self-derogation at T_1 were increasingly likely to affirm at T_3 that they frequently told lies (65), that they had a better chance of doing well if they cut corners than if they played it straight (94), and that to be liked, one has to tell others what they want to hear even if it is not the truth (132), after having denied the items at T_2. Also consistent with the expectation were increasingly greater rates of denial of the following items at T_3 (after affirmation at T_2) with increasingly greater initial (T_1) self-derogation: "I do what I think is right even when I'm criticized for it" (97) and "When I do something wrong, I usually admit it and take my punishment" (134).

DEVALUING THE BASIS FOR SELF-REJECTION

The observations that follow are consistent with the expectation that the more self-derogating subjects would be more likely subsequently to reject the social bases of their self-devaluation (whether specific groups such as the family that engendered self-rejection or devaluing people in general). Subjects characterized by increasingly greater levels of self-rejection at T_1 were increasingly likely at T_3 to affirm (after having denied at T_2) that they disobeyed their parents (21); that they would respond to insults by thinking, "who cares what he thinks" (153); that they did not care much about other people's feelings (178); and that their experiences outside the home made them wonder whether or not their parents' ideas were right (168). Furthermore, among subjects who *affirmed* the items at T_2, those characterized by initially greater levels of self-derogation were more likely at T_3 to *deny* that what their parents thought of them was important (93), and that being kind to others was important (150).

AVOIDING THE BASIS FOR SELF-DEVALUATION

The occasions for self-devaluation may be avoided in any of a number of ways—by refusing to recognize the reality of one's obligations (and thereby avoiding the risk of one's failure to live up to them); by avoiding groups or individuals who are implicated in the genesis of self-rejection by their offering negative emotional responses or lofty expectations; and by structuring one's life in a way that decreases the requirement for responses not within one's repertoire. Consistent with the hypothesis, self-derogation level was associated with the rate of subsequent adoption of all of these mechanisms. The refusal to face the reality of obligations is reflected in the observed greater tendency for increasingly more self-rejecting persons to affirm (after denying at an intermediate time) that they sometimes wished they were little kids again (13), that they would like to travel with a circus or carnival (98), and that they spent a lot of time daydreaming (196). The predisposition to avoid interpersonal situations having self-devaluing implications is reflected in the greater tendency on the part of the more self-derogating subjects subsequently to indicate the desire to quit school (51), avoid competitive situations (71), spend a lot of time alone (80), avoid talking to those who insult them (121), and leave home (149) after having denied these predispositions at an earlier time. The tendency of more self-derogating subjects to structure their lives so as to forestall events requiring novel responses (and thereby increasing the risk of failing to make the required response) is suggested by the observation that initially greater levels of self-rejection are associated with increasingly greater rates of subsequent affirmation of the item "I get nervous when things aren't just right" (182).

SUBSTITUTING RELATIONSHIPS AND VALUES

To the extent that subjects have a need to enhance self-attitudes (particularly where self-acceptance is problematic) and insofar as self-rejecting attitudes stem from an inability to defend against self-perceptions of possessing disvalued attributes, performing disvalued behaviors, and being the object of negative attitudes expressed by valued others in one's membership groups, it is to be expected that highly self-rejecting persons would seek to enter into alternative group relationships and adopt alternative values that offer greater promise of evoking positive attitudes from (now) valued others and of approximating the newly adopted values.

That more self-rejecting subjects do change group relationships was suggested by the observation that (among subjects who denied the item at T_2) the more self-rejecting subjects at T_1 were more likely at T_3 to indicate that most of their friends were older than they were (32). The increasing tendency to interact with older friends might reflect the subjects' anticipation that less would be expected of them so it would be easier to conform to expectations and evoke positive responses. Also, among subjects who affirmed at T_2 that most of their close friends were also friends with each other (60), persons with increasingly greater levels of self-rejection at T_1 were increasingly likely to deny the statement at T_3. Consistent with the more general theory of deviant behavior outlined in the first chapter, as well as with the more specific postulate of the self-esteem motive, were the observed associations between antecedent self-derogation and subsequent reports of entering into deviant group relationships. Among subjects denying the items in question at T_2, persons with increasingly greater levels of self-rejection at T_1 were increasingly likely to report at T_3 that many of their good friends smoked marijuana (62), that many of their good friends took narcotic drugs to get high (79), and that most of their close friends were the kinds of kids who got into trouble a lot (176).

The adoption of new values as a response to self-rejection appeared to be reflected in the following relationships. Among subjects who denied (at T_2) that the values in question were significant ones, subjects with increasingly greater levels of self-derogation at T_1 were increasingly likely to report at T_3 that they thought it was important to be good at drawing or painting (115), to get good grades (135), and to be good at sports (139). These associations are consistent with the interpretation that people with a greater need for self-acceptance will be more likely to adopt new values that offer greater promise of self-enhancement through greater ease of approximating the values and/or increased likelihood of evoking positive responses from those who endorse the values.

In short, one implication of the assertion that the self-esteem motive is prevalent is that people with the greatest need for positive self-attitudes (that is, the most self-rejecting subjects) would be most likely to adopt self-protective responses. The expectation that antecedent self-rejection would be related to subsequent adoption of self-protective responses that would function to forestall or diminish in intensity the experience of self-rejecting feelings appears to be warranted. Subjects characterized by increasingly greater initial levels of self-derogation were increasingly likely to report 2 years later each of 42 items said to reflect a self-protective pattern (after having denied the item at an intermediate point in time), whether the pattern took the form of reduced levels of self-expectations, justification of self-acceptance in the face of failure to manifest desirable attributes or behaviors and evoke favorable responses from valued others, presentation of self to others in ways that would disguise self-perceived faults and evoke positive responses, rejection of the basis for self-devaluation, avoidance of circumstances having self-devaluing implications, and/or substituting new social relationships and values that offer greater promise of self-enhancement than previous ones.

Summary

A number of specific hypotheses based on implications of the postulated self-esteem motive were tested and supported. Although it might have been argued that the postulated prevalence of the self-esteem motive requires no further evidence beyond the universal recognition that people do behave in ways that are expected to maximize the experience of positive self-attitudes and to minimize the experience of negative self-attitudes, the assumption of the self-esteem motive indeed has been questioned. Webster and Sobieszek (1974, p. 153) have termed the belief that people seek to maximize their self-evaluations a "myth." They argue that "no convincing empirical support for the intuitively appealing idea that individuals attempt to maximize their levels of self-evaluations" exists. These investigators performed a number of tests, using data from their own experiments (none of which they note was designed specifically to test the various versions of the postulate), in order to determine whether there was evidence of effects that "might reasonably be expected" if the maximization postulate was warranted. They concluded that no strong or moderate evidence of maximization effects was observed. It is of course arguable as to whether such findings from the other studies described earlier are "convincing"; similarly, it is problematic whether or not the procedures and formulations employed by Webster and Sobieszek constituted an appropriate analysis of the postulated prevalence of the self-esteem motive. Within the context of the general theory guiding the present analysis, I regard as highly questionable many of their formulations by which specific effects were said to be expected if a need to maximize self-evaluations did exist. I also question whether subjectively perceived ability to judge whether a pattern of randomly arranged black and white rectangles contains a greater area of black or white is a valid indicator of salient self-evaluations (as was suggested by Webster and Sobieszek). It is also problematic whether the resolution of disagreements in this regard in favor of self is necessarily indicative of seeking to maximize self-evaluations.

Although I believe the evidence cited against the justifiability of the postulate of the self-esteem motive to be highly questionable, both the raising of the question and the strategic significance of the postulate for the general theory under consideration required, so far as it was possible, the presentation of empirical justification for the postulated prevalence of the self-esteem motive. Toward this end the hypotheses translating implications of the postulate were tested.

Consistent with the postulate, it was observed that the mean self-derogation score among subjects present for all three testings decreased from the first to the second, and from the second to the third, testings. The consideration of characteristic levels of, and changes in, self-evaluation associated with particular ages or grade levels in cross-sectional studies suggested that the decrease in self-rejection over time was to be accounted for by the subjects' own behaviors (presumably stimulated by the self-esteem motive), rather than by increasingly benign effects of the environment or maturation over the same time span.

In conformity with the expectation that subjects who were more highly motivated to restore or attain self-esteem would be more likely to behave in ways calculated to achieve acceptable levels of self-esteem, it was observed that persons having initially more negative self-attitudes manifested significantly greater subsequent decreases in self-rejecting attitudes than did those having initially less negative self-attitudes. The increase in self-derogation observed for the initially low self-derogation subjects was accounted for in terms of environmental and/or maturational changes having self-devaluing implications being experienced by subjects who were least motivated to behave in ways that would reduce the experience of self-rejecting feeling. Analyses involving the use of residual gain scores and stability coefficients over variable time intervals suggested that the relatively greater decreases in self-derogation on the part of the initially more self-rejecting subjects could not be accounted for solely in terms of consequences of the measurement process. Rather, they reflected true changes presumably influenced by the greater intensity of the self-esteem motive among those subjects.

Arguing that initially more self-rejecting individuals, being more motivated to achieve greater self-esteem, would be both more quick to respond with self-protective responses to self-devaluing circumstances *and* more sensitive to the self-devaluing implications of life events, it was expected that these subjects would be more likely than less self-rejecting subjects to display unstable self-attitudes. As anticipated, antecedent level of self-rejection was related to subsequent instability of self-attitudes.

As expected, the subjects tended to endorse socially desirable self-descriptions and to deny socially disvalued self-descriptions. This outcome was consistent with the postulated prevalence of the self-esteem motive, whether it reflected successful striving for qualities and behaviors that would earn self-approval, unconscious perceptual distortion as a way of avoiding self-rejection, or conscious dissimulation toward the goal of presenting a favorable image to others thereby evoking positive attitudinal responses.

Consistent with the expectation that the absence of self-esteem is a subjectively distressful state, it was hypothesized that self-rejecting attitudes would be associated with subsequent experiences of each of 16 indicators of subjective distress. As anticipated, increasingly greater antecedent levels of self-derogation were related to subsequent reports of symptoms among subjects who had earlier denied the symptoms.

Finally, compatible with the implication of the postulated prevalence of the self-esteem motive that people who are more highly motivated to reduce feelings of self-rejection would be most likely to adopt self-protective responses calculated to forestall or reduce the adverse effects of self-devaluing experiences, antecedent level of self-rejection was related to the subsequent adoption of each of several apparently self-protective responses. Among subjects who earlier had denied performing the responses in question, initially more self-derogating persons were significantly more likely subsequently to affirm items indicative of revised self-expectations, justification of disvalued attributes and behaviors, dissemblance, devaluation of the basis for self-rejection, avoidance of the basis for self-rejection, and substitution of new relationships and values offering greater promise than earlier ones of self-enhancing experiences.

Attempts to gainsay the prevalence of the self-esteem motive might take either of two forms. First, implications of the postulate might be drawn (that have not been drawn here) that are without empirical foundation. For example, it might be argued that the self-esteem motive implies that people would continue to decrease in level of self-rejection and that initially more self-rejecting individuals would ultimately achieve the same level of self-acceptance as that achieved by more self-accepting subjects—expectations that are clearly at variance with the data presented. However, such implications are here regarded as unwarranted in the context of the general theory guiding this analysis. The existence of the self-esteem motive implies that more self-rejecting individuals will be more highly motivated to so behave as to enhance self-attitudes and, so behaving, will decrease in self-rejection over the short term at a faster rate than initially self-rejecting subjects. But it is also implied that the enhanced self-attitudes will weaken the need for subsequent self-enhancement. Furthermore, continuing self-enhancement is not expected, since the same inability to defend against adverse life circumstances that was responsible for the genesis of self-rejecting attitudes in the first place will probably still be operative.

Second, it might be argued that the failure to observe greater magnitudes of association speaks against the prevalence of the self-esteem motive. However, questions about the validity and stability of measures aside, this circumstance is quite compatible with the postulate. For example, the significant but low-order associations between earlier self-rejection and subsequent adoption of self-protective mechanisms may simply reflect the broad range of mechanisms that are available, as well as the range of individual preferences for these mechanisms. Similar associations between self-derogation and subsequent distress may merely reflect the obscuring of the relationship by the operation of self-protective responses.

In any case, although the postulated prevalence of the self-esteem motive may not be said to have been demonstrated, the empirical support for the range of hypotheses implied by the postulate certainly is compatible with the assertion that human beings universally seek to attain, maintain, or restore feelings of self-acceptance and seek to avoid the experience of self-rejecting attitudes.

Chapter 4

Antecedents of Self-derogation

According to the general theory of deviant behavior outlined in the first chapter, people are more likely to develop negative self-attitudes when their participation in membership groups has been characterized by three analytically distinguishable but empirically interdependent sets of experiences:

1. Self-perceptions of failure to possess personally valued attributes or to perform personally valued behaviors (and self-perceptions of the possession of personally disvalued attributes or the performance of disvalued behaviors)
2. Self-perceptions of failure to be the object of positive attitudes by personally valued others (and self-perceptions of being the object of negative attitudes by personally valued others)
3. The failure to possess and employ self-protective response mechanisms that function to preclude the experience, or mitigate the effects, of the first two sets of experiences

This general proposition is compatible with a broad range of research findings, which will be reviewed in conjunction with the results to be presented here. Indeed, the proposition was in part derived from a consideration of this literature. However, these studies were characterized by a number of limitations. In some investigations both the indices of self-rejection and those of the characteristics of membership group experiences were determined at the same point in time, thus rendering it difficult to conclude whether the membership group experiences were antecedents or consequences of negative self-attitudes and, indeed, whether both were independently related to some third variable. In other investigations the study groups tended to be small and of unknown representativeness. In still other studies, notably many of the experimental studies, the groups were such that they could not reasonably be assumed to have exercised early, extended, lasting, or pervasive influences upon the person's psychosocial development.

In view of these and other limitations, the present analysis was undertaken. Indices of each of the three sets of membership group experiences determined at the time of the first testing were related to three measures of self-derogation determined at subsequent points in time. The three outcome measures refer to level of negative self-attitudes (self-derogation) at the second testing, 1 year following the first testing (SD 2); level of self-derogation at the third testing, 2 years following the first testing (SD 3); and residual gain in self-derogation from the first to the second testing (Rch SD 1–2).

The outcome measures SD 2 and SD 3 permit demonstration of the predictive value of the antecedent variables over two periods of time and, at the same time, under two degrees of sample representativeness, since sample attrition was greater from T_1 to T_3 than from T_1 to T_2. The use of Rch SD 1–2 permits partial resolution of certain problems of interpretation posed by the use of the first two measures (some of the very problems involved in the determination of independent and dependent variables at the same point in time) or that would have been posed by the use of simple difference scores to measure change, since the residual gain score in effect removes from the gain that portion of the gain that could have been predicted linearly from the earlier score. These issues will be considered later.

The measures of self-derogation were as described in earlier chapters. The indices of membership group experiences will be described together with the presentation of results. The findings concerning self-perceptions of valued or disvalued qualities and behaviors, attitudes of others toward the subject, and self-protective patterns as these relate to level of, and changes in, self-attitudes will be considered in turn.

Valued and Disvalued Qualities and Behaviors

A number of reports have indicated associations between the nature of self-attitudes on the one hand and any of a wide variety of qualities and behaviors on the other, particularly where there was reason to believe that the attributes or behaviors in question were affectively significant within the context of the subject's need–value system. These attributes or performances (variously determined by self-report, independent observation, or experimental induction) included physical attributes, intellectual ability, classroom performance, interpersonal influence, political success, educational and occupational attainments, as well as a number of other personal traits and behavior patterns.

With regard to physical attributes, Gunderson (1965) reported that among young navy men short–underweight and short–overweight groups tended to manifest the most unfavorable self-images. Rosen and Ross (1968) reported a correlation of .52 between satisfaction with physical appearance and self-concept, a correlation that was appreciably higher (.62) when only those items that tended to be rated by the subjects as more important were considered. Data from several studies have indicated that, for both genders, early physical maturation was related to more positive self-conceptions (H. H. Davidson & Gottlieb, 1955; Mussen & Jones, 1957; Smith and Lebo, 1956). This relationship is likely to be mediated by the responses of significant others in the environment to the subjects. Thus, in a follow-up study of adolescent boys when they were in their thirties, the retrospective reports indicated that the early maturers tended to recall pleasurable memories, whereas the late-maturing boys tended to recall peer rejection and unpleasantness (Jones, 1965).

With regard to perceived intellectual ability and classroom performance, the experimental induction of success on an IQ test has been related to an increase in overt self-ratings (Diller, 1954). Experimentally induced failure on an English grammar test has been related to reduced self-evaluations and to a reduction in the extent to which subjects believed they were valued by significant others in their lives (Gibby & Gibby, 1967). Furthermore, a longitudinal study of low-income black children revealed that teacher evaluation of academic performance in kindergarten is positively associated with self-esteem at grade 6 (Slaughter, 1977). In general, overachievers tended to be characterized in terms of higher self-esteem and such associated phenomena as good peer relationships and controlled anxiety (Taylor, 1964).

Traits relating to interpersonal influence, whether in the context of small group interaction or in the more inclusive sociopolitical arena, have also been related to self-esteem. A comparison of winning and losing political candidates revealed that those who were elected to office tended to gain in self-esteem, whereas those who were not elected were less likely to increase in self-esteem and were more likely to decrease in self-esteem. Those candidates who increased in self-esteem despite being defeated (all nonincumbents), it was suggested, may have received gratification from the publicity associated with candidacy (Ziller & Golding, 1969).

Consistent with the idea that a person's relative power, dominance, or influence in a small group predicts the direction of change in self-concept that person experiences as a function of participation in the group, members who were high in power were observed to change toward a more positive self-concept. Those low in power changed toward a more negative self-concept. These changes may be due to (as the investigator suggests) differential feelings of competence resulting from subjects' efforts at contribution to group discussions, differential perceptions of them and their ideas by other group members, or differential perceptions of receiving a disproportionate amount of the attention of other group members (Archer, 1974). Consistent with these results, others have noted the relationship of leadership abilities to self-esteem (Petersen & Kellam, 1977).

Numerous reports have indicated that occupational status was related to self-esteem (Jacques & Chason, 1977; Luck & Heiss, 1972), although it has been difficult to interpret the meaning of the association between the two variables. However, on the basis of data derived from a longitudinal study of tenth-grade boys, Bachman and O'Malley (1977) concluded, after controlling background factors and earlier self-esteem, that having a high-status job made a direct contribution to higher self-esteem. Educational attainment has also been related to self-esteem (Jacques & Chason, 1977; Purkey, 1970), although Bachman and O'Malley (1977) indicated that post–high school educational achievement, at least, had no direct impact on self-esteem and only a minor indirect impact by way of occupational status.

A variety of other manifestly valued attributes and behaviors have been related to self-esteem. Rosenberg (1965, pp. 234–248) reported that low self-esteem subjects, relative to subjects with medium and high levels of self-esteem, were appreciably less likely to indicate that they possessed the specified qualities considered essential for a young person to get ahead. Among subjects who rated themselves poor in terms of a number of qualities, those who indicated that they cared a great deal about the quality were more likely to manifest low self-esteem than those who indicated that they cared less than a great deal about the quality.

Congruent with the expectation that individuals who perceive themselves as having traits that are appropriate to their roles will have higher self-esteem, "masculine" males were observed to score higher on a measure of self-esteem than "feminine" males (Sappenfield & Harris, 1975). However, a parallel prediction that females who were more "feminine" would have higher self-esteem than females who were "masculine" was not supported. Apart from explanations of the sex-specific validity of the measure of masculinity/femininity, it is possible that current changes in female attitudes toward the feminine role may be such that "masculinity" now tends to be perceived as a socially desirable characteristic for females as well as males.

Even qualities that might appear to be less than basic in one's hierarchy of values have been associated with indices of self-attitudes. Data presented by Schneider (1974) suggest that the perception of one's mode of dress may influence positiveness of self-concept. An examination of two groups of subjects differing in mode of dress but not in prior self-concept indicated that well-dressed subjects, in comparison with more casually dressed subjects, manifested more socially desirable self-descriptions in an interview situation. Finally, consistent with the view that self-perceptions of having valued attributes and performing valued behaviors are related to the genesis of self-esteem are the results of a study in which subjects were induced to write self-descriptive essays involving the marshaling of arguments designed to convey an extremely favorable impression of themselves. Presumably the ideation involved in the preparation and organization of these arguments would facilitate the enhancement of self-attitudes. In an experiment in which half the subjects wrote about their personality attributes and half wrote about social propositions, the subjects who wrote the self-laudatory essays subsequently rated themselves more favorably than did the subjects who wrote in support of the social propositions (Mirels & McPeek, 1977). Although these data are consistent with a number of interpretations, they are certainly compatible with the view that the induction of self-perceived favorable qualities (by virtue of the required consciousness-raising activities involved in writing the essays) is related to increased self-acceptance.

With regard to the relationship between self-attitudes on the one hand and such attributes as those related to gender, race, and socioeconomic status on the other, the literature has failed to report consistently any significant relationships *in the absence of conditions suggesting the personal and social significance of the attributes.* Studies have variously reported that males had more positive self-attitudes than females, females had higher levels of self-esteem than males, and there was no significant difference between males and females with regard to level of self-acceptance (Jacques & Chason, 1977; Petersen & Kellam, 1977; Rosenkrantz, Voge, Bee, Broverman, & Broverman, 1968; Simmons & Rosenberg, 1975). In part this finding may be due to the variable bases of self-esteem among female and male subjects (Douvan & Adelson, 1966) and the differential probability that subjects of each gender will be able to display the respectively valued attributes and behaviors at the point in the developmental process at which the self-attitudes are measured. Thus, male and female adolescents appear to identify different achievement areas with specific genders and think it more important to achieve in the areas associated with their own gender (Stein, 1971). However, at specific developmental stages girls may be less able to approximate their gender-specific values. For example, during adolescence white girls may be more likely than boys to emphasize the importance of being good-looking and, therefore, to be much less satisfied with pubertal changes than are boys (Simmons & Rosenberg, 1975), a dissatisfaction that would be reflected in lowered self-esteem. Not only is the possibility of achieving valued qualities and behaviors variable with developmental sequence, but the value placed on different attributes may also change with developmental stage. Thus, Bachman and O'Malley (1977) reported that a number of dimensions showed the strongest correlation with self-esteem during high school and weaker correlations with later self-esteem. Such findings may indicate that there is a developmental shift in the value placed on certain attributes and behaviors as a basis for self-esteem whether or not they also indicate a reevaluation by society in general of the attributes and behaviors in question.

A similar situation has been observed with regard to race. Far from observing the frequently hypothesized advantage with regard to self-esteem said to accrue to white subjects, a number of investigations have observed either that there is no difference between black and white subjects or that black subjects have higher self-esteem (Hulbary, 1975; Hunt & Hunt, 1977; Jacques & Chason, 1977; Rosenberg & Simmons, 1972). Part of the explanation for this situation may again be in the circumstances influencing the values placed upon the racial statuses. In an insulated environment where to be black is the norm, self-esteem need not be adversely affected by that social fact. In an environment where to be white is the norm, to be black may result in self-rejection. Rosenberg (1975) has noted the maleficent influence of dissonant social contexts with regard to self-rejecting attitudes. At the junior-high level, black children attending white schools had lower self-esteem than blacks attending predominantly black schools. This difference was even greater at the senior-high level (Rosenberg & Simmons, 1972). These findings are consistent with the report by Powell and Fuller (1970) in a study of black and white students in grades 7 through 9. Black students in segregated schools were observed to have higher self-esteem than black students in integrated schools. Bachman (1970), in a nationwide study of tenth-grade boys, also observed blacks in segregated schools to have higher self-esteem scores than blacks in integrated schools; the differences became even stronger when controlling on socioeconomic status and intelligence.

Findings concerning the relationship between social class position and self-attitudes were similarly variable (H. B. Kaplan, 1971b). In some instances, the relationship was positive, in other instances it was negative; in still other studies no significant relationship was observed. Apparently a major condition for observing a significant relationship between self-acceptance and social class position is the value placed upon class membership within the personally and socially defined value systems (H. B. Kaplan, 1971b). The personal values placed upon social class positions will be determined in part by the consonance of the position with the more inclusive social context. For example, Rosenberg (1975) has noted that middle- or upper-class children attending lower-class schools had significantly lower self-esteem than middle, or upper middle-class children attending higher-class schools. Lower-class children in higher-class schools had lower self-esteem than lower-class children in lower-class schools.

Thus, even in the instances of attributes that have not consistently been associated with self-attitudes, such relationships have tended to be observed in circumstances where the personal valuation of the attributes is apparent. There is then a substantial empirical as well as theoretical basis for the expectation that the subjective perception of possessing valued attributes and performing valued behaviors will be related to self-attitudes. The following analysis considers whether this expectation is warranted in the context of the present research.

84

ANALYSIS

At the time of the first test administration the subjects indicated whether or not each of 12 descriptive qualities or behavior patterns were self-descriptive. They also indicated whether or not they considered each of the qualities or behavior patterns to be important. By combining the judgments of whether or not the items were self-descriptive and whether or not they were important it was possible, for each item, to distribute the subjects among four groupings: self-descriptive/important; self-descriptive/not important; not self-descriptive/ important; not self-descriptive/not important. The four groupings could then be compared with regard to mean self-derogation score at the time of the second test administration, mean self-derogation score at the time of the third test administration, and mean residual gain in self-derogation between the first and second testings.

The "desirable" items were selected on an a priori basis. In general, the choices appear to be justified in view of the very high percentages of subjects who endorsed the items as self-descriptive and as important. In only two instances was the endorsement highly equivocal. Only a small minority endorsed the item "having a rich family" as either self-descriptive or important, suggesting either the low value relevance of the item and/or the existence of a democratizing influence that prohibited the endorsement of such an elitist item. Only a slim majority endorsed the item that concerned painting or drawing well, and only a small minority judged the item to be important. In the instances of the other 10 items (being kind to others, having good manners, usually obeying teachers, being a fairly honest person, being patriotic, getting good grades, having a lot of friends, being liked by kids of the opposite sex, being good-looking, and being good at sports), the clear majority of the subjects endorsed the items as self-descriptive and important. The exact wording of the items is presented in Tables 4.1, 4.2, and 4.3. In any case, the major hypothesis was tested by holding judged importance constant.

RESULTS

The major hypothesis to be tested was this: Among subjects who judged an item to be important, those who endorsed the item as self-descriptive relative to those who denied that the item was self-descriptive would manifest significantly lower self-derogation scores at the times of the second and third test administrations and would display significantly greater residual decreases (or smaller residual increases) in self-derogation between the first and second testings. The results with regard to each of the outcome variables will be considered in turn.

The findings with regard to self-derogation at T_2 are summarized in Table 4.1. For each of the 12 items, among subjects who judged the item to be important, those who indicated at T_1 that the item was self-descriptive com-

85

TABLE 4.1

Mean Self-derogation Score at Second Testing (T_2), by Self-descriptions and Judgment of Importance of Presumably Valued Qualities and Behaviors at First Testing (T_1)

Items indicating quality or behavior $(T_1)^{a,b}$	Favorable quality or behavior is self-descriptive (yes)^c		Favorable quality or behavior is not self-descriptive (no)^c	
	Important	Not important	Important	Not important
1. Are you usually kind to others?/ I think it is important to be kind to others. (a,b)	32.91 27.90 3942	38.36 27.07 197	38.31 27.89 251	37.12 29.49 56
2. Do you usually have good manners?/I think it is important to have good manners. (a,b,c)	32.68 27.60 3900	40.50 29.71 174	38.72 29.65 243	40.66 28.90 109
3. Do you usually obey your teachers?/I think it is important to obey the teachers. (a,b,c)	32.40 27.61 3598	38.93 28.42 334	37.32 28.14 259	38.78 29.37 191
4. Are you a fairly honest person?/I think it is important to be honest. (a,b,c)	32.49 27.76 3846	38.82 27.53 207	42.38 28.95 280	38.84 26.40 109
5. Are you patriotic?/I think it is important to be patriotic. (a,b,c)	32.02 27.73 2873	36.34 29.25 393	34.82 25.94 351	36.72 28.55 734
6. Do you usually get good grades?/ I think it is important to get good grades. (a,b,c,d)	31.62 27.35 3433	36.96 26.32 204	41.39 29.66 652	42.00 28.89 118
7. Do you have a rich family?/I think it is important to have a rich family. (a,b,d,f)	35.47 27.60 206	31.56 27.22 486	40.90 27.79 490	32.48 27.86 3221
8. Do you have a lot of friends?/I think it is important to have a lot of friends. (b,c,d,e,f)	32.57 27.59 3244	30.79 26.29 646	44.82 29.75 342	37.37 30.82 199

(Continued)

pared to those who indicated that the item was not self-descriptive at that time (column 1 compared to column 3) manifested significantly lower self-derogation scores a year later at T_2. Thus, self-perceptions of personally valued attributes or behaviors were predictive of subsequent self-attitudes. Those who perceived themselves as *not* possessing personally valued qualities or performing personally valued behaviors displayed significantly greater (subsequently measured) levels of self-derogation than those who perceived themselves as possessing the personally valued traits or performing the personally valued behaviors. Con-

TABLE 4.1—*Continued*

Items indicating quality or behavior $(T_1)^{a,b}$	Favorable quality or behavior is self-descriptive (yes)^c		Favorable quality or behavior is not self-descriptive (no)^c	
	Important	Not important	Important	Not important
9. Are you liked by kids of the opposite sex?/I think it is important to be liked by kids of the opposite sex. (a,b,c,d,e,f)	32.52	29.73	44.84	36.22
	27.85	25.91	29.23	27.28
	3078	656	393	255
10. Are you fairly good looking?/I think it is important to be good looking. (a,b,c,d,e)	33.25	29.86	43.38	40.11
	27.22	26.59	31.12	29.88
	2206	1448	394	347
11. Are you good at sports?/I think it is important to be good at sports. (b,c,d,e,f)	31.95	31.90	43.50	36.28
	27.09	27.12	29.54	30.11
	2537	923	408	563
12. Do you paint or draw well?/I think it is important to be good at drawing or painting. (a,b,d,e,f)	33.45	31.18	41.13	33.49
	27.32	27.71	27.59	28.25
	1043	1193	413	1708

[a] Numbers differ from actual test-item numbers.

[b] Parenthetical entries indicate significant difference ($p < .05$, one-tailed test) between paired columns: a = 1 versus 2; b = 1 versus 3; c = 1 versus 4; d = 2 versus 3; e = 2 versus 4; f = 3 versus 4.

[c] Initial entry indicates mean score; second entry indicates standard deviation; third entry indicates cell N.

versely, those subjects who reported possessing personally valued attributes or performing personally valued behaviors displayed significantly more self-accepting attitudes than those subjects who reported not possessing the personally valued attributes or not performing the personally valued behaviors.

Among subjects who judged the items to be important, self-descriptions of having the desirable trait or performing the desirable behavior were significantly associated with lower self-derogation scores *for all 12 items,* but this relationship was not so consistently observed among subjects who denied that the traits or behaviors were important (column 2 compared to column 4). Considering only subjects who did not judge the item to be important, for only 5 of the items was the self-description of having the quality or performing the behavior associated with significantly lower self-derogation scores (having a lot of friends, being liked by kids of the opposite sex, being good-looking, being good at sports, painting or drawing well). For these items, whether or not the subject valued it, the self-perceptions of the trait or behavior were associated with more self-accepting attitudes. It was of course expected that where a quality or behavior was personally valued that the self-perception of having the quality or performing the behavior would enhance the subject's self-attitudes. However, certain traits apparently have self-enhancing consequences whether or not the subject values them. The 5 items in question suggest that, for example, the subjects characterized by them will evoke positive attitudinal response from others because of their looks, talent, or general likability, which in turn will influence the genesis of positive self-attitudes. This is not to exclude the possibility of other self-enhancing correlates of such traits, as the feeling of competence associated with being good at sports that might generalize to other areas of achievement.

However, the possession of other personally *nonvalued* traits does not necessarily have such benign consequences for self-attitudes. To perceive oneself as kindly, well-mannered, obedient to teachers, honest, and patriotic when one does not value these virtues is not to enhance self-attitudes, perhaps because such patterns are so nearly universally expected that to manifest the pattern does not excite praise, and to violate the expectation evokes criticism. This might account for the relatively high self-derogation scores among those who did not describe themselves in terms of these particular qualities, regardless of whether or not the item was felt to be important.

In addition to being explained in terms of the failure to evoke positive responses from others (despite the widespread social endorsement), the failure of subjects who describe themselves in terms of such "not important" virtues as the first five listed in Table 4.1 to display more self-accepting attitudes may also be explicable in terms of the deviant implications of the judgment of these virtues as unimportant. The acts of judging such widely endorsed virtues as unimportant may themselves evoke negative attitudinal responses from significant others and/or may be correlated with other deviant acts, which in turn evoke responses that influence the exacerbation of self-rejecting attitudes.

In any case, such self-descriptive qualities and behaviors as these appear to be relevant to enhancement of self-attitudes only insofar as they are judged to be important.

It may also be noted that those traits and behaviors that are associated with more self-accepting attitudes, regardless of judgment of importance (notably items 8–12), tend to be those that are associated with the peer value system. Those qualities that are associated with self-appreciation only where they are valued as important tend to be those that are endorsed particularly by parents and teachers. Thus, at a developmental stage where peer interaction is so prevalent, it is resonable to conclude that peer responses to subject traits and behaviors might have independent effects (by virtue of responses to subject qualities and behaviors) on subject self-attitudes, regardless of subject evaluation of the importance of the self-descriptive traits and behaviors, and that parent–teacher attitudes toward self-described traits and behaviors are more likely to influence adolescent self-attitudes only where such values are internalized, that is, judged to be important.

However, regardless of the nature of the influence of self-described traits and behaviors on subsequent self-attitudes among subjects who evaluate the traits and behaviors as not important, it remains clear that, in accordance with the major hypothesis, where traits and behaviors are judged to be important self-descriptions in such terms tend to be associated with lower levels of self-rejection.

Similar conclusions were warranted when self-derogation scores were measured 2 years, rather than 1 year, following the initial self-descriptions and self-judgments of the importance of qualities and behaviors. These findings are summarized in Table 4.2. For each of the 12 attributes and behaviors under consideration, among those subjects who considered the trait or behavior important, those who indicated that the item was self-descriptive had lower self-rejection scores than those who indicated that the item was not self-descriptive. In 10 of the 12 comparisons (Column 1 versus Column 3), the differences were statistically significant. Only in the instances of kindness and good manners did the differences fail to reach significance, perhaps indicating a change in these areas of personal value systems during the developmental stage between the seventh and ninth grades. Again, it would appear that the self-description of not being characterized in terms of valued qualities and behaviors is antecedent to more self-rejecting attitudes.

In contrast, where the item was judged to be not important, in only six of the comparisons (between Column 2 and Column 4) were there significant differences in self-derogation between those who judged themselves to be characterized by the item and those who judged that the item was not self-descriptive. Again, these items for the most part (items 8–12) appeared to reflect the peer value system and could be expected to have benign consequences for self-attitudes (in large measure because of positive responses from others in the context of omnipresent peer interaction), independent of the subjective judgment of importance. In short, these qualities could have been related to self-acceptance in part because the subject judged himself to be more praiseworthy by virtue of self-perceptions of valued attributes and behaviors, and in part by virtue of positive responses of others to socially valued attributes independent of personal judgments of importance.

In addition to items 8–12, getting good grades was significantly related to self-attitudes at T_3 even among subjects who judged the item to be unimportant. (The same item was appreciably but not significantly related to self-

TABLE 4.2

Mean Self-derogation Score at Third Testing (T_3), by Self-descriptions and Judgment of Importance of Presumably Valued Qualities and Behaviors at First Testing (T_1)

| Items indicating quality or behavior (T_1)[a,b] | Favorable quality or behavior is self-descriptive (yes)[c] | | Favorable quality or behavior is not self-descriptive (no)[c] | |
	Important (1)	Not important (2)	Important (3)	Not important (4)
1. Are you usually kind to others?/I think it is important to be kind to others. (a,d)	28.97 27.62 2749	36.13 27.53 135	29.52 25.38 163	33.78 27.78 40
2. Do you usually have good manners?/I think it is important to have good manners. (c)	29.15 27.52 2732	29.69 26.28 116	31.42 29.14 155	35.08 28.74 74
3. Do you usually obey your teachers?/I think it is important to obey the teachers. (b,c)	28.72 27.51 2551	31.35 27.16 222	32.40 26.79 166	35.87 27.88 113
4. Are you a fairly honest person?/I think it is important to be honest. (a,b,c)	28.33 27.17 2726	35.50 28.47 126	38.22 29.37 179	34.41 28.72 68
5. Are you patriotic?/I think it is important to be patriotic. (b,c)	28.32 28.16 2059	29.64 25.51 271	31.44 24.68 234	32.30 27.24 470
6. Do you usually get good grades?/I think it is important to get good grades. (b,c,d,e)	27.94 26.88 2459	30.68 27.56 147	36.69 29.82 400	41.66 31.22 67
7. Do you have a rich family?/I think it is important to have a rich family. (b,d,f)	29.39 26.05 146	26.90 26.47 353	37.53 29.41 320	28.62 27.41 2246
8. Do you have a lot of friends?/I think it is important to have a lot of friends. (b,c,d,e,f)	28.65 27.04 2242	26.56 25.41 487	40.51 32.41 228	32.96 30.01 128

(*Continued*)

derogation at T_2). Again, this item might be expected to have self-enhancing consequences independent of personal judgment of importance, perhaps as a result of evoking positive responses from others (parents, teachers).

Again, in contrast to these, items 1–5 and 7 are clearly only related to self-rejection or acceptance by virtue of self-perceptions of being—or not being—characterized by personally valued attributes or behaviors. Self-descriptions in terms of these items were not predictive of self-attitudes where

TABLE 4.2—*Continued*

Items indicating quality or behavior $(T_1)^{a,b}$	Favorable quality or behavior is self-descriptive (yes)^c		Favorable quality or behavior is not self-descriptive (no)^c	
	Important (1)	Not important (2)	Important (3)	Not important (4)
9. Are you like by kids of the oppo-site sex?/I think it is important to be liked by kids of the opposite sex. (a,b,c,d,e,f)	28.47 26.91 2136	26.26 26.06 477	41.02 30.59 253	32.72 30.33 193
10. Are you fairly good looking?/I think it is important to be good looking. (a,b,c,d,e,f)	29.14 27.04 1547	26.76 26.38 1027	39.24 30.58 247	33.94 30.59 235
11. Are you good at sports?/I think it is important to be good at sports. (b,c,d,e,f)	27.84 26.65 1737	27.31 26.43 647	38.20 30.17 274	33.49 29.91 416
12. Do you paint or draw well?/I think it is important to be good at drawing or painting. (a,b,d,e,f)	29.48 26.84 715	26.31 26.28 833	34.91 28.55 291	30.52 28.44 1196

^{a} Numbers differ from actual test-item numbers.

^{b} Parenthetical entries indicate significant ($p < .05$, one-tailed test) differences between paired columns: a = 1 versus 2; b = 1 versus 3; c = 1 versus 4; d = 2 versus 3; e = 2 versus 4; f = 3 versus 4.

^{c} Initial entry indicates mean score; second entry indicates standard deviation; third entry indicates cell N.

the items were judged not to be important. As suggested earlier, perhaps the possession of these traits and the performance of these behaviors *in themselves* are not sufficient to evoke positive responses because of their near-universal (with the exception of item 7) prevalence—that is, the attribute or behavior is to be expected. Rather, the *absence* of the item would evoke negative responses. However, the effect would not be strong enough to render subjects who lacked the items significantly more self-derogatory than those characterized by the "unimportant" item, since such a deviant judgment (or its correlates) might evoke negative responses, which in turn would increase the level of self-rejection among these subjects.

In the case of having a rich family (Item 7), *not* having a rich family was associated with higher subsequent levels of self-derogation *among subjects who judged the quality to be important.* However, among those who reported that having a rich family was *not* important, there was no difference in self-derogatory attitudes between the group that reported that they had a rich family and the group that reported that they did not. Similar findings were observed for self-derogation scores 1 year later (Item 7 in Table 4.1). Although having a rich family might be expected to have certain advantages with regard to self-enhancement (such as providing resources that permit the avoidance or assuagement of the effects of self-devaluing experiences), even if the item was judged to be not important, apparently the effects were not sufficient greatly to outweigh any advantages implicit in the normatively defined circumstances, whereby having a rich family is both rare and judged to be unimportant.

In summary, as in the earlier analysis where self-derogation level at T_2 was observed to be consistently related to self-descriptions (at T_1) of having qualities and performing behaviors judged by the subject to be important, so was self-derogation at T_3 related to self-descriptions in terms of items subjectively judged to be important. In general, among subjects who judged an item to be important, those subjects who reported that they were not characterized by the item later had significantly higher self-derogation scores than those subjects who indicated that the item was self-descriptive.

Consistent with this conclusion are the findings related to residual gains in self-derogation between the first and second test administrations. These results are summarized in Table 4.3.

Among subjects who judged the items to be important, for 11 of the 12 items those subjects who indicated that an item was not self-descriptive showed greater residual increases (or lower residual decreases) in self-derogation between the first and second test administrations than those subjects who indicated that the item was self-descriptive. For 6 of the items the differences (between Column 1 and Column 3) were statistically significant. Why there should have been more appreciable and significant differences among this set of items rather than among the remaining set of items is problematic. A number of explanations suggest themselves, including the possibility that the absence of certain of the traits is highly visible and therefore is more likely to evoke negative responses from significant others, which would exacerbate the already relatively high levels of self-rejection resulting from self-perceptions of not being characterized by the subjectively valued item (for example, not being a fairly honest person). The absence of other items, in addition to constituting disvalued circumstances, implies the deprivation of personal resources (for example, not having a lot of friends) that might have functioned to assuage the adverse effects of other self-devaluing circumstances. The judgment that certain items are not self-descriptive (not being liked by kids of the opposite sex, for example) suggests continuing interpersonal rejection. Finally, the failure to describe oneself as good at sports, or at painting or drawing, might imply the absence of areas of achievement that might have served as compensatory responses for an otherwise pervasively self-devaluing life-style. In short, in addition to inducing the subject to disvalue himself increasingly by virtue of self-perceptions of not being characterized by personally valued attributes and behaviors (or of being characterized by personally disvalued attributes and behaviors), the self-perceptions, in varying kinds and degrees, may have other implications for changes in self-attitudes.

In any case the judgment that the behavior or quality is important appears to be a relevant condition for the influence of the self-perceptions on residual gains in self-attitudes. When only subjects who judged the quality or behavior to be not important were considered, self-perceptions of only 1 of the 12 items (being fairly good-looking) significantly differentiated between those who did (Column 2) and did not (Column 4) describe themselves as characterized by the quality or behavior. Indeed for the first 7 of the items the differences in residual gain in self-derogation were not even in the direction that would have been predicted on the basis of the self-description alone, perhaps reflecting sequelae of the deviant nature of the judgments that these items were not important in addition to sequelae of not possessing, in general, socially (if not personally) valued characteristics.

Thus, as in the analyses predicting self-derogation scores at T_2 and T_3, residual gains in self-derogation between T_1 and T_2 were related to antecedent self-description in terms of important (but not, consistently, unimportant) qualities or behaviors. Among subjects who judged the qualities or behaviors to be important, those who described themselves (at T_1) as not possessing the important quality or not performing the personally valued behavior tended to be more self-rejecting 1 year (T_2) and 2 years (T_3) later and to display relatively greater residual increases in self-derogation between T_1 and T_2 than subjects who described themselves as possessing the quality or behavior in question.

Attitudes of Significant Others

A basic theoretical premise of the study under consideration is that the expressed attitudes of significant others toward the subject influence the nature of the subject's self-attitudes. To be sure, all "others" are not equally influential. A person cares more about the opinions of some than about the opinions of others. Indeed, to some extent how important a person's attitudes are will be determined by the nature of the attitudes expressed by that person toward the subject in the past. By way of self-protection the person, within limits, may come to value less those who reject him and to value more those who are emotionally supportive. The significance of others' attitudes toward us at a given point in time or over time is apparently influenced also by their positions in the social structure (Rosenberg, 1973). Thus, older children are said to be

TABLE 4.3

Mean Residual Change in Self-derogation between the First (T₁) and Second (T₂) Testings, by Self-descriptions and Judgment of Importance of Presumably Valued Qualities and Behaviors at First Testing (T₁)

Items indicating quality or behavior $(T_1)^{a,b}$	Favorable quality or behavior is self-descriptive (yes)^{c,d}		Favorable quality or behavior is not self-descriptive (no)^{c,d}	
	Important (1)	Not important (2)	Important (3)	Not important (4)
1. Are you usually kind to others?/I think it is important to be kind to others.	−.09 24.64 3918	2.54 24.69 195	−.08 25.78 248	−2.49 29.55 55
2. Do you usually have good manners?/I think it is important to have good manners. (a,c)	−.37 24.43 3875	4.68 26.52 174	.59 27.14 241	4.16 26.50 108
3. Do you usually obey your teachers?/I think it is important to obey the teachers. (a)	−.47 24.41 3573	3.82 26.13 332	.82 25.06 259	.85 27.04 191
4. Are you a fairly honest person?/I think it is important to be honest. (b)	−.31 24.59 3823	1.82 24.90 206	3.51 25.95 279	.54 26.82 108
5. Are you patriotic?/I think it is important to be patriotic. (d,f)	−.50 24.68 2866	1.60 26.99 391	−1.45 22.88 348	1.12 24.91 73
6. Do you usually get good grades?/I think it is important to get good grades. (a,b)	−.50 24.32 3409	2.54 24.52 204	1.65 26.76 646	2.51 26.80 116
7. Do you have a rich family?/I think it is important to have a rich family. (f)	1.44 23.98 205	.42 24.46 483	1.98 25.55 484	−.55 24.73 3210
8. Do you have a lot of friends?/I think it is important to have a lot of friends. (b,d)	−.41 24.70 3222	−.96 23.59 642	4.24 26.35 342	.52 27.04 197

(*Continued*)

less likely than younger children to care what their parents think of them, and among white children there is a decline with age in concern with what adults (mother, father, teachers) think of them, although among black children such a reduction is not at all or only modestly apparent. Furthermore, among white (but not among black) children there is an increase with age in caring about their friends' opinions. With regard to sex, by way of further illustration, girls

TABLE 4.3—*Continued*

Items indicating quality or behavior $(T_1)^{a,b}$	Favorable quality or behavior is self-descriptive (yes)[c,d]		Favorable quality or behavior is not self-descriptive (no)[c,d]	
	Important (1)	Not important (2)	Important (3)	Not important (4)
9. Are you liked by kids of the opposite sex?/I think it is important to be liked by kids of the opposite sex. (b,d,f)	−.47 24.96 3068	−1.57 23.02 650	4.74 25.91 390	.42 24.36 253
10. Are you fairly good looking?/I think it is important to be good looking. (c,d,e)	.05 24.44 2192	−1.00 23.45 1441	1.77 28.08 391	3.05 26.95 346
11. Are you good at sports?/I think it is important to be good at sports. (b,c,d)	−1.04 24.10 2514	0 23.96 919	3.31 27.35 406	2.14 26.49 563
12. Do you paint or draw well?/I think it is important to be good at drawing or painting. (b,d,f)	−.58 24.65 1035	−.24 24.12 1184	2.83 25.70 411	−.16 25.06 1700

[a] Numbers differ from test-item numbers.

[b] Parenthetical entries indicate significant ($p < .05$, one-tailed test) difference between paired columns: a = 1 verus 2; b = 1 versus 3; c = 1 versus 4; d = 2 versus 3; e = 2 versus 4; f = 3 versus 4.

[c] Initial entry indicates mean score, second entry indicates standard deviation, third entry indicates cell N.

[d] Negative value of mean score indicates relative decrease in self-derogation. Positive value of mean score indicates relative increase in self-derogation.

are more likely to care about what their teachers think of them and, after age 12, become more concerned than boys with the attitudes of friends and classmates. With regard to position in the social structure differentiated according to socioeconomic status, higher-class children are more likely to care about what their mothers, fathers, and friends think of them than lower-class children. This holds true controlling on race, but it is *especially true of higher-class blacks* (Rosenberg, 1973).

However, though much variability in the nature of the influence of others' attitudes on self-attitudes may be noticed, it is rare that others have been reported to have *no* influence on self-attitudes, regardless of whether the social context involved familial, school, peer, or other relationships. With regard to familial attitudes, Rosenberg (1965) noted a relationship between low self-esteem and perceived lack of parental interest; Medinnus (1965) observed self-acceptance to be associated with subjects' perceptions of parents as loving, nonneglectful, and nonrejecting; and Coopersmith (1967) reported high self-esteem to be associated with parental acceptance of the child and with well-defined and enforced limits on the child's behavior—but within those limits, there was respect for the child and some latitude for the child's behavior. In a nationwide sample of tenth-grade boys, Bachman (1970) observed that self-esteem was positively related to perceptions of affection among family members and to reports of inclusion of children in family decision-making activities. Sears (1970) used measures of parental attitudes obtained from interviews with the subjects' mothers 7 years earlier and concluded that parental warmth significantly influenced the child's self-esteem. Thomas and his associates (1974) reported that a measure of parental support was strongly and consistently related to self-esteem among their adolescent subjects, although parental control was not strongly or consistently related to adolescent self-esteem (Thomas, Gecas, Weigert, & Rooney, 1974). Matteson (1974) reported support for the hypothesis that adolescents with low self-esteem received more dysfunction in the way their parents communicated with them than other adolescents with high self-esteem. Petersen and Kellam (1977) indicated that quality and quantity of affectional resources in the family were related to self-esteem.

In the context of the schools, self-attitudes were observed to vary appropriately in response to the experimental manipulation of ratings by a "visiting speech expert" of students' reading performance in introductory speech classes (Videbeck, 1960), and ratings by a "physical development expert" of male high-school students' performance of physical tasks (Maehr, Mensing, & Nafzger, 1962), and in relationship to the child's perception of the teacher's perception of him (H. H. Davidson & Lang, 1960).

In the context of peer groups, Rosenberg (1965), for example, reported that among high-school students low self-esteem students were least likely to be nominated as leaders and were most likely to report never having held an office.

A variety of other reports have concurred in the conclusion that the perceived attitudes of others influence self-esteem. Thus, subjects who report experiences of discrimination are more likely to have low self-esteem, and with decreasing levels of self-esteem high-school juniors and seniors were increasingly likely to report that most people thought poorly of them (Rosenberg, 1965). Consistent with these results are experimental studies (e.g., Tippett & Silber, 1966) reporting that subjects tend to show lower self-esteem in response to fictitious research-staff evaluations that consistently altered subjects' self-ratings in a less favorable direction on certain items.

Thus, as in the case of perceived values and behaviors, there is a substantial empirical as well as theoretical basis for the hypotheses to be considered subsequently.

ANALYSIS

In general, each of five indices of subjects' perceptions of others' attitudes toward them (measured at T_1) was hypothesized to be related to subsequently measured indices of self-attitudes (self-derogation score at T_2, self-derogation score at T_3, and residual gain in self-derogation between T_1 and T_2) such that subjects who were "high" in perception of negative attitudes expressed by others toward them would manifest higher subsequent self-derogation scores and increases in self-derogation than those who were "low" on the indices.

The first three independent variables refer to attitudes by peers, family, and school authorities, respectively. The fourth measure is a summary measure based on the first three indices. The fifth measure refers to generalized "other" responses to specified ascribed qualities of the subjects. All of the indices (except the fourth) were derived by factor analysis. The items are presented in decreasing order of magnitude of the orthogonal factor loadings (indicated parenthetically following the item).

Perceived devaluation of peers was measured in terms of the number of "true" responses to the following items:

The kids at school are usually not very interested in what I say or do. (.70)

Most of the kids at school do not like me very much. (.66)

More often than not I feel put down by the kids at school. (.60)

I am not very good at the kinds of things the kids at school think are important. (.55)

For purposes of the analysis the person was considered "high" in perceived devaluation in peer groups if he answered "true" to one or more of the items, and "low" on this variable if he answered "false" to all of the items. In this as in the following instances, cutting points were selected as close to the median value as was permitted by the distribution of responses.

Perceived devaluation by family was measured in terms of the number of "true" responses to the following items:

I would like to leave home. (.70)

My parents do not like me very much. (.64)

At home I have been more unhappy than happy. (.63)

As long as I can remember my parents have put me down. (.61)

My parents are usually not very interested in what I say or do. (.40)

My parents hardly ever trust me to do something on my own. (.35)
My family can't give me the chance to succeed that most kids have. (.32)

For purposes of the analysis the person was considered to be "high" in perceived devaluation by family if he answered "true" to·one or more of the items, and "low" on this variable if he answered "false" to all of the items.

Perceived devaluation by school was measured in terms of the number of affirmative ("yes" or "true") responses to the following items:

Would you like to quit school as soon as possible? (.61)
I have never been very happy in school. (.52)
My teachers do not like me very much. (.48)
My teachers are usually not very interested in what I say or do. (.35)
I probably will not go to college and graduate. (.34)
My teachers usually put me down. (.28)
By my teachers' standards I am a failure. (.25)

For purposes of the analysis the person was considered "high" on perceived devaluation by the school if he answered affirmatively to two or more of the items, and "low" on this variable if he answered affirmatively to only one or none of the items.

Perceived devaluation by membership groups was measured by the number of instances in which the person was "high" on the first three measures. For purposes of the analysis the person was considered "high" on perceived devaluation by membership groups if he was "high" on one or more of the first three variables, and "low" on this variable if he was "low" on all of the first three variables.

Perceived devaluation by people for ascribed characteristics was measured in terms of the number of affirmative responses to the following items:

People often put me down because of my color. (.54)
Is your family a member of a minority group? (.48)
People often put me down because of my religion. (.35)
People often put me down because my family is poor. (.28)

For purposes of the analysis the person was considered "high" on perceived devaluation by people for ascribed characteristics if he responded affirmatively to one or more of the items, and "low" on this variable if he responded in the negative to all of the items.

For this variable, as for all of the others, the median value differentiated the "high" and "low" groups. These groups were then compared with regard to the mean self-derogation scores at T_2 and T_3, and mean residual gain in self-derogation between T_1 and T_2.

RESULTS

The findings are summarized in Table 4.4. All hypotheses were supported. Subjects who scored high on perceived devaluation by peers, family, school, membership groups in general, and on perceived devaluation by others because of specified ascribed characteristics at T_1, compared to subjects who scored low on these measures, manifested higher self-derogation scores at T_2 and T_3 and greater increases (or smaller decreases) between T_1 and T_2 in residualized changes in self-derogation. All differences were significant at the .001 level, with the exception of mean residual change in self-derogation $T_1 - T_2$ for the last variable. Perhaps the failure to achieve significance in this instance suggests that the self-devaluing influence of others' negative attitudes toward the specified ascribed characteristics had already reached its outer limit by this stage in the developmental sequence.

In any case the data generously support the expectation that the subjectively perceived expression of negative attitudes toward the subject by others will be related to higher future levels of, and greater future increases in, self-derogation, and the subjectively perceived expression of positive attitudes toward the subject by others will be related to lower future levels of, and greater future decreases in, self-derogation.

Self-protective Patterns

The relationship between self-attitudes and self-protective patterns has been suggested by several categories of research findings. In one category, results have been reported in which self-rejecting attitudes were associated with the apparent *inability* to forestall the experience of self-devaluing circumstances or to redefine and thereby reduce the self-devaluing implications of such circumstances. Results in this category would include Rosenberg's (1965) reports indicating that low self-esteem subjects are more likely to score high on a "sensitivity to criticism" scale and are more likely to be described by others as "touchy and easily hurt." Also included are Leventhal and Perloe's (1962) findings that, where a communication was apparently from a source who was dissimilar in personality characteristics, low self-esteem subjects were more influenced by threatening than by optimistic communications, whereas the reverse was true for high self-esteem subjects.

Into a second category fall those studies in which self-rejecting attitudes are associated with patterns of response to self-devaluing circumstances that are unlikely to forestall or reduce the experience of self-rejecting feelings (perhaps

99

TABLE 4.4

Mean Self-derogation Scores at T_2 and T_3 and Mean Residual Change in Self-derogation T_1-T_2, by Selected Antecedent (T_1) Indices of Devaluation by Others[a]

	Mean self-derogation[b]		Mean residual change in self-derogation,[b,c]
	T_2	T_3	T_1-T_2
Perceived devaluation by peers			
Low	25.4	22.9	−2.4
	25.2	24.8	23.1
	1713	1206	1700
High	38.6	33.9	1.5
	28.4	28.4	25.6
	2750	1853	2740
Perceived devaluation by family			
Low	26.8	24.7	−2.2
	25.5	25.6	23.3
	2324	1651	2306
High	40.8	35.2	2.3
	28.5	28.6	26.1
	2155	1418	2146
Perceived devaluation by school			
Low	28.9	26.1	−1.6
	26.5	26.5	23.8
	2935	2104	2922
High	42.4	37.2	3.1
	28.4	28.5	26.3
	1512	942	1504

(*Continued*)

because of their near-complete divorcement from reality) and/or are likely to evoke further circumstances with self-devaluing implications (perhaps because of the social judgments of deviance attached to the patterns in question). Thus, Washburn (1962) reported support for the hypothesis that self-evaluations of inadequacy would be associated with more retreating defenses (marked by the avoidance of coming to grips with problems, or by denial of reality) and hostile defenses (marked by critical, suspicious behavior and lack of identification with others). Retreating defenses were indicated by a Reality Rejection subtest reflecting the attempt to detach oneself from potentially threatening situations by refusing to accept and face existing circumstances, and included such defenses as suppression, regression, withdrawal, and negativism. The pattern correlated negatively with empathy.

TABLE 4.4—*Continued*

	Mean self-derogation[b]		Mean residual change in self-derogation,[b,c]
	T_2	T_3	T_1-T_2
Perceived devaluation by membership groups			
Low	21.7	20.4	−3.5
	23.7	23.8	22.3
	1036	760	1028
High	37.1	32.5	1.0
	28.1	28.1	25.4
	3393	2275	3384
Perceived devaluation by people for ascribed characteristics			
Low	32.2	27.9	−.2
	28.0	27.4	25.0
	3026	2082	3011
High	36.4	33.0	.4
	27.4	27.7	24.2
	1452	985	1442

[a] Part of this table, drawn from Table 2 of "Antecedents of Negative Self-attitudes: Membership Group Devaluation and Defenselessness," by Howard B. Kaplan, is reprinted with stylistic changes from *Social Psychiatry*, 1976, *11* (2), pp. 15–25, by permission of the publisher, Springer-Verlag.

[b] The three values in sequence are mean, standard deviation, and N. All low versus high comparisons are significant, $p < .001$ (one-tailed) for t test assuming unequal variances (Welch, 1947) with the exception of mean residual change in self-derogation T_1-T_2 for the last variable.

[c] Negative values indicate decrease in self-derogation.

Hostile defenses, indicated by a Self–Other Distortion subtest, reflected both exaggeration of threats in the external environment and use of symptoms of physical illness to excuse the subject's behavior. Included among the hostile defenses were projection, displacement of hostility, substitution, and conversion. This pattern was inversely related to sublimation, fantasy, and identification.

Consistent with the view that these defenses were deviant in nature was the observation that delinquents were more likely than nondelinquents to display both the denial and externalization type clusters of defenses (Washburn, 1963). In this connection it may also be noted that "maladjusted" children classified as externalizers (those who were hyperaggressive, acted out in class, or committed antisocial acts such as stealing)—the very children who appear to be least tolerated in school and family contexts—had a particularly depressed sense of self-worth (Katz, Zigler, & Zalk, 1975). Although both externalizers and internalizers (those characterized by fears, phobias, general anxiety, depression, or social withdrawal) had a poorer real self-image than normal children, the difference was significant only for the externalizer–normal comparison. It was also observed that externalizing children had lower ideal-self scores than the internalizers and normals, thus suggesting that the lower self-image disparities also observed for the externalizing children were "due not only to a lower real self-image but also to an attenuated aspiration to emit socially valued behaviors [Katz *et al.*, 1975, p. 550]."

A third category would include results relating to the association of self-accepting attitudes (or their correlates, such as reduced anxiety) with response patterns that (*a*) were interpretable as effectively functioning to forestall self-devaluing circumstances or reduce the intensity and duration of consequent self-rejecting feelings and (*b*) were not likely in themselves to evoke further circumstances with self-devaluing implications, such as might be evoked by socially unacceptable patterns that might otherwise have functioned to forestall or reduce the experience of self-rejecting feelings. Into this category would fall the report of findings indicating that subjects with less anxiety tended to possess more defensive attitudes, which avoided blame and justified unacceptable behavior (Washburn, 1962). More specifically, subjects with a relatively low level of anxiety (compared to those whose anxiety level was relatively high) scored significantly higher on a measure of guilt deflection, labeled *vindication* in a later report (Washburn, 1963). This measure was said to reflect an attempt to avoid blame and to maintain manifest *conformity to socially approved standards,* and involved such defenses as rationalization, reaction formation, and compensation. In the present context it is particularly interesting to note that this measure was negatively related to nonconformance. Also falling into this category are such diverse studies as those that show positive self-attitudes to be related to such measures of defensiveness as the K scale of the MMPI (Wylie, 1961)—said to indicate a disposition to deny, among other things, feelings of inferiority and to look at others and oneself through rose-tinted glasses (Marks & Seeman, 1963)—and those that suggest self-attitudes to be related to realistic self-appraisal and constructive attempts to adjust to the environment. In this last connection, contrasting upwardly and downwardly mobile boys, Douvan and Adelson (1958) reported that upwardly mobile boys showed high self-acceptance and confidence in social situations, whereas self-rejection and demoralization were more likely to be found in downwardly mobile boys. In response to a question about what they would like to change about themselves if they could, the downwardly mobile boys more often desired major changes that indicated alienation from self, and were more likely to wish for changes unlikely to occur. In contrast, the upwardly mobile boys more often cited changes they had the power to effect themselves. In short, they were less self-rejecting and more *realistically* critical of themselves.

These findings, along with many other results cited in Chapter 3, are consistent with the hypothesis that self-rejecting attitudes would be associated with the *absence* of self-protective mechanisms that (*a*) function to forestall or reduce self-rejecting feelings and (*b*) would not evoke new circumstances (circumstances that might not otherwise have arisen were it not for the nature of the self-protective response) having self-devaluing implications. Conversely, these results are compatible with the hypothesis that self-accepting attitudes are related to the *presence* of self-protective patterns that (*a*) function to forestall or reduce self-rejecting feelings and (*b*) do not evoke new circumstances having self-devaluing sequelae. Unlike these reports, however, the following analysis permitted a demonstration of the temporal relationship between the indices of self-protective attitudes and the subsequent measurement of self-attitudes. It also permitted, to a limited extent, disentanglement of questions regarding whether the observed association reflected the need for self-rejecting subjects subsequently to adopt self-protective patterns and/or the effectiveness or ineffectiveness of dysfuntional consequences of the self-protective patterns with regard to increasing or decreasing self-rejecting attitudes.

ANALYSIS

The three indices of self-protective attitudes employed in the present analysis parallel the three categories of findings reviewed earlier. The three measures were derived by factor analysis. As before, the items comprising the measure are presented in descending order of the magnitude of the orthogonally rotated factor loadings (indicated parenthetically following the item). Individuals who were "high" and "low" respectively on each of the indices at T_1 were compared with regard to each of the outcome measures (self-derogation score at T_2, self-derogation score at T_3, and residual gain in self-derogation T_1-T_2). The subjects were distributed into "high" and "low" categories with reference to the median value of the distribution.

Defenselessness/vulnerability was measured by the number of affirmative responses to the following items:

Are you often bothered by nervousness? (.56)

Do you often get angry, annoyed, or upset? (.54)

I get nervous when things aren't just right. (.54)

Do you often feel downcast and dejected? (.54)

Do you often have difficulty keeping your mind on things? (.52)

I spend a lot of time daydreaming. (.47)

Do you often have trouble sitting still for a long time? (.43)

When the kids at school dislike something I do, it bothers me very much. (.39)

Do you become deeply disturbed when someone laughs at you or blames you for something you have done wrong? (.32)

Do you have a lot of accidents? (.31)

When my parents dislike something I do it bothers me very much. (.31)

When my teachers dislike something I do it bothers me very much. (.24)

These items may be thought of as falling into two subsets—those indicative of subjective distress, and those suggesting extreme sensitivity to negative attitudes expressed by others. Thus, high scores on this variable are understood to be indicative of defenselessness/vulnerability in the sense that the individuals are apparently unable to forestall or reduce the experience of subjective distress associated with sensitivity to negative attitudes expressed toward them by others.

For purposes of the analysis subjects were considered to be "high" in defenselessness/vulnerability if they responded affirmatively to six or more of the items, and "low" on this variable if they responded affirmatively to only five or fewer items.

This variable appeared to have good construct validity. Consistent with its interpretation as the inability to forestall or reduce the experience of self-rejecting feelings through normatively prescribed patterns is the pattern of modest but significant correlations observed between this variable and a number of others measured at T_1 for all subjects present at the first testing. Some of these variables have been defined. Others will be described in other connections. Most relevant in the present context are the positive relationships observed between this variable and perceived devaluation by peers (.36), by family (.29), by school (.22), by others because of ascribed characteristics (.12), and between the variable and indices of contranormative patterns (.21) and awareness of deviant patterns in the environment (.26).

The second index is interpreted as the attempt to avoid personal responsibility for self-devaluing circumstances through the adoption of ineffective or deviant response patterns. The ineffectiveness of the responses in part results from the surrendering of control over personal outcomes to the environment ("It's mostly luck if one succeeds or fails." and "You can do very little to change your life") and in part from escaping into fantasy ("I would like to travel with a circus or carnival."). The deviant nature of the responses is reflected in the person's cynical detachment from reigning moral codes ("I don't care much about other people's feelings." and "Do you tell lies often?").

The items comprising the index are as follows:

It's mostly luck if one succeeds or fails. (.58)

I don't care much about other people's feelings. (.49)

You can do very little to change your life. (.44)

When I do something wrong, it's almost like it's someone else who is doing it, not me. (.42)

Do you tell lies often? (.39)

Often I feel that I don't have enough control over the direction my life is taking. (.38)

If someone insulted me I would probably avoid talking to him in the future. (.37)

I would like to travel with a circus or carnival. (.36)

Do you often lose track of what you were thinking? (.34)

Are most of your friends older than you? (.31)

People often talk about me behind my back. (.27)

Do you try to avoid situations in which you have to compete with others? (.24)

Subjects were considered "high" on the variable if they responded affirmatively on four or more items, and "low" on the variable if they responded affirmatively to only three or fewer items.

This measure appears to encompass two patterns of protective attitudes discussed previously in the review of the relevant literature. These two patterns were identified by Washburn (1962) in a cluster analysis of 15 defense mechanisms. One of these patterns, *self–other distortion,* is said to involve "exaggeration of threats in the external environment . . . to excuse one's own behavior [p. 88]." The defenses involved in this pattern include projection, displacement of hostility, substitution, and conversion or symptom formation. The second pattern, *reality rejection,* "involves seeking to detach oneself from potentially threatening situations by refusing to accept and face things as they are [p. 88]." This pattern includes suppression, regression, withdrawal, and negativism, and is negatively correlated with empathy.

Consistent with the fact that both of these clusters, labeled *externalization* and *denial* respectively in a later report (Washburn, 1963), appeared on the same factor in the present study, Washburn (1962, p. 89) reported a correlation of .28 between measures of these two patterns for a grouping of 100 high-school students, thus suggesting a common underlying factor.

This variable also appears to have good construct validity, significantly correlated as it is with subjective perceptions of self-devaluing experiences in peer (.41), family (.45), and school (.44) settings, and with subjective perceptions of rejection by others for one's ascribed characteristics (.31). This index was also positively correlated with a measure of contranormative attitudes (.56), awareness of deviant patterns in the environment (.31), and with the index of defenselessness/vulnerability introduced earlier (.44). This is just the pattern that would be expected if the index reflected ineffective/deviant attempts to avoid (forestall or reduce) the experience of self-rejecting feelings.

The third variable was labeled *guilt deflection* after Washburn (1962, p. 88), who described this pattern of self-protective attitudes as "an attempt to avoid blame and maintain the experience of conforming to socially approved standards of behavior." Guilt deflection was inversely related to nonconformance and involved such defenses as rationalization, reaction formation, and compensation. The index was here interpreted broadly as the use of socially acceptable mechanisms to forestall or reduce the experience of self-rejecting feelings. From the nature of the factor sturcture it would appear that much the same mechanisms were reflected in the component items as were said to be involved in Washburn's guilt-deflection cluster. The items comprising the measure were as follows:

> By the time I am 30 I will probably have a good job and a good future ahead of me. (.51)
>
> If someone insulted me I would probably figure, "Who cares what he thinks." (.48)
>
> If someone insulted me I would probably figure it was his own problems that made him do it. (.44)
>
> When things aren't going too well for me I try to think that things will be better in the future. (.42)
>
> If someone insulted me I would probably try to joke about it. (.41)
>
> I usually like to have friends with me when I go somewhere new. (.40)
>
> If someone insulted me I would probably try to forget about it. (.40)
>
> When I do something wrong I usually admit it and take my punishment. (.36)
>
> When things are going wrong for me, I try to think of my strong points and my past successes. (.36)
>
> Does your memory seem to be all right (good)? (.36)
>
> I do what I think is right even when I'm criticized for it. (.31)
>
> I know what I want out of life. (.29)

A subject was categorized as "high" on this factor if he responded affirmatively to 10 or more items and as "low" if he responded affirmatively to less than 10 items. The items reflect a number of socially acceptable patterns through which the person may redefine the situation so as to mitigate its self-devaluing implications. Notable among the patterns are compensation by reference to future ("By the time I am 30 I will probably have a good job and a good future ahead of me.") and past accomplishments ("When things are going wrong for me, I try to think of my strong points and past successes."). The desire to have friends along in novel experiences may reflect a similar attempt to balance possibly self-devaluing experiences with positive social support. Other patterns include expiation ("When I do something wrong I usually admit it and take my punishment".), attribution of fault to characteristics of the source rather than the self ("If someone insulted me I would probably figure it was his own problems that made him do it."), and minimization of the significance of the source or the event in response to personal insult ("I would probably figure,

'Who cares what he thinks.'. . . I would probably try to joke about it. . . . I would probably try to forget about it").

These interpretations appear warranted in view of the pattern of significant correlations observed. That the patterns are somewhat effective in forestalling or reducing the experience of self-rejecting feelings is suggested by the inverse relationships between guilt deflection and perceived self-devaluation in the context of peer ($-.11$), family ($-.25$), and school ($-.29$) settings and by others for ascribed characteristics ($-.12$). That the patterns are normative is suggested by the inverse relationship between this index on the one hand, and a measure of contranormative attitudes ($-.17$) and the measure of attempted avoidance of personal responsibility through the use of self-defeating/deviant response patterns ($-.14$) on the other. Although it might have been expected that the index would have also been related to the index of defenselessness/vulnerability, no relationship was observed ($-.02$). This is attributed to the fact that the index reflects a positive orientation to others in the normative structure. Thus any inverse relationship with the subjective distress component of defenselessness/vulnerability would have been counterbalanced by the positive correlation with the component reflecting responsiveness to the attitudes of others in the normative structure. Indeed guilt deflection was positively correlated ($.22$) with a measure of identification with the normative structure ("It is very important what my parents [teachers, the kids at school] think of me"; "When my parents [teachers, the kids at school] dislike something I do it bothers me very much").

RESULTS

Interpreting the index of defenselessness/vulnerability as reflecting the absence of effective/socially acceptable patterns for the avoidance or mitigation of self-rejecting feelings, the index of avoidance of personal responsibility as the adoption of ineffective/deviant attempts to forestall or mitigate self-rejecting feelings, and the index of guilt deflection as the adoption of effective/socially acceptable patterns in order to forestall or assuage the experience of self-rejecting feelings, it was hypothesized that high scores on the first two variables and low scores on the third variable at T_1 would be related to significantly higher self-derogation scores at T_2 and T_3 and significantly greater increases (or smaller decreases) in self-derogation between T_1 and T_2. Conversely, it was hypothesized that low scores on the first two variables and high scores on the third variable would be related to significantly lower self-derogation scores at T_2 and T_3 and significantly lower increases (or greater decreases) in self-derogation between T_1 and T_2.

The results of the analysis are summarized in Table 4.5. All hypotheses were supported at the $p < .05$ level. Subjects who were "high" on defenselessness/vulnerability, "high" on avoidance of personal responsibility, and "low" on guilt

TABLE 4.5
Mean Self-derogation Scores at T_2 and T_3 and Mean Residual Change in Self-derogation T_1-T_2, by Indices of Antecedent (T_1) Defensive/Adaptive Dispositions[a]

	Mean self-derogation[b]		Mean residual change in self-derogation,[b,c]
	T_2	T_3	T_1-T_2
Defenselessness/vulnerability			
Low	26.0	23.4	−2.4
	25.0	25.0	22.8
	2269	1553	2249
High	41.3	35.8	2.5
	28.6	28.7	26.4
	2211	1514	2201
Avoidance of personal responsibility			
Low	26.0	24.0	−2.7
	25.8	25.7	23.5
	2234	1563	2216
High	41.1	35.3	2.6
	27.9	28.2	25.7
	2247	1505	2238
Guilt deflection			
Low	36.0	30.9	.8
	28.3	28.4	25.0
	2367	1572	2353
High	30.9	28.1	−.8
	27.3	26.7	24.4
	2107	1492	2098

[a] Part of this table, drawn from Table 2 of "Antecedents of Negative Self-attitudes: Membership Group Devaluation and Defenselessness," by Howard B. Kaplan, is reprinted with stylistic changes from *Social Psychiatry*, 1976, *11* (2), pp. 15–25, by permission of the publisher, Springer-Verlag.

[b] The three values in sequence are mean, standard deviation, and N. All low versus high comparisons are significant, $p < .05$ (one-tailed) for t test, assuming unequal variances (Welch, 1947).

[c] Negative values indicate decrease in self-derogation.

deflection at T_1 (compared with those who were "low" on defenselessness/ vulnerability and avoidance of personal responsibility and "high" on guilt deflection) manifested significantly higher self-derogation scores at T_2 and T_3 and significantly greater increases (or smaller decreases) in self-derogation between T_1 and T_2.

Thus, consistent with theoretical and empirical indications, the absence of effective and socially acceptable self-protective patterns that might function to forestall or mitigate self-rejecting feelings, or the adoption of ineffective/deviant patterns, is associated with relatively high subsequently measured self-derogation scores and relatively greater subsequently determined residual gains in self-derogation.

Summary

The results reported in this chapter provide further empirical support for the theoretical position that self-attitudes are influenced by three categories of analytically distinguishable but empirically interdependent sets of variables: self-perceptions of possessing valued qualities and performing valued behaviors; self-perceptions of being the object of positive or negative attitudes by presumably valued others; and self-protective attitudes that more or less effectively forestall or mitigate the experience of self-rejecting feelings. The present analysis goes somewhat beyond cross-sectional studies insofar as it establishes relationships between independent variables measured earlier in time and subsequently determined outcome measures. However, such relationships, though they lend greater credibility to this conclusion, do not lead unequivocally to the interpretation that self-perceived valued qualities and behaviors, self-perceived attitudinal responses by others toward the subject, and the nature of self-protective patterns influence the genesis of self-accepting or self-rejecting attitudes—particularly when the self-rejecting attitudes are reflected in self-derogation scores at T_2 and T_3. Since it is known that self-derogation at T_2 and T_3 is positively related to self-derogation at T_1, and since the independent variables are also related to self-derogation at T_1 (although these data need not be reported here), it is possible that the relationships between the independent variables (self-perceptions as characterized by qualities and behaviors, self-perceptions of being the object of positive or negative attitudinal responses by others, and self-protective responses) and the subsequently determined (dependent variables) self-derogation scores (at T_2, T_3) are accounted for by the common association of the "independent" and "dependent" variables with self-derogation at T_1, thereby permitting the interpretation that both the "independent" and "dependent" variables are either reflections or consequences of preexisting self-derogation. Thus, self-derogation—rather than (or in addition to) being a consequence of the three independent variables—may have been an influence in the genesis of the self-perceptions and self-protective patterns. Alternatively, it may simply have these self-perceptions as its phenomenal expression.

What is under consideration here is not whether or not self-derogation does in fact lead to these outcomes and/or phenomenal expressions. Indeed these outcomes are to be expected on theoretical grounds. Rather what is at issue is whether or not the possibility of these alternative interpretations renders less credible the conclusion that self-attitudes are influenced by the earlier self-perceptions and self-protective patterns. The position taken here is that although these interpretations might be congruent with the data neither is as parsimonious an explanation as the presently preferred one, since neither can account for some of the other findings in the present study, namely those concerning the relationship between the independent variables and subsequent increases in self-derogation. The employment of this particular change measure obviates the potentially confounding influence, upon interpretation of the longitudinal findings, that might obtain from any relationship existing between the independent variables and self-derogation level at the same point in time by expressing the change in a way that removes from the gain that portion of the gain that could have been predicted linearly from the earlier score.

Thus, although self-attitudes may indeed influence or be reflected in particular self-perceptions and self-protective patterns, the data from the present analysis lend support to the conclusion that self-attitudes are influenced by the ability to forestall or assuage self-rejecting feelings stemming from self-perceptions of not possessing valued qualities and performing valued behaviors (or possessing disvalued qualities and performing disvalued behaviors) and of being the object of negative attitudes expressed by valued others.

Chapter 5

Self-attitudes and Deviant Behavior

According to the theory under consideration, the operation of the self-esteem motive in conjunction with the development of negative self-attitudes in the course of membership experiences influences the later adoption of deviant responses by two routes: first, by leading to the experience of conformity to membership group patterns as intrinsically distressing, and, second, by influencing the person's need to seek alternatives to the now intrinsically disvalued normative patterns in order to satisfy the self-esteem motive. In Chapter 3 evidence was presented in support of the postulated prevalence of the self-esteem motive. In Chapter 4 hypotheses were tested regarding the determinants of negative self-attitudes in the course of membership group experiences. This chapter considers the general proposition that relatively high levels of negative self-attitudes or increases in negative self-attitudes are associated with subsequent adoption of deviant responses. First the related literature will be reviewed, and then the relevant findings from the present study will be given.

Related Literature

There are few (if any) modes of psychosocially defined deviance that have not been observed (or asserted) to be associated with self-rejecting attitudes. The implication of these reports is that the negative self-attitudes preceded the deviant responses, and/or that the adoption of the deviant responses was consciously or unconsciously motivated by subjective anticipation of self-enhancing consequences of the deviant patterns. More frequently than not justification for these assumptions was not apparent. Nevertheless, the literature taken as a whole was at least consistent with the assumptions, occasional contradictions and proffered qualifications notwithstanding.

The range of deviant patterns considered in this literature includes the partly overlapping categories of informally sanctioned dishonesty, formally sanctioned modes of delinquency and criminality, drug addiction and abuse, alcoholism and alcohol abuse, a range of psychiatric disorders, violence and aggression, suicidal behavior, social protest, and the establishment (or reestablishment) of institutional forms that are regarded as deviant in the context of contemporary social institutions—notably in the area of religion. These categories will be illustrated in turn.

Dishonesty

In a number of experimental studies self-attitude was observed to be associated with subsequent cheating or dishonest behavior.

In one such investigation Aronson and Mettee (1968) investigated the effects of differential levels of induced self-esteem upon cheating behavior. The subjects (female psychology students) were led to believe that the study in which they were participating concerned the relationship between personality test scores and extrasensory perception (ESP). The latter ability was said to be determined through the use of a modified game of blackjack. After taking a personality test the subjects were provided with false feedback, which was intended to induce a temporary increase or decrease or no change in self-esteem. The subjects were randomly assigned to one of the three self-esteem conditions. During the blackjack game that followed they were placed in situations in which they could cheat and win, on the one hand, or not cheat and lose the game, on the other hand. The results tended to be congruent with the hypothesis that individuals having low self-esteem are more likely to engage in immoral behavior than are individuals having high self-esteem. People who received uncomplimentary feedback about themselves (the low self-esteem condition) were significantly more likely to cheat than were subjects who received more positive information about themselves.

Similar results were reported by Graf (1971). As in the preceding investigation, experimental induction of self-esteem levels was attained through false feedback of personality test scores to the subjects. Dishonest behavior was determined in terms of whether or not the subject kept a dollar bill left on the floor near the door of the testing room following completion of the feedback of the positive, negative, or neutral personality descriptions. The results indicated a significant relationship between low self-esteem and dishonest behavior. Thus, in both studies the induction of low self-esteem appeared to increase the probability of subsequent dishonest behavior.

Other studies reported somewhat inconsistent results, which may be attributable to methodological variations or to role-related differences in definitions of deviant behavior. Thus, Eisen (1972) found a relatively strong correlation between self-esteem and honesty for sixth-grade boys but a nonsignificant relationship between these variables for girls. Mussen and his associates, on the other hand, found that for girls high self-esteem was associated with honesty, whereas for boys low self-esteem was associated with honesty (Mussen, Harris, Rutherford, & Keasey, 1970).

Delinquency and Criminality

The relationship between self-rejecting attitudes and deviant responses has been observed in cultures other than that of the United States. A greater tendency toward a history of self-devaluing experiences on the part of criminal offenders as opposed to nonoffenders may be inferred from data reported by Wood (1961) for Ceylon. The data were collected by personal interviews with two groupings of subjects. One grouping consisted of males, 17 years of age or older, who had committed personal assault or property felonies during the preceding 5 years. The second grouping consisted of a representative sample of nonoffenders who were living in the same three Sinhalese Low-Country villages. Data concerning the felonies were collected from police records and local informants. A comparison of the offender and nonoffender groupings suggested that, with reference to evaluative standards that appeared to be meaningful in that particular cultural context, the offenders were appreciably more likely to have had the kinds of experiences that were compatible with receiving negative evaluations from others and evoking self-rejecting attitudes.

Relative to the nonoffenders, the offenders were less likely to be regularly employed, have an English-language education, or hold a relatively prestigious occupational position. When the subjects were compared with their fathers regarding land ownership and occupational rank, the offenders were more likely than the nonoffenders to have lost status. The offenders were also less likely than the nonoffenders to manifest consistency between career aspiration, occupational achievement, and educational level. Wood (1961, p. 748) summarized the situation as follows: "Cumulative evidence suggests a self-image of relative failure for the offender group."

Numerous studies carried out in the United States are also consistent with this conclusion, whether the dependent variable reflected a predisposition to deviance, delinquent behavior, or delinquent status.

Reed and Cuadra (1957) reported findings indicating a significant association between delinquency proneness and apparently self-derogatory attitudes. Among a group of student nurses, those who scored higher on a delinquency scale indicated their expectations of peer descriptions in terms of more unfavorable adjectives than those who scored lower on the scale. This difference was observed despite the fact that there were no objective differences in the adjectives actually used by the group to describe high and low scorers. In a study of young, healthy navy men, measures of self-evaluation were observed to be correlated with delinquency proneness (Gunderson & Johnson, 1965). Subjects who manifested more positive self-regard tended to score lower on a delinquency scale, whereas subjects having more negative self-attitudes tended to score higher on the delinquency scale.

Also illustrative of studies that relate current self-evaluation and concurrent delinquency proneness is an investigation reported by Schwartz and Tangri (1965). The sixth-grade teachers as well as the principal and assistant principal in an all black inner-city school in the highest delinquency area of Detroit were asked to nominate boys who, in their opinion, would never have police or court contacts ("good" boys) and boys who would have such contacts ("bad" boys). When comparing the good and bad boys with regard to their scores on a semantic differential measure of self-evaluation, it was observed that the bad boys had less positive self-concepts than the good boys.

With regard to self-reports of delinquent behavior, Jensen (1973) reported a significant inverse relationship between self-esteem and delinquency, although the relationship was stronger under certain conditions than others.

Illustrative of studies reporting a relationship between concurrent measures of delinquency and self-devaluation is that of Scarpitti (1965). Inmates of a boys' industrial school, all of whom had been committed for delinquency, were compared with white ninth-grade boys from a junior high school in a lower-class area of a city and with white ninth-grade boys from a junior high school in a middle-class area of a city with regard to responses to a questionnaire. One part of the questionnaire consisted of 11 items previously developed "to assess interpersonal competence or feelings of personal worth [p. 401]." Whether more inclusive groupings of delinquent boys or only white ninth-grade delinquent boys were considered, the delinquent group received the least favorable scores, the white ninth-grade lower-class boys received more favorable scores, and the white ninth-grade middle-class boys received the most favorable scores on this measure.

Again, however, exceptions and qualifications are noted for the generally observed relationship between self-attitudes on the one hand and delinquency (proneness) or criminality on the other. For example, Schwartz and Stryker (1970) observed, for boys attending a Midwest school in an urban area characterized by high social disorganization and a lower-class population, that the black subjects who were nominated as potentially delinquent did tend to display more negative self-evaluation than their nondelinquent counterparts. However, also among the findings was the observation that white bad boys did not differ significantly in level of self-evaluation from white good boys. And Deitz (1969) noted no significant tendency for delinquent subjects to rate themselves lower (using semantic differential measures) on the concept "me as I really am" than the nondelinquent subjects.

Drug Addiction and Drug Abuse

Whether dealing with clinical observations or survey-type data, available reports lead to the conclusion that negative self-attitudes are associated with drug abuse and/or addictive outcomes. Hoffman's observation is not uncommon in the clinical literature:

> The most striking clinical finding which I noted during my experience in conducting psychoanalytic psychotherapy with drug addicts is their abysmally low self-esteem. Behind the facade of their various ego defenses and their basically depressed affect, lies this low feeling of self-value which never fails to be revealed at the core of the addiction prone personality [Hoffman, 1964, p. 265].

Illustrative of cross-sectional survey studies is that of H. B. Kaplan and Meyerowitz (1970). They compared drug addicts and "normal" subjects along a variety of psychosocial dimensions. The addict subject grouping consisted of the first 300 persons with recent histories of addiction who were released into a previously defined target area in Texas by either the Texas Department of Corrections or the U.S. Public Health Service Hospital at Fort Worth following initiation of the study. The "normal" subject grouping consisted of a nonrandom selection of subjects from various sources such as industrial work groups who were not excluded from consideration by virtue of being younger than 17 years of age, having less than a fifth-grade education or more than a year of college, not being a United States citizen, having been hospitalized or treated for mental illness, having a police record for other than traffic offenses, or having ever illegally used addictive drugs. The data consisted of responses for the most part to structured and semistructured questionnaire items.

Support for the hypothesis that self-derogation is associated with the adoption of drug abuse patterns was provided more or less directly by several discrete findings, each of which was based on observations of the differential responses of the addict and nonaddict subjects to a series of instruments of widely differing format, all of which were manifestly related to self-evaluation. These instruments included single-item measures of self-satisfaction and self-respect, a multiple-item measure of self-estrangement, semantic differential evaluations of the concept "me," and a "What kind of person am I?" test calling for unstructured responses. On all of these tests the addict subjects were significantly more likely than the "normal" subjects to provide self-devaluing responses. These group differences could not be accounted for by observed differences in age or social class of origin between the two groups of subjects.

Alcoholism and Alcohol Abuse

Whether comparing diagnosed alcoholics with control subjects or studying nonalcoholic subjects having variable drinking patterns, the literature suggests a consistent association between negative self-attitudes and alcoholism or alcohol abuse. In the former category, Berg (1971) compared alcoholic male subjects (consecutive admissions to the alcoholism unit of a psychiatric hospital, characterized by a psychiatric diagnosis of alcoholism and a history of abundant drinking, alcohol dependency, and difficulties in functioning due to alcohol use) with a control group consisting of male employees of a penitentiary who were defined as social drinkers—that is, they consumed less than the equivalent of 10 ounces of absolute alcohol per week and responded in the negative to all of the items on the drinking questionnaire. The control group was so selected as to be comparable to the alcoholic subjects in age, education, and measures of neuroticism and extraversion. Self-concept was measured by self-ideal discrepancy using a Q sort technique and by a number of scores derived from responses to the adjective checklist.

The alcoholic subjects manifested significantly greater self-ideal discrepancy scores than the control subjects. This difference was accounted for by the more derogatory self-descriptions of the alcoholic subjects relative to those of the control subjects, since both groups expressed similar ideal-self descriptions. The alcoholic subjects were also significantly more likely to endorse unfavorable adjectives as self-descriptive, were significantly less likely to endorse favorable adjectives as self-descriptive, and were significantly more likely to express "feelings of inferiority through social impotence, guilt and self-criticism [Berg, 1971, p. 445]" than the control subjects. These differences were not likely to be accounted for by variability in perceptual distortion, in view of the observation that the groups did not differ significantly in scores on the defensiveness scale.

Among nonalcoholic subjects, Williams (1965) reported for male college students that scores on an index of problem drinking were significantly associated with higher scores on the self-criticality index, lower scores on a self-acceptance index, and lesser correspondence between real-self and ideal-self descriptions. In another investigation, Maddox (1968) also observed associations between self-derogation and drinking behavior at the same point in time. In a study of black male college students, drinking behavior was related to scores on a measure of self-derogation in such a way that subjects who were categorized as abstainers were least likely to be self-derogatory, subjects who were categorized as lighter drinkers were somewhat more likely to be self-derogatory, and subjects who were categorized as heavier drinkers were most likely to be self-derogatory. Maddox also reported that *changes* in drinking pattern from the freshman to sophomore year were related to changes in self-derogation. Increases in drinking were accompanied by increases in self-derogation and decreases in drinking were associated with decreased self-derogation.

Other studies are consistent with the view that self-rejection, rather than motivating the use of alcohol to assuage self-rejecting attitudes, is a condition for the use of alcohol to reduce subjective distress. Thus, Pearlin and Radabaugh (1976) suggest that those experiencing economic strain are more likely to experience intense anxiety, which predisposes them to use alcohol to alleviate the anxiety. The use of alcohol in such circumstances is most likely to occur for low self-esteem people who presumably are less able to bear distress without resorting to alcohol use.

Psychiatric Disorders

A number of studies reported that mixed psychiatric patient groupings tend to display relatively higher levels of self-rejection than nonpsychiatric groupings. For example, when the self-ratings of 34 adolescent and young adult psychiatric patients were compared with those of 20 "normal" control subjects of similar age and educational level, it was observed that the self-ratings of the patients were significantly poorer than those of the comparison group (Harrow, Fox, Markhus, Stillman, & Hallowell, 1968). The patient grouping was mixed, consisting of 15 schizophrenics, 7 depressives, 6 having character disorders, and 6 having varied diagnoses. However, 16 of the 34 cases had either a primary or a secondary diagnosis of depression.

Data regarding the differential self-attitudes of normal subjects and of apparently variously diagnosed psychiatric patients were also provided by Wilson and his associates (Wilson, Miskimins, Braucht, & Berry, 1971). Although the investigators were primarily interested in those who attempted suicide they administered the Miskimins Self–Goal–Other Discrepancy Scale to psychiatric controls and normals as well. These groups were matched for sex, age, and education. Among the scores derived from responses to the scale was the "self–other plus discrepancy." This factor, which is highly correlated with depression, was said to reflect self-derogation. In addition to manifesting higher scores than the normals on other derived factors, the psychiatric patients showed higher self–other plus discrepancy. Thus, relative to the normal controls, the psychiatric patients apparently valued themselves less than they felt others valued them.

Long and her associates cited an earlier study in which male adult patients in a neuropsychiatric ward of a veterans' hospital displayed lower self-esteem than normal controls. They reported similar results in a comparison of institutionalized adolescents with a control group (Long, Ziller, & Bankes, 1970). The institutionalized grouping consisted of 58 adolescents in a state residential treatment center. The classifications of the adolescents by the staff psychiatrists were said to range from mildly neurotic to psychotic (childhood schizophrenia). The control subjects consisted of "a random selection of public school students from a nearby community of the same age and sex as the institutionalized group [p. 44]." Among the findings was the observation that the mean value on a measure of self-esteem was significantly lower for the institutionalized grouping relative to the control grouping. The authors speculated that this finding might be accounted for by the stigma associated with institutionalization as well as by differences in socioeconomic background between the two subject groupings.

Katz and her associates (1975) observed that emotionally disturbed children had more negative real self-images than nonmaladaptive children, and Wylie (1961, pp. 205–218) has cited several studies in which neurotic subjects and/or mixed psychiatric patient groups were compared with presumably normal control subjects on some measures of self-regard. In general, the neurotic and/or mixed psychiatric patient subjects displayed significantly lower levels of self-acceptance than did normal controls.

Finally, H. B. Kaplan (1978b) has considered numerous studies implicating painful self-feelings in the genesis of schizophrenia.

Violence and Aggression

The significance of self-derogation as an antecedent of aggressive behavior is apparent in Leon's (1969) discussion of the characteristics of criminals who committed "atrocious crimes" (those crimes characterized by an "excess of aggression and cruelty") during the period known as "La Violencia" in the recent history of Colombia. The author argued "that the most ferocious of these criminals are probably individuals overwhelmed by fear and guilt, who perceive themselves as weak and worthless and hate themselves and their environment for that [p. 1573]."

Among the characteristics of the bandits are those indicating a strong vulnerability to self-devaluing attitudes. An underlying self-derogation is suggested both by the bandits' defensive postures and by their earlier socialization experiences. They are described as boastful about their aggression and sexual abilities, easily flattered, and at the same time quick to react to provocation, suspicious, impulsive, and unpredictable. Negative self-attitudes might also be expected on the basis of characterizations of the bandits' early cultural and familial settings. Their early broad environment is said to have imposed a variety of social, economic, religious, and cultural restrictions that did not permit the children "to channel their impulses and biological needs so as to achieve self-expression and self-realization [Leon, 1969, p. 1571]." For instance, within one family the child was unable to establish a satisfactory self-image in the face of a brutal father who attempted to impose rigid moral demands on his son while himself violating the code. The repressive attempts by the father are said to have been particularly heavy in the areas of aggression and sexuality. Thus, the repressive behavior ultimately led to "feelings of inadequacy, impotence, bitterness, helplessness, and worthlessness [p. 1571]."

An association between self-rejecting attitudes and aggressive behavior is suggested also by a study of 53 homicide offenders (Tanay, 1969). On the basis of interview and history data, the investigator reported that 68% of the offenders could be classified as having severe superegos. Self-punishment was said to be easily seen in these individuals "in the nature of interpersonal relations and self-abusive behavior." However, only 7% of the homicide offenders could be described as having a supportive superego as indicated by a positive self-image and the absence of self-punitive behavior.

Consistent with these findings is the report by Miller (1968) that a grouping of wife-murderers as well as a grouping of attempted suicides, when statistical controls were introduced, differed from a presumably normal control group in being more self-derogating and scoring higher on a self-estrangement measure, as well as in a number of other respects such as scoring lower on an ego-strength scale and manifesting less closeness in interpersonal relationships.

Suicidal Behavior

Self-attitudes have long been viewed as playing a significant role in the development of suicidal behavior. Gould (1965, p. 236) notes that the common factor underlying the wide variety of events that appear to precipitate suicide attempts in children and adolescents is (fear of) rejection and deprivation that is the consequence of loss of love and support. The feelings of being abandoned and rejected signifies to subjects that this is their punishment for being bad persons. A decrease in self-esteem and a sense of worthlessness follow.

Self-rejecting attitudes were also implicated by Glaser (1965, p. 255). In a report based on the study of 15 children and adolescents who made suicide threats or attempts and were subsequently referred for psychiatric evaluation and/or treatment he asserted, "Low self-esteem and a feeling of being unwanted was a common characteristic."

A number of studies are available comparing suicidal and nonsuicidal persons with regard to the nature of their self-attitudes. Hattem (1964), for example, reported that, in comparison with the responses of their spouses, suicidal individuals manifested a greater discrepancy between their self and ideal self on the dominance scale of the Leary Interpersonal Adjective Check List. In a similar vein, Braaten and Darling (1962), having compared suicidal college students with a nonsuicidal group, suggested that the suicidal subjects were characterized by self-hate as well as by a number of other traits, including anger, hostility, and dependence. Miller (1968) contrasted the self-attitudes of attempted suicides with those of a group of suicide prevention workers. Miller, in addition to reporting that attempted suicides and wife-murderers were alike in a number of respects, indicated that these individuals differed from a normal comparison group along several specified dimensions. Among the differences noted were the greater tendencies on the part of the suicidal subjects and wife-murderers to be more self-derogating, to score higher on a self-estrangement measure, and to score lower on an ego-strength scale.

In the course of investigating the effectiveness of self-concept measurement in the prediction of suicidal behavior, Wilson and his associates (1971) concluded, in a comparison of the attempted suicides with psychiatric and normal controls, that the person who attempts suicide "apparently values himself considerably less than he feels others value him and is not able to relieve this discrepancy [p. 309]."

Social Protest and Deviant Social Institutional Forms

Although the characterization of "deviant" applied to social protest and similar activities might be arguable, nevertheless negative self-attitudes have been implicated in activities that aim at reordering or reformulating the institutionalized goals and means thereto in the more inclusive society. With regard to social protest, a study of psychological variables in student activism (Isenberg, Schnitzer, & Rothman, 1977), using projective tests, differentiated between radicals and moderates on the basis of such variables as "negative identity" and "masochistic surrender."

Consistent with these findings, self-rejecting attitudes were associated with deviant religious response patterns. Guided by the same theoretical formulation outlined in Chapter 1, Freemesser and Kaplan (1976), in a cross-sectional study, investigated the relationships between self-attitudes and the adoption of membership in any of a variety of charismatic religious movements existing in the contemporary world, such as the Catholic and Protestant charismatic communities, "Jesus freaks," and evangelistic communities. It was hypothesized that members of the charismatic religious communities relative to comparison subjects would have reported high levels of self-derogation referring to the time at which they accepted membership in the charismatic group. Furthermore, individuals who adopted membership in the charismatic cults were expected to have displayed a significantly greater tendency to decrease the level of self-rejection between the earlier point in time and the point in time at which they were interviewed. Finally, the significantly greater decreases in self-rejection on the part of the charismatic cult subjects were expected to have resulted in comparable levels of self-derogation for the charismatic and comparison groups at the time of the interview. These hypotheses were based upon the general theory of deviant behavior (H. B. Kaplan, 1975b) that deviant patterns are adopted as alternative routes to self-esteem when normative response patterns have been associated with the genesis of negative self-attitudes. Adoption of membership in a charismatic religious group is a form of deviant behavior in the sense that it contrasts with normative expectations of the person's predeviance membership groups. Thus, individuals who joined charismatic religious groups were expected to be motivated by an experience of negative self-attitudes and to have anticipated salutary effects on level of self-esteem. Furthermore, it was expected that joining charismatic religious groups would give individuals the opportunity to avoid and/or attack the values of the predeviance membership groups in which self-rejecting attitudes were developed and would offer alternative responses that would permit the development of self-accepting attitudes—for example, by permitting self-perceptions of serving a higher power, by identification with a worthy set of standards, and by the experience of group acceptance through approximation of these shared goals. Support was obtained for all hypotheses, consistent with the reports of others who describe self-enhancing effects of the religious conversion experience. Although the data were compatible with the hypotheses, the results were interpreted with caution in view of the cross-sectional nature of the research design.

The literature that has been reviewed is generally congruent with the expected relationship between self-attitudes and deviant behavior. The findings were interpretable as support for the theory that any of a broad range of deviant patterns are motivated by the conscious or unconscious expectation that the responses will reduce the person's preexisting self-rejecting attitudes. However, each of the studies reviewed was characterized by one or more of the following deficits, which rendered the conclusions suspect. First, the research generally (but not exclusively) employed cross-sectional rather than prospective longitudinal research design. Therefore, it was not possible to establish a temporal relationship between antecedent self-attitudes and deviant behavior. Although the results were compatible with the hypothesized relationship between antecedent self-attitudes and later adoption of deviant response patterns, the data could as easily have been interpreted as supporting a hypothesized relationship between the adoption of deviant response patterns and consequent increases in self-rejecting attitudes. Second, the generalizability of the findings was limited because of the frequent use of small, unrepresentative, and uncontrolled samples. Third, the frequent use of institutionalized or otherwise under treatment samples introduced the possibility of other interpretations of the data. Thus, institutionalization might have resulted in negative self-attitudes by virtue of the stigma associated with institutionalization or by virtue of the institutionalization or mode of treatment having deprived the person of the varied (deviant) response patterns that might have assuaged preexisting self-rejecting attitudes. Fourth, the reported research generally dealt with only one or a few modes of deviant response. Since self-attitudes were said to predispose an individual to the adoption of any of a range of deviant responses, the theoretical proposition could not be properly tested in the context of any of the specific studies. Only by simultaneously considering the broad range of studies could the proposition be said to have been supported. Fifth, even where longitudinal research designs were employed, the analysis of the data was such that they did not permit exclusion of alternative interpretations of the data. For example, any observed relationships between antecedent self-rejection and subsequent adoption of deviant response patterns might have permitted the interpretation that the later performance of deviant patterns was associated with earlier performance of deviant patterns antedating the self-rejecting attitudes. That is, the self-rejection might have been a consequence of the earlier deviant behavior and correlated self-devaluing circumstances.

These limitations, along with the observed exceptions and qualifications in the literature, precluded acceptance of these conclusions as demonstration of the validity of the theoretical model. The analyses to be reported subsequently were considered a more appropriate test of the hypothesized relationship between antecedent self-rejection and subsequent adoption of any of a broad range of deviant responses.

Test of the Hypothesis

The hypothesized relationship between antecedent self-attitudes and subsequent adoption of deviant response patterns was tested in separate analyses of (a) the relationship between antecedent levels of self-attitudes and subsequent adoption of deviant response patterns, (b) the relationship between antecedent level of self-attitudes and subsequent adoption of deviant response patterns according to the social class of the subject, and (c) the relationship between antecedent *change* in self-attitudes and subsequent adoption of deviant response patterns.

Self-attitude Level and Deviant Responses

In the first analysis, the initial level of self-attitudes was related to each of 28 indices of deviant responses.

HYPOTHESIS

The hypothesis was stated as follows: Among persons presumed not to have already adopted the deviant response patterns in question, those with higher levels of negative self-attitudes would be significantly more likely to perform subsequently each of a range of specified deviant acts.

No such relationship was expected for persons who apparently had already adopted the deviant responses, for two reasons. First, prior performance of the act in question might imply that it was not *deviant* in the context of the person's current membership groups. Since the theoretical statement implicates antecedent negative self-attitudes in the subsequent adoption of *deviant* responses, there was no reason to anticipate the relationship if the act was not in fact deviant. Second, whether or not the acts were truly deviant, the relationship between self-attitudes and subsequent performance might be obscured by the self-enhancing or self-derogating implications of consequences of *prior* performance of the acts. That is, the earlier performance of the act might have evoked negative attitudinal responses from significant others, which in turn influenced negative self-attitudes and thus spuriously enhanced the observed relationship between self-derogation and deviant behavior. Or, the earlier performance of the deviant act might have increased positive self-attitudes (congruent with theoretical expectations), thus accounting for any observed association between low self-derogation and deviant responses. Insofar as both forces were operative, a relationship between earlier self-derogation level and subsequent reports of deviant behavior might have been obscured.

ANALYSIS

The distinction between those who had and had not already adopted the deviant pattern prior to the first testing was operationally drawn in terms of affirmation or denial of having performed the deviant act during the specified time interval (generally 1 month) prior to that testing. As noted in Chapter 2, the relatively brief time-period reference at the first administration was employed on this assumption: There was a greater probability that students indicating performance of an act during that brief period would already have adopted a deviant response pattern, in contrast to students not indicating recent performance of the act. Conversely, the probability was greater that students indicating nonperformance of the act relative to those indicating recent performance of the act would not already have adopted a motivationally relevant deviant response pattern.

To have used a more extended time period might have introduced factors that could have obscured the hypothesized relationship. Although the use of a longer time period as a time reference might exclude persons for whom the "deviant" act was a normative pattern, it would also exclude persons who only occasionally—perhaps as an experiment, or by accident—performed the deviant act. The result might be an overrepresentation in the sample of persons who conform out of timidity rather than out of the lack of motivation to deviate or the positive motivation to conform.

Thus, the hypothesis was tested for all students present for the first two testings for whom the appropriate data (self-derogation level at the first administration and self-reports of the deviant behavior in question) were available *and who reported not performing the deviant behavior during the specified period prior to the first testing.*

The operational definitions of self-attitudes and deviant behavior were provided in Chapter 2.

The self-derogation scores of the students responding to the first test were arbitrarily divided into three groupings: low (0–20), medium (21–50), and high (above 50). Students in these groupings at the time of the first administration were compared with regard to the relative frequency with which they reported (at the time of the second administration) performing each of the deviant behaviors under consideration between the first and second test administrations. Gamma was employed as a measure of association (Goodman & Kruskal, 1954). The relationship between self-attitudes and deviant behaviors was examined separately for each of the 28 indices of deviant behavior.

The analysis thus permitted the establishment of a temporal relationship between earlier self-derogation level (at T_1) and later reports (at T_2) of each of a broad range of essentially uncorrelated deviant patterns. The method used minimized the possible obscuring influence of earlier adoption of the deviant response by including in the analysis only those instances where the subject denied performance of the deviant act prior to the first testing.

RESULTS

The results of the analysis summarized in Table 5.1 are clearly in support of the hypothesis. For each of the deviant behaviors in question, among students reporting nonperformance of the deviant behavior during the specified period prior to the first testing, students in the low self-derogation category at the first testing relative to those in the high and/or medium self-derogation groupings were less likely to report (at the second testing) having performed the deviant behavior in the period between the first and second testing. For 26 of the 28 comparisons the association between antecedent self-derogation and subsequent reports of the deviant behavior was statistically significant. For example, 8% of the low, 11% of the medium, and 14% of the high self-derogation subjects (at the time of the first testing) reported (at the time of the second testing) having taken things worth between $2 and $50 during the preceding year. Also, 5% of the low, 7% of the medium, and 9% of the high self-derogation subjects reported suspension or expulsion from school subsequent to the first testing. Corresponding figures for having thought about or threatening to commit suicide were 9, 14, and 23%. With regard to getting angry and breaking things, 21% of the low, 27% of the medium, and 31% of the high self-derogation subjects reported subsequent adoption of the pattern. For cheating on exams the corresponding percentages were 32, 38, and 43%, and for using narcotics the corresponding percentages were 8, 11, and 14%. Corresponding percentages of students indicating damaging or destroying public or private property were 5, 9, and 10 for the three self-derogation groupings. Similar linear relationships were observed for selling drugs, getting failing grades, attempting suicide, starting fistfights, skipping school without an excuse, participating in gang fights, using force to get valuables from another person, stealing from someone else's desk or locker, beating up someone who did nothing to the person, smoking marijuana, and other patterns.

A number of possible explanations suggest themselves for the two nonsignificant relationships. It is possible that participating in social protest (item 48) was not subjectively defined as deviant. With regard to coming to the attention of the authorities (item 11), this outcome might well have been an unanticipated one independent (at least in part) of the subject's purpose. Although the acts that evoked the attention of the authorities might have been adopted in response to self-derogation, the association between the performance and detection of the act might have been too weak to reflect the association between self-attitudes and deviant behavior. That is, the factors influencing detection may have been independent of those influencing performance of the act. Such considerations might have depressed what would have been even stronger relationships (although they were significant in any case) between self-attitudes and the indicator of deviant response in the cases of being suspended or expelled from school (item 5), being sent to a therapist (item 56), and being taken to the office for punishment (item 68). In these cases the significant relationship might suggest that the subject, in response to greater self-derogation, intended such outcomes for self-enhancing purposes, and/or that there was a closer association between subject behaviors and these responses than there was in the case of coming to the attention of the authorities.

Although the gammas reflecting the degree of association between self-derogation and the deviant behaviors were generally significant, their magnitudes were generally low. The average gamma was .17; the highest one observed was .34. However, perhaps more impressive than the magnitudes of the associations is the consistency of the pattern of associations by which antecedent self-derogation was observed to be related to subsequent reports of each of a range of essentially uncorrelated deviant acts, thus lending strong support to the hypothesis. In further support of the hypothesis, for reasons stated earlier, it was not anticipated that antecedent self-derogation would be related to subsequent deviant responses for subjects who reported the deviant acts during the specified periods prior to the first testing. Therefore these relationships will not be reported here in detail. However, as these data were a by-product of the computer analysis used to test the hypothesis, it is noted in passing that, as expected, for these subjects antecedent self-derogation was generally unrelated to subsequent reports of deviant responses. For only two items (14 and 31) was gamma significant.

TABLE 5.1

Percentage of Students Reporting Performance of Deviant Behaviors between T_1 and T_2, by Self-derogation Level at T_1, among Students Indicating Nonperformance of the Behavior during a Specified Period Prior to T_1[a]

Test item[b]	Self-derogation level at T_1[c]		
	Low	Medium	High
3. Took things worth between $2 and $50 (.22***)	7.8 (1672)	10.7 (1452)	14.2 (1265)
5. Was suspended or expelled from school (.20***)	4.8 (1644)	7.0 (1410)	8.6 (1216)
7. Took things worth less than $2 (.09**)	19.5 (1547)	21.9 (1248)	24.1 (1022)
10. Thought about or threatened to take own life (.34***)	9.4 (1624)	13.9 (1306)	22.9 (1025)
11. Had something to do with police, sheriff, juvenile officers for something subject did or was thought to have done (.05)	7.8 (1584)	9.1 (1335)	8.9 (1143)
14. Became angry and broke things (.17***)	21.0 (1462)	27.3 (1185)	30.8 (917)
17. Carried a razor, switchblade, or gun as a weapon (.15***)	7.3 (1626)	11.5 (1397)	11.1 (1217)
24. Sold narcotic drugs (dope, heroin) (.18**)	3.1 (1661)	4.4 (1461)	5.3 (1279)
26. Received a failing grade in one or more school subjects (.16***)	15.9 (1408)	22.8 (1047)	23.0 (831)
28. Used wine, beer, or liquor more than two times (.12***)	18.2 (1574)	23.1 (1318)	23.8 (1143)
29. Cheated on exams (.16***)	31.7 (1528)	37.7 (1283)	42.6 (1043)
31. Attempted suicide (.30***)	5.0 (1688)	7.5 (1390)	11.5 (1163)
33. Started a fistfight (.11**)	11.5 (1536)	12.8 (1296)	15.5 (1104)
38. Took narcotic drugs (.19***)	8.1 (1638)	11.1 (1455)	13.5 (1250)
44. Skipped school without an excuse (.15***)	13.9 (1637)	19.8 (1427)	20.0 (1212)
48. Took an active part in social protest either at school or outside of school (.04)	10.5 (1560)	12.4 (1314)	11.6 (1142)
50. Took part in gang fights (.14**)	6.1 (1651)	8.2 (1410)	9.1 (1228)

(Continued)

DISCUSSION

To test the hypothesis, subjects were used who were presumed not to have previously adopted the deviant pattern under consideration, as indicated by the students' denial that they had performed the deviant act during a specified period (usually a month) prior to the first testing. Of course the denial of deviant performance during that period is no guarantee that the students had not already adopted the behavior pattern. They may already have performed the act repeatedly prior to the specified period. Furthermore, even if they had not previously performed the act, the behavior in question might not constitute deviant behavior for some subjects. Rather, the students might have learned

TABLE 5.1—*Continued*

	Self-derogation level at $T_1{}^c$		
Test item[b]	Low	Medium	High
56. Was sent to a psychiatrist, psychologist, or social worker (.13*)	3.0 (1617)	4.9 (1396)	4.4 (1190)
57. Used force to get money or valuables (.25***)	3.0 (1651)	5.7 (1427)	6.4 (1243)
61. Broke into and entered a home, store, or building (.16**)	3.2 (1656)	5.6 (1464)	5.2 (1295)
64. Damaged or destroyed public or private property on purpose (.24***)	5.3 (1652)	9.1 (1414)	10.4 (1213)
68. Was taken to the office for punishment (.13***)	18.1 (1358)	23.0 (1141)	24.6 (915)
69. Stole things from someone else's desk or locker (.18***)	10.0 (1608)	12.3 (1374)	16.4 (1155)
72. Used a car without the owner's permission (.21***)	4.3 (1666)	5.9 (1457)	7.9 (1279)
75. Beat up someone who did nothing to subject (.19***)	5.0 (1633)	7.3 (1393)	8.5 (1198)
78. Took things worth $50 or more (.14*)	2.6 (1677)	4.6 (1471)	3.9 (1297)
82. Smoked marijuana (.12***)	11.8 (1617)	13.8 (1430)	16.3 (1222)
84. Took part in a strike, riot, or demonstration (.14**)	4.2 (1625)	6.3 (1421)	6.3 (1240)

[a] Part of this table, drawn from Table 3 of "Self-attitudes and Deviant Response," by Howard B. Kaplan, is reprinted with stylistic changes from *Social Forces*, 1976, 54 (4), pp. 788–801, by permission of the publisher, the University of North Carolina Press.

[b] Parentheses indicate Goodman and Kruskal's (1954) gamma: *$p < .05$; **$p < .01$; ***$p < .001$.

[c] Parenthetical entries indicate cell N.

the behavior as an appropriate one to be performed at some future time, that is, by the way of anticipatory socialization. However, the probability is greater that students had not already adopted the behavior as a normatively endorsed membership group response if they indicated prior nonperformance than if they indicated prior performance of the act during the period in question. By this assertion it would be appropriate to speak of the *adoption* of a deviant response to preexisting self-derogation associated with past experiences in the membership group. The fact that this relationship was observed for persons who had not reported prior performance of the act but was not observed for persons who had reported prior performance of the act fits this assumption. In any case, the failure to have successfully excluded those who had earlier adopted the deviant pattern would have weakened the hypothesized relationship, for reasons noted previously.

The decision to exclude those who indicated early performance of the deviant act mitigated the possible biases introduced by the sample attrition. The attrition of the sample was disproportionately accounted for by subjects who had already engaged in deviant behavior by the time of the first test administration as indicated by self-reports of having recently performed the acts in question. Since the hypothesis presumed that the students had not yet adopted deviant response patterns, those reporting the performance of the act during the month prior to the first testing would have been excluded from the analysis in any event. Therefore the lesser representation of these students did not constitute as serious a bias in the sample as would have been the case if they had been included in the analysis. In any case, since dropping out of the study was related to prior performance of the deviant acts but was not significantly related to self-attitudes (see Chapter 2), it would appear that the earlier performance of the act would not have the same significance in relationship to negative self-attitudes as initial adoption of the deviant responses.

An alternative explanation of the observed relationship between antecedent self-derogation and subsequent adoption of deviant responses might assert that self-derogation influences not the *performance* of deviant behaviors so much as the willingness to confess it, perhaps by way of self-reproach or as a reflection of the absence of self-protective patterns. However, such an explanation would have to account for the fact that the students used in this analysis all reported *not* performing the act during the period prior to the first testing.

These considerations notwithstanding, the observation of significant associations between antecedent self-derogation on the one hand and the subsequent performance of each of several virtually uncorrelated dissimilar deviant patterns on the other hand lends strong support both to the thesis that negative self-attitudes are a common predisposing influence in the adoption of a range of deviant response patterns and to the general theory of deviant behavior from which it was derived.

Social Class, Self-derogation, and Deviant Response

A basic assumption of the present study is that deviant behaviors are responses to the genesis of negative self-attitudes in the course of membership group experiences. Insofar as the behaviors that are characterized as deviant in the present study are indeed deviant from the point of view of the subjects' membership groups, the relationship between antecedent self-rejection and subsequent adoption of deviant behaviors would be expected. However, where these acts are in fact normative or consistent with the norms of segments of the population, it is not to be expected that for those segments of the population the behaviors would be consequences of the genesis of self-rejection in the membership groups.

Although in the analysis just reported the relationship between antecedent self-rejection and subsequent adoption of deviant responses was documented, it is argued here that this relationship is accounted for primarily by middle-class subjects for whom the behaviors in question indeed represented departures from previously accepted membership group norms, not by lower-class subjects for whom the behaviors were consonant with the standards of their subculturally defined membership groups. If the behaviors are indeed clearly defined as deviant for middle-class membership groups and compatible with the standards of lower-class membership groups, in accordance with the general theory negative self-attitudes would be expected to increase the probability of subsequent "deviant" responses for the middle-class subjects but not for the lower-class subjects.

The position taken here does not demand the assertion that behaviors defined as deviant in the middle class are normative in the lower class or in a segment of the lower class (e.g., the youth subculture) in the sense that the behavior is prescribed in these presumed subcultures. The assertions that behaviors defined as deviant in the middle class may be defined as normative in the lower class and that delinquency may represent conformity to the norms of delinquent subcultures appear to be highly problematic. See, for example, the discussions of the relevant literature by Hewitt (1970, pp. 84–87, 93–95), Hirschi (1969, pp. 11–15), and Jessor et al. (1968, pp. 32–38).

The compatibility of the behaviors under consideration with lower-stratum norms need not take the form of prescriptions for such behavior the absence of which evokes negative sanction. Rather, the compatibility may take the form of the decreased proscription of such behaviors that may be prominent in the lower class (cf. Short & Strodtbeck, 1965). Alternatively, the compatibility of these behaviors with the normative system of the lower-stratum adolescents might take the form of a system of rationalizations that permit justification of the violation of norms supported by the broader society (cf. Sykes & Matza, 1957). Finally, the deviant responses might represent extreme examples of adaptive responses that are normative in lower-class subcultures (H. B. Kaplan, 1972a, pp. 141–180).

In short, the propositions under consideration here were derived not from the assumption that deviant behaviors were necessarily normative in the lower class but rather that they were compatible with the normative structure of the lower class in the sense of either being extreme extensions of acceptable patterns or of not being proscribed (that is, being tolerated) in the lower classes. This distinction is implicit in the discussion by Jessor and his associates (1968, pp. 36–37) who reject the proposal that deviance is generally normative in the lower class, but note a study by Gordon and his associates that indicates an inverse relationship between tolerance of deviant behavior and social level in the face of a general acceptance of middle-class proscriptive norms (Gordon, Short, Cartwright, & Strodtbeck, 1963).

In the present study, the compatibility of the deviant behaviors under consideration with lower-class subcultures is suggested by observation of the following relationship, among others. For both male and female subjects, lower-class subjects were significantly more likely than middle-class subjects to score high (four or more affirmative responses on a factorially derived 11-item scale) on a measure of the tendency to devalue the normative structure and to value positively contranormative patterns. Many of the component items were like those employed in earlier delinquency scales (Gough & Peterson, 1952) and measures of value orientation and awareness of limited access to opportunity (Landis, Dinitz, & Reckless, 1963). The items and the factor loadings (indicated parenthetically) were as follow:

If you want people to like you you have to tell them what they want to hear even if it isn't the truth. (.65)

The kids who mess up with the law seem to be better off than those who play it straight. (.52)

I would like to take a more active part in social protest groups. (.49)

I have a better chance of doing well if I cut corners than if I play it straight. (.48)

There isn't much chance that a kid from my neighborhood will ever get ahead. (.48)

Most of the adults I know got what is important out of life without getting an education. (.46)

As long as I stay with the straight life I will never make it. (.43)

I have never been able to accomplish as much as my family wanted me to. (.40)

A smart lawyer can usually get a criminal free. (.28)

The law is always against the ordinary guy. (.28)

If you stick to law and order you will never fix what is wrong with this country. (.24)

Considering subjects who were present for all three test administrations, among males, 47% of the lower-class subjects ($N = 228$) compared to only 29% of the middle-class subjects ($N = 1042$) received high scores. Among females, 33% of the lower-class subjects ($N = 318$) compared to only 23% of the middle-class subjects ($N = 1336$) received high scores on the measure.

Insofar as the deviant patterns under consideration are indeed compatible with lower-class subcultures, highly self-derogating subjects in the lower class should not be expected to adopt such patterns with greater frequency than low self-derogation subjects in response to the genesis of self-rejection or in anticipation of reduction of self-rejecting feelings, since the lower-class way of life is in fact (and presumably subjectively) associated with the genesis of the high levels of self-derogation in question. For middle-class subjects, on the other hand, these deviant patterns are not compatible with the subcultural norms. Hence these patterns represent, for self-derogating middle-class subjects who associate the normative structure with the genesis of their self-rejecting attitudes, true alternative patterns that might be adopted as more or less functional attempts to assuage self-rejecting feelings.

HYPOTHESIS

For each of the indices of deviant response it was hypothesized that for both male and female middle-class subjects who denied performance of the act during specified periods prior to the first testing (T_1), high (relative to medium and low) self-derogation subjects at T_1 would be significantly more likely to report at T_2 (a year later) performance of the behavior during the intervening year. For male and female lower-class subjects significant relationships between antecedent self-derogation and subsequent deviant responses were not expected.

Social class, for present purposes, was defined in terms of the mother's educational achievement. Students whose mothers did not graduate from high school were defined as lower class, whereas those whose mothers did graduate from high school were defined as middle class. The mother's, rather than the father's, educational achievement was selected because subjects were less likely to be ignorant of the mother's educational level, and where subjects were raised by one parent that parent was appreciably more likely to be the mother.

ANALYSIS

As in the preceding analysis, from the pool of students present for the first two testings, students who scored high, medium, and low, respectively, in self-derogation at T_1 were compared with regard to the relative frequency with which they reported (at T_2) performing each of the deviant behaviors under consideration between the first and second test administrations (considering only students who denied performing the act during the specified period prior to the first testing). Gamma was again employed as a measure of association (Goodman & Kruskal, 1954). However, in the present analysis the relationship was examined separately for each of the four sex by social class subgroupings.

RESULTS

The results are summarized in Tables 5.2 and 5.3. In all cases only those students who denied recent performance of the acts in question prior to T_1 were considered. Considering the *male, middle-class* students first, for 27 of the 28 indices of deviant response initial level of self-derogation was related to subsequent adoption of deviant response, with initially high self-derogation

TABLE 5.2

Percentage of Male Students Reporting Performance of Deviant Behaviors from T_1 to T_2, by Self-derogation Level at T_1 and Mother's Education, among Male Students Indicating Nonperformance of the Behavior Prior to T_1[a]

| Test item | Mother had less than high-school education | | | | Mother was high-school graduate | | | |
| | Self-derogation at T_1[b] | | | | Self-derogation at T_1[b] | | | |
	Low	Medium	High	Gamma	Low	Medium	High	Gamma
3. Took things worth between $2 and $50	14.3 (98)	17.5 (114)	9.7 (124)	-.15	11.2 (634)	15.0 (492)	21.1 (380)	.24***
5. Was suspended or expelled from school	7.0 (100)	6.7 (104)	7.3 (110)	.02	6.5 (618)	8.5 (496)	7.3 (386)	.06
7. Took things worth less than $2	28.4 (95)	30.6 (85)	18.8 (96)	-.17	27.1 (546)	28.7 (425)	33.2 (277)	.09
10. Thought about or threatened to take own life	5.9 (101)	8.7 (104)	14.4 (111)	.32*	6.1 (625)	10.9 (479)	20.8 (337)	.43***
11. Had something to do with police, sheriff, or juvenile officer	12.9 (93)	13.5 (96)	10.6 (104)	-.08	12.7 (565)	14.7 (415)	15.0 (319)	.07
14. Became angry and broke things	29.6 (81)	27.6 (98)	30.5 (95)	.02	25.4 (531)	32.0 (387)	34.7 (262)	.16**
17. Carried a razor, switchblade, or gun as a weapon	12.4 (97)	22.1 (104)	14.9 (114)	.04	11.8 (593)	20.9 (465)	21.1 (356)	.24***
24. Sold narcotic drugs (dope, heroin)	5.0 (100)	2.6 (116)	4.7 (129)	.00	4.4 (635)	7.0 (512)	5.7 (386)	.11
26. Received a failing grade in one or more school subjects	30.6 (72)	31.9 (72)	34.6 (81)	.06	17.1 (527)	23.9 (356)	26.0 (262)	.19**
28. Used wine, beer, or liquor more than two times	23.9 (92)	27.0 (100)	21.7 (115)	.05	21.1 (589)	27.2 (452)	29.3 (341)	.15**
29. Cheated on exams	35.8 (95)	40.9 (93)	34.5 (113)	-.02	34.0 (594)	36.3 (460)	43.6 (335)	.12**
31. Attempted suicide	2.9 (103)	6.2 (113)	8.8 (114)	.34*	3.1 (647)	5.6 (497)	9.2 (368)	.37***
32. Started a fistfight								

47. Skipped school without an excuse								
48. Took an active part in social protest either at school or outside of school	8.1 (99)	12.9 (101)	6.7 (105)	−.06	12.7 (606)	12.1 (461)	10.7 (354)	−.06
50. Took part in gang fights	12.1 (99)	14.2 (106)	11.3 (115)	−.03	9.3 (611)	12.2 (482)	12.9 (372)	.13
56. Was sent to a psychiatrist, psychologist, or social worker	4.1 (98)	4.8 (104)	3.6 (112)	−.05	3.4 (613)	7.1 (490)	5.8 (347)	.20*
57. Used force to get money or valuables	2.0 (101)	9.9 (111)	8.1 (123)	.30*	4.8 (625)	9.0 (501)	10.3 (370)	.27***
61. Broke into and entered a home, store, or building	8.9 (101)	5.4 (112)	7.0 (129)	−.08	5.1 (624)	9.5 (507)	9.5 (399)	.22**
64. Damaged or destroyed public or private property	10.5 (95)	10.1 (109)	8.5 (118)	−.08	8.2 (623)	14.2 (478)	18.2 (352)	.30***
68. Was taken to the office for punishment	31.6 (76)	24.7 (73)	14.3 (70)	−.31**	23.2 (453)	30.6 (350)	29.7 (249)	.13*
69. Stole things from someone else's desk or locker	19.4 (93)	14.0 (100)	22.4 (107)	.08	13.9 (595)	19.0 (462)	23.8 (328)	.22***
72. Used a car without the owner's permission	6.0 (100)	2.6 (115)	9.5 (126)	.24	7.2 (623)	7.9 (507)	10.0 (389)	.11
75. Beat up someone who did nothing to subject	8.4 (95)	13.3 (105)	7.8 (116)	−.04	8.8 (613)	12.1 (471)	13.9 (345)	.17**
78. Took things worth $50 or more	6.9 (102)	8.4 (107)	4.0 (125)	−.18	3.8 (633)	7.5 (520)	8.1 (397)	.26***
82. Smoked marijuana	18.8 (101)	17.0 (112)	16.5 (109)	−.05	14.3 (600)	13.7 (502)	20.2 (376)	.12
84. Took part in a strike, riot, or demonstration	8.7 (103)	9.3 (107)	5.2 (115)	−.17	4.9 (608)	7.8 (503)	8.5 (376)	.20*

a Part of this table, drawn from Table 1 of "Social Class, Self-derogation, and Deviant Response," by Howard B. Kaplan, is reprinted with stylistic changes from *Social Psychiatry*, 1978, 13, pp. 19–28, by permission of the publisher, Springer-Verlag.

b Parenthetical entries indicate cell N.

*$p < .05$

**$p < .01$

***$p < .001$

TABLE 5.3

Percentage of Female Students Reporting Performance of Deviant Behaviors from T_1 to T_2, by Self-derogation Level at T_1 and Mother's Education, among Female Students Indicating Nonperformance of the Behavior during a Specified Period Prior to T_1[a]

Test item	Mother had less than high-school education				Mother was high-school graduate			
	Self-derogation at T_1[b]				Self-derogation at T_1[b]			
	Low	Medium	High	Gamma	Low	Medium	High	Gamma
3. Took things worth between $2 and $50	3.0 (135)	9.5 (148)	8.4 (155)	.26*	4.6 (735)	7.2 (572)	11.5 (521)	.32***
5. Was suspended or expelled from school	5.3 (133)	10.6 (141)	9.2 (152)	.16	3.3 (725)	4.7 (557)	9.2 (488)	.36***
7. Took things worth less than $2	15.5 (129)	24.0 (129)	20.5 (132)	.10	13.5 (705)	15.9 (533)	21.5 (447)	.18***
10. Thought about or threatened to take own life	10.2 (127)	19.5 (123)	29.5 (122)	.40***	12.4 (700)	17.1 (491)	25.8 (395)	.29***
11. Had something to do with police, sheriff, or juvenile officer	3.1 (130)	6.9 (145)	8.9 (158)	.32*	4.4 (728)	5.5 (568)	5.9 (491)	.11
14. Became angry and broke things	18.0 (122)	34.7 (118)	26.1 (115)	.14	17.0 (666)	22.3 (476)	27.8 (381)	.21***
17. Carried a razor, switchblade, or gun as a weapon	1.5 (132)	6.1 (147)	6.3 (160)	.33*	4.0 (731)	3.8 (560)	5.1 (509)	.08
24. Sold narcotic drugs (dope, heroin)	1.5 (134)	3.5 (143)	3.2 (158)	.20	2.4 (719)	3.2 (568)	5.6 (519)	.30**
26. Received a failing grade in one or more school subjects	21.6 (116)	28.3 (106)	30.8 (91)	.16	11.1 (642)	18.0 (445)	14.8 (359)	.14*
28. Used wine, beer, or liquor more than two times	16.7 (132)	19.0 (137)	18.1 (149)	.03	14.9 (693)	20.2 (511)	22.1 (457)	.17***
29. Cheated on exams	24.6 (122)	38.8 (121)	36.2 (130)	.17*	31.2 (651)	39.4 (495)	47.6 (391)	.23***
31. Attempted suicide	6.0 (134)	14.2 (134)	21.3 (141)	.42***	6.7 (735)	7.8 (530)	11.4 (465)	.19***
33. Started a fistfight	6.9 (131)	9.2 (142)	8.3 (144)	.06	4.8 (704)	5.8 (528)	9.7 (691)	.21***

48. Took an active part in social protest either in school or outside of school	10.4 (125)	20.2 (124)	16.4 (134)	.15	9.0 (663)	10.5 (516)	10.9 (466)	.07
50. Took part in gang fights	4.4 (135)	9.1 (143)	8.7 (150)	.20	3.1 (736)	3.8 (558)	5.7 (506)	.21*
56. Was sent to a psychiatrist, psychologist, or social worker	1.5 (131)	4.9 (144)	3.2 (155)	.16	3.4 (706)	2.9 (545)	4.0 (494)	.05
57. Used force to get money or valuables	4.5 (134)	3.6 (140)	2.0 (150)	−.26	1.5 (723)	2.7 (564)	3.7 (513)	.29**
61. Broke into and entered a home, store, or building	1.5 (132)	2.6 (152)	2.5 (161)	.14	1.1 (724)	3.5 (567)	2.5 (512)	.25*
64. Damaged or destroyed public or private property	3.6 (113)	4.9 (147)	4.5 (155)	.06	2.8 (725)	5.9 (563)	6.8 (498)	.30***
68. Was taken to the office for punishment	12.4 (121)	21.0 (124)	25.8 (128)	.28**	14.4 (647)	17.7 (503)	21.5 (418)	.16**
69. Stole things from someone else's desk or locker	5.1 (137)	7.6 (144)	10.5 (153)	.08	6.9 (710)	7.4 (544)	12.5 (487)	.22**
72. Used a car without the owner's permission	.7 (135)	5.3 (151)	3.1 (161)	.23	2.9 (732)	4.3 (561)	7.2 (515)	.32***
75. Beat up someone who did nothing to subject	2.3 (132)	3.4 (146)	4.5 (156)	.22	2.1 (729)	3.4 (557)	5.0 (500)	.30**
78. Took things worth $50 or more	.7 (136)	2.0 (150)	1.9 (160)	.24	1.5 (734)	2.3 (571)	1.7 (524)	.26***
82. Smoked marijuana	12.0 (133)	15.8 (146)	17.1 (152)	.13	9.3 (711)	13.4 (545)	14.5 (496)	.17**
84. Took part in strike, riot, or demonstration	3.1 (130)	3.6 (140)	5.9 (153)	.24	3.2 (717)	4.9 (550)	4.9 (508)	.15

[a] Part of this table, drawn from Table 2 of "Social Class, Self-derogation and Deviant Response," by Howard B. Kaplan, is reprinted with stylistic changes from Social Psychiatry, 1978, 13, pp. 19–28, by permission of the publisher, Springer-Verlag.
[b] Parenthetical entries indicate cell N.

*p < .05
**p < .01
***p < .001

subjects being in general most likely to report performance of the deviant response between T_1 and T_2. The measure of association (gamma) was significant for 18 of the behaviors. These results were expected on the assumption that for middle-class subjects the deviant behaviors represented attempts to enhance self-attitudes that were adopted as alternatives to normatively endorsed patterns that came to be disvalued by virtue of their association with the genesis of negative self-attitudes. In contrast, for the lower-class male subjects antecedent self-derogation was significantly associated with subsequent deviant responses in only 3 of the 28 instances (items 10, 31, 57). These results were also expected on the assumption that the deviant responses were compatible with the lower-class subcultures and therefore, given the association of the subcultural patterns with the genesis of negative self-attitudes, would not be likely to be adopted by self-derogating subjects in an attempt to reduce their levels of self-derogating feelings.

For the middle-class females comparable results were observed (Table 5.3). In all 28 cases initial level of self-derogation was positively associated with subsequent reports of deviant responses such that higher initial levels of self-derogation were associated with higher probabilities of subsequent adoption of the deviant response. In 23 of the 28 instances the degree of association was statistically significant.

In sharp contrast, among the lower-class female subjects in only 8 cases was a significant association between earlier level of self-derogation and subsequent reports of deviant response observed (items 3, 10, 11, 17, 29, 31, 38, 68).

In general, then, the results are supportive of the expectation that earlier self-derogation is associated with subsequent deviant response among middle-class subjects but not among lower-class subjects.

DISCUSSION

Although the theory from which the hypotheses under consideration were derived is one of a number of views of delinquency as responses to frustration of the self-esteem motive (cf. Wells, 1978), these various theoretical positions come to quite different conclusions about the probable relationship between social class, self-esteem, and deviant behavior. Hewitt (1970, p. 69), for example, asserts that "the lower class child is less likely than the working class child to find any adult context of socialization within which self-esteem can be constructed." Thus he is more likely to turn exclusively to his peers in order to bolster his self-esteem. These circumstances increase the probability of law violations. This position implies that lower-class subjects who are more self-derogating (that is, have lower self-esteem) would be more likely than higher-class self-derogating subjects to adopt deviant responses (or correlated patterns) in anticipation of assuaging their self-rejecting attitudes. However, the data indicate quite the reverse. The relationship between antecedent self-derogation and subsequent adoption of specified deviant responses appears to be strongest and most consistent among upper-stratum subjects and is least likely to be observed among lower-stratum subjects. Rather, these findings are quite consistent with the view stated earlier that the behaviors that we have been calling deviant are compatible with lower-class subcultural systems. To the extent that individuals develop severe self-rejecting attitudes in the context of these subcultures they would thus be unlikely to adopt such behaviors in an attempt to reduce the level of intrinsically distressful self-rejecting feelings. Instead, we would expect them to adopt responses directed toward the goal of improving self-acceptance that were not associated with the way of life in which severe self-rejecting attitudes were developed. For lower-class subjects, therefore, it would be expected that no relationship would be obtained between self-attitudes and subsequent performance of these responses. Alternatively, the relationship would be such that more self-rejecting subjects would be least likely subsequently to adopt deviant responses (since these deviant responses were associated with the way of life that led to the distressful self-attitudes and thereby became intrinsically disvalued). Indeed, reference to Table 5.2 will indicate that for lower-class males those having high self-derogation relative to those having low and/or medium self-derogation were subsequently *less* likely to indicate adoption of the deviant response in 16 of the 28 instances (items 3, 7, 11, 29, 38, 44, 48, 50, 56, 61, 64, 68, 75, 78, 82, 84). However, these relationships were statistically significant in only one instance (item 68).

Among lower-class females, only one such relationship (item 57) was observed. In any case, the observed consistency of the relationship between antecedent self-derogation and subsequent deviant response among middle-class subjects but not among lower-class subjects (regardless of sex) is more compatible with the conclusion that "deviant" behaviors will only be adopted as responses to antecedent self-derogation insofar as these responses are not viewed as compatible with the way of life that is subjectively and in fact associated with the genesis of negative self-attitudes.

The observation that differential levels of self-derogation are associated with the probability of subsequently adopting deviant responses among middle-class but not among lower-class subjects does not imply that lower-class subjects are not more self-derogating than middle-class subjects. Indeed it has been demonstrated for adult subjects that under specified conditions the probability of higher self-derogation scores progressively increases as position on the social class scale decreases (H. B. Kaplan, 1971b). In the present study, data retrievable from Tables 5.2 and 5.3 will also reveal that, for both males and females, lower-class subjects are more likely to manifest high self-derogation scores than are middle-class subjects. What is asserted, however, is that for lower-class subjects the deviant behaviors under consideration are not responses to their relatively greater self-derogation. For these subjects the "deviant" responses are in fact compatible with the values and normative standards of their membership groups. Although the postulate of the self-esteem motive (see Chapter 3) leads to the expectation that the lower-class subject would experience a need to respond in ways that might be expected to enhance self-attitudes, by the reasoning described earlier such self-enhancing responses would be those that were alternative responses to the patterns endorsed by, or compatible with, the normative structure of the groups in which the individual developed his intrinsically distressful negative self-attitudes. This would presumably preclude the kind of behaviors considered here as deviant for the lower-class subjects and would indicate the adoption of such responses by highly self-derogating middle-class subjects.

A further issue to be considered concerns the relationship between prevalence of deviant behaviors and social class. One assumption leading to the hypotheses stated earlier is that the deviant behaviors are more compatible with lower-class subcultural standards than middle-class standards. If this is the case, should not the deviant responses be more prevalent in the lower class than in the middle class? In point of fact, in the present study as well as in numerous other studies (Hirschi, 1969, pp. 66–75), the relationship between social class and deviant behavior is neither consistent nor appreciable. Does this not imply that the behaviors in question are equally incompatible with the normative standards of both social classes? The position here is that the failure to observe significant differences in deviant responses between the classes does not necessarily imply that these responses are equally acceptable within the respective normative frameworks of the class subcultures. It is possible that the failure to observe differences in the frequencies of deviant acts might be due to the ages of the subjects. It is conceivable that these acts were learned in the lower class as appropriate ones ordinarily to be performed at some future time, that is, by way of anticipatory socialization. Furthermore, the failure to observe differences in self-reports of deviant behaviors might be accounted for by the differential sample attrition among those segments of the population who were most predisposed to deviance. In point of fact, subjects were less likely to continue participation in the study if they reported prior performance of deviant acts and if they were in the lower-class segment of the population. But, finally, and most important, even if the acts in question were equally prevalent (or rare) in the two social classes, they might still be more or less acceptable according to the standards of the subgroup. For the lower-class subjects the acts might represent acceptable extrapolations of normative response patterns, whereas for the middle-class subjects they might represent deviant responses that are adopted in an attempt to reduce high levels of self-derogation. Such differential meanings of the "deviant" acts for the two class subcultures would indeed be consistent with the results reported previously that for middle-class subjects high levels of self-derogation anticipated deviant responses but for lower-class subjects antecedent level of self-derogation was unrelated to subsequent deviant response.

The data presented in Tables 5.2 and 5.3 provide another opportunity to test the hypothesis that in segments of the population where the behavioral indices are more likely to be interpreted as deviant responses, the relationship between antecedent level of self-derogation and subsequent adoption of deviant behavior will be stronger than among segments of the population where the behavioral indices are less likely to be interpreted as deviant responses. As mentioned earlier, it was observed as expected that among males, upper-stratum subjects manifested stronger relationships between antecedent self-derogation and subsequent adoption of deviant responses (mean gamma = .17) than lower-stratum subjects (mean gamma = −.02). Among females as well, upper-stratum subjects manifested a stronger relationship between antecedent self-derogation and subsequent adoption of deviant responses (mean gamma = .21) than lower-stratum subjects (mean gamma = .17). Furthermore, a literature to be cited in Chapter 7 in another connection also leads to the expectation that the behaviors in general are more likely to be regarded as deviant if performed by females than if performed by males. That is, in the subjects' membership groups the behaviors are viewed as in greater contravention of female-appropriate than male-appropriate roles. Thus, if deviant definition is a precondition for the relationship, then regardless of social class the relationship between antecedent level of self-derogation and subsequent adoption of deviant behavior should be stronger for females than for males. Consistent with this expectation, upper-stratum females (mean gamma = .21) generally displayed a stronger relationship than upper-stratum males (mean gamma = .17), and lower-stratum females generally displayed a stronger relationship (mean gamma = .17) than lower-stratum males (mean gamma = −.02). This last group, which was least likely to define the behaviors as deviant, displayed the weakest and most inconsistent relationship between self-attitudes and subsequent adoption of responses presumed to be deviant.

These findings lend further support to the assertion that self-rejecting attitudes lead to the adoption of responses that are defined as deviant in the context of the person's predeviance membership groups.

Self-attitude Change and Deviant Behavior

The analyses that have been presented observe a relationship between antecedent *level* of self-derogation and subsequent adoption of deviant responses (particularly among subjects who could be expected to define the acts as deviant in the context of their predeviance membership groups). The question remains, however, as to whether change in self-attitudes, regardless of level of self-attitudes, anticipates the adoption of deviant responses. Individuals with initially low *or* initially high levels of self-rejection could have relatively small or great changes in self-attitudes—do these variable changes make a difference in the subsequent adoption of deviant behavior?

The following analyses consider the relationship between antecedent increases in self-rejecting attitudes and subsequent adoption of the range of deviant responses. The issue of whether self-rejecting attitudes are associated with more (continued) and/or less (discontinued) stable deviant response patterns is also considered. The latter issue is raised for this reason: Although the theoretical statement leads to the expectation that the genesis of negative self-attitudes would be associated with deviant responses *regardless of the stability of the response over time* (the degree to which a person becomes *confirmed* in a deviant response, on the other hand, would be a function of the complex interaction among variables affecting the net self-enhancing *consequences* of the deviant response), other outcomes are possible. It might be argued, for example, that only short-lived deviant responses are likely to be responses to the earlier genesis of negative self-attitudes, since continuing deviant responses are likely to reflect conformity to patterns that are expected of the person once he reaches an appropriate age. Alternatively, it might be argued that only continuing deviant responses would be responses to the earlier genesis of negative self-attitudes, insofar as the continuity is a reflection of continuing adverse experiences in the normative membership groups. In contrast, the argument proceeds, the more ephemeral responses are likely to be instances of "characteristic" adolescent experimentation and as such are not likely to be responses to the earlier genesis of self-rejecting attitudes.

The first question is addressed by comparing those who had and had not adopted the various deviant acts with regard to earlier change in self-attitudes. The second issue is addressed by considering the association between the adoption of each of two categories of deviant responses—responses that are adopted and continued, and responses that are discontinued—and increases in negative self-attitudes.

The measurement of change poses a number of general problems, as was indicated in Chapter 2. Other issues are more relevant to the measurement of change in self-attitudes in particular. Thus, modes of response to self-attitude change are apparently a function of characteristic level of self-attitudes (Dittes, 1959a, 1959b; Frankel, 1969; McGuire, 1968, pp. 1158–1160; Silverman, 1964; Stotland, Thorley, Thomas, Cohen, & Zander, 1957). Also, congruent with expectations based on the postulate of the self-esteem motive (see Chapter 3), the amount and direction of self-attitude change are reported to be a function of initial level of self-acceptance (Brownfain, 1952; Clifford & Clifford, 1967; Engel, 1959; French, 1968, p. 149; Rosenberg, 1965, pp. 152–154). Therefore, in order to investigate the "independent" relationship between adoption of deviant responses and antecedent change in self-attitudes, it was necessary to "factor out" the predictive utility of initial level of self-attitudes. Given these considerations, change in self-derogation from the first to the second testing was measured by a residual change score (as defined in Chapter 2), the effect of which is to remove from the change that portion that could have been predicted linearly from the first score.

Unlike the earlier analyses reported in this chapter, which were based on data provided by the more inclusive set of subjects present for the first two testings (see Chapter 1), the present analyses were based necessarily (in view of the requirements for observations at three points in time) on data provided by subjects present for all three testings.

For reasons indicated earlier, those subjects who reported the occurrence of the deviant act during the specified period prior to the first testing were excluded from the analysis.

ANALYSES

To test the general hypothesis that the adoption of deviant responses is preceded by an increase in self-derogation, only students who indicated that they had not performed the act in question up to (but not including) the year period covered by the third questionnaire were retained in the analysis. These included students who denied performing the act between the first and second test administrations as well as prior to the first testing. The students who were thus retained in the analysis were distributed among two groupings: (a) those who reported at T_3 that they had performed the deviant act during the preceding year and (b) those who reported not performing the act during the same time period. The two groupings were then compared with regard to the mean residual change in self-derogation between T_1 and T_2. It was hypothesized that, for each deviant act, the former group would manifest significantly greater residual gains, thus indicating that those who "initially" adopted a deviant response relative to those who continued not to do so had experienced significantly greater than expected *antecedent* (to the period of the deviant response) increases (or less than expected decreases) in self-derogation.

The issue of stability of deviant response was considered by comparing each of two subject groupings with a third with regard to mean residual gain in self-derogation between T_1 and T_2. Again, only those who denied performance of the deviant act during the specified period prior to the first testing were included in the analysis. The first grouping consisted of those who adopted and continued the deviant act, that is, subjects who reported the act at both the second and third testing. The second grouping consisted of those who adopted but discontinued the act, that is, affirmed the act at T_2 but denied the act at T_3. The third grouping consisted of all subjects who continued to deny the deviant act at T_2 and T_3 (the same comparison group as in the earlier change analysis).

Comparisons between groupings in both sets of analyses were made in terms of mean differences in residual gain scores. As in the analyses previously reported in this chapter, the comparisons were made separately for each of the 28 indices of deviant responses. In all comparisons significance of difference between mean change scores was treated by a t test assuming unequal variances in the two groups (Welch, 1947).

RESULTS

The results of the two sets of analyses are summarized in Table 5.4. The data relevant to the first analysis involve a comparison of columns 3 and 4. This comparison permits consideration of the relationship between adoption of deviant responses and antecedent increases in self-rejection. The results relevant to a consideration of the second issue require a comparison of each of the first two columns with column 4. Such comparisons address the issue of the association between increase in self-derogation and continuity or discontinuity of deviant responses.

It should be emphasized that positive scores indicate greater than expected increases (or smaller than expected decreases) in self-rejection between T_1 and T_2, whereas negative scores indicate smaller than expected (on the basis of initial scores) increases (or greater than expected decreases) in self-derogation between T_1 and T_2.

With regard to the first question, a comparison of columns 3 and 4 indicates that in each of the 28 comparisons, differences were in the hypothesized direction. Among students denying performance of the act prior to T_2-T_3, students who reported performing the act during T_2-T_3 relative to those who denied performing the behavior during the same period had manifested higher $Rch\ SD$ 1–2 scores during the antecedent period T_1-T_2. The differences were statistically significant in 22 of the 28 comparisons.

The data appear to provide strong support for the hypothesized relationship between adoption of deviant responses and antecedent increases in self-rejecting attitudes. Individuals who (presumably) initially adopted a deviant response during a given time period relative to those who continued to refrain from performing the deviant act over the same period manifested significantly greater than expected increases (or lower than expected decreases) in self-rejecting attitudes during the preceding period. In short, the results support the position that an antecedent condition of deviant responses is the experience of increased negative self-attitudes.

These results, by virtue of the change measure employed, cannot be accounted for in terms of the relationship between initial level of self-attitudes and amount or direction of change in self-attitudes. Nor can they be reinterpreted in terms of reversal of the hypothesized causal sequence by virtue of the mutually exclusive time periods employed in the analysis. However, the relationship might be explained in terms of increased willingness to report deviant acts rather than in terms of adoption of the acts. That is, increased self-rejection could be associated with decreasing defensiveness, and therefore an increased willingness to report acts that had previously been denied. Although not completely obviating this argument, three observations suggest its tenuous nature. First, significant relationships were observed between self-reports and an external validating criterion (school personnel reports). This observation cannot be accounted for by the students' reporting acts that they knew had been observed, since far more acts were reported than were known to school personnel. Second, only persons who previously denied the acts in question were included in the analysis. These included an appreciable portion of high self-derogation subjects who denied prior performance of the act. Such an occurrence would not have been observed if the relationship between high self-derogation and willingness to admit to a deviant act were a very strong one. Third, and perhaps most significant in this connection, although these findings were not hypothesized and therefore are not reported here (and in any case, did not permit establishment of a temporal relationship), with few exceptions greater increases in self-derogation from T_1 to T_2 were consistently observed for persons who admitted performing the deviant act at all three points in time relative to those who denied the performance at all three points in time. Since for the former grouping the admission of the act was constant for periods both prior and subsequent to the observed changes in self-derogation (T_1-T_2), the increase in self-derogation by itself cannot account for subsequent willingness to admit to (as opposed to valid self-reports of) deviant acts. As noted earlier, the consistency of the relationship over the range of deviant acts cannot be accounted for in terms of the interdependence of the deviant acts. On the other hand, this relationship between deviant response and antecedent increase in self-derogation, consistently observed for a variety of highly independent deviant acts, does provide support for the general theory of deviant behavior, a central tenet of which is the assertion that the genesis of negative self-attitudes is a common influence mediating between adverse social experiences and the adoption of any of a broad range of deviant responses.

With regard to the second issue, whether considering only students who adopted and continued performance of the deviant acts or those who adopted and discontinued performance of the deviant acts, the results were generally the same. For each deviant act, students who adopted deviant responses manifested greater than expected increases (or less than expected decreases) in self-derogation between T_1 and T_2 than students who did not adopt deviant responses. All of the 56 comparisons were in the predicted direction. For the students who continued performance of the deviant act (Column 1), 19 of the 28 comparisons with Column 4 were statistically significant. For the students who discontinued performance of the act (Column 2), 21 of the 28 comparisons

TABLE 5.4

Mean Residual Change in Self-derogation between the First (T_1) and Second (T_2) Test Administrations, by Adoption of Deviant Response Patterns among Students Indicating Nonperformance of the Deviant Response Prior to T_1[a]

Test item[b]	Deviant response performed during[c,d]			
	T_1–T_2 and T_2–T_3 (1)	T_1–T_2 but not T_2–T_3 (2)	T_2–T_3 but not T_1–T_2 (3)	Neither T_1–T_2 nor T_2–T_3 (4)
3. Took things worth between $2 and $50 (a,b,c,e,f)	9.3 27.2 102	3.4 26.8 147	3.1 27.9 209	-1.6 24.2 2368
5. Was suspended or expelled from school	3.8 24.8 43	.9 24.9 84	2.6 26.0 153	-.3 24.8 2478
7. Took things worth less than $2 (b,c,e,f)	6.6 27.6 258	5.2 24.4 229	2.4 25.3 257	-2.7 23.7 1783
10. Thought about or threatened to take own life (a,b,c,d,e,f)	18.0 27.1 143	9.7 26.0 207	3.9 27.3 206	-4.2 22.6 2020
11. Had something to do with police, sheriff, or juvenile officers for something subject did or was thought to have done (c,e,f)	6.3 24.2 83	4.3 26.6 98	4.2 25.6 178	-1.2 24.2 2299
14. Became angry and broke things (a,b,c,e,f)	6.7 26.7 264	2.8 24.6 282	2.1 25.3 256	-3.8 23.0 1525
17. Carried a razor, switchblade, or gun as a weapon (c,e,f)[e]	6.2 24.2	4.0 26.6	2.3 27.6	-1.1 24.5

Item	(1) diff	(1) mean	(1) N	(2) diff	(2) mean	(2) N	(3) diff	(3) mean	(3) N	(4) diff	(4) mean	(4) N
		28.1	39		25.1	47		26.3	170		24.6	2583
26. Received a failing grade in one or more school subjects (c,f)	3.2	26.4	203	-.5	24.5	185	2.8	25.3	243	-1.8	24.2	1575
28. Used wine, beer, or liquor more than two times (a,b,e,f)	-.5	24.7	249	3.4	24.8	237	4.4	25.8	383	-2.0	24.2	1733
29. Cheated on exams (b,c,d,e,f)	3.2	26.2	561	2.6	26.7	317	-.7	24.2	464	-3.2	23.0	1143
31. Attempted suicide (b,c,d,e,f)	18.2	26.3	51	13.5	26.5	125	5.5	28.7	139	-2.4	23.6	2426
33. Started a fistfight	2.3	26.1	107	2.1	25.7	184	.5	26.6	180	-.8	24.4	2106
38. Took narcotic drugs (c,e,f)	6.2	26.1	157	8.4	24.2	90	5.9	27.0	294	-1.9	24.0	2263
44. Skipped school without an excuse (c,e,f)	4.8	26.3	255	4.7	26.9	150	3.3	25.3	385	-2.4	24.2	1983
48. Took an active part in social protest either at school or outside of school (e)	.8	22.3	75	3.6	26.8	195	1.4	26.7	162	-.7	24.7	2165

(Continued)

TABLE 5.4—*Continued*

Test item[b]	Deviant response performed during[c,d]			
	T_1–T_2 and T_2–T_3 (1)	T_1–T_2 but not T_2–T_3 (2)	T_2–T_3 but not T_1–T_2 (3)	Neither T_1–T_2 nor T_2–T_3 (4)
50. Took part in gang fights (e)	3.1 28.7 53	4.4 28.2 111	-.1 25.2 138	-.9 24.5 2471
56. Was sent to a psychiatrist, psychologist, or social worker (b,c)	13.6 27.2 22	4.2 29.0 60	-.8 27.0 90	-.8 24.5 2551
57. Used force to get money or valuables (b,c,e,f)	14.0 21.9 25	7.5 24.4 91	4.6 27.1 124	-1.0 24.5 2562
61. Broke into and entered a home, store, or building (c,d,e,f)	6.9 25.6 42	12.1 26.8 71	3.7 27.1 103	-1.1 24.5 2633
64. Damaged or destroyed public or private property on purpose (c,e,f)	8.7 27.3 66	4.2 27.3 130	4.2 27.4 154	-1.1 24.2 2411
68. Was taken to the office for punishment (c,f)	4.5 25.1 233	.7 24.6 199	2.1 25.6 261	-1.2 24.4 1566
69. Stole things from someone else's desk or locker (b,c,e,f)	10.0	6.0	3.0	-2.0

	Column 1	Column 2	Column 3	Column 4
(partial row)	22.? / 45	89	178	2524
75. Beat up someone who did nothing to subject (c,e,f)	4.7 / 25.2 / 53	9.4 / 27.0 / 110	7.3 / 25.6 / 155	−1.5 / 24.3 / 2418
78. Took things worth $50 or more (e,f)	.7 / 19.0 / 25	8.4 / 24.8 / 65	4.6 / 26.7 / 115	−.8 / 24.7 / 2676
82. Smoked marijuana (c,e,f)	3.9 / 26.0 / 217	4.8 / 27.5 / 94	2.5 / 26.5 / 406	−1.7 / 24.0 / 2044
84. Took part in a strike, riot, or demonstration	2.7 / 22.7 / 25	.9 / 27.0 / 92	.4 / 26.6 / 154	−.5 / 24.7 / 2492

[a] Parts of this table, reprinted with stylistic changes by permission of the publisher, Plenum Publishing Corporation, are drawn from Table 1 in "Increase in Self-rejection as an Antecedent of Deviant Responses," by Howard B. Kaplan [*Journal of Youth and Adolescence*, 1975, *4* (3), pp. 281–292] and Table 1 in "Increase in Self-rejection and Continuing/Discontinued Deviant Response," by Howard B. Kaplan [*Journal of Youth and Adolescence*, 1977, *6* (1), pp. 77–87].

[b] Parenthetical entries indicate significant ($p < .05$) difference between column pairs by t test (one-tailed), assuming unequal variances (Welch, 1974): a = 1 versus 2; b = 1 versus 4; c = 1 versus 3; d = 2 versus 3; e = 2 versus 4; f = 3 versus 4.

[c] The series of three entries in each column indicate the mean of the residual change score, the standard deviation, and N.

[d] Positive signs indicate relative increases in mean self-derogation from T_1 to T_2. Negative signs indicate relative decreases in mean self-derogation from T_1 to T_2.

[e] p column 3 versus column 4 = .054.

[f] p column 2 versus column 4 = .052.

with Column 4 were statistically significant. For 16 of the deviant acts both groups manifested significantly greater *Rch* 1–2 scores than nonadopters.

Although an analysis of the differences in scores between the two groups is reported in Table 5.4 (Column 1 versus Column 2), these results are not relevant to the present hypothesis and will not be discussed here. It may be noted in passing, however, that only four of the comparisons (Items 3, 10, 14, and 28) were significant.

Unlike the earlier analyses, which established a temporal relationship between adoption of deviant patterns and antecedent change in self-derogation, the present analyses pose some problems in this regard. Although the results are interpreted as indicating that an increase in self-derogation is an antecedent condition of the adoption of deviant responses regardless of whether or not continuation of the response occurs, the circumstances of limiting the data collection to three points in time in conjunction with the operational definition of adoption of deviant responses serve to permit alternative explanations, since the period over which change in self-attitudes is observed (T_1–T_2) is the same period during which adoption of the deviant pattern is said to have occurred. Consequently, it is difficult to establish the direction of the temporal relationship that is said to exist. To be sure, in the case of those subjects who continued the deviant response, the period that defines the continuity of the response (T_2–T_3) follows the period over which self-attitude change is measured (T_1–T_2). However, for subjects who discontinued the deviant responses, the period of self-attitude change and the period of adopting the deviant response are both T_1–T_2. Although the earlier analysis indicated that increase in self-derogation is temporally prior to adoption of deviant responses, it might be argued that this relationship is accounted for only by instances of continuing deviant responses. For the instances of discontinued deviant responses now under consideration, the observed relationship might be accounted for in terms of the increase in *Rch SD* 1–2 being a consequence (mediated by negative attitudinal responses by significant others) of adopting the deviant response. However, the earlier established temporal relationship between antecedent increase in self-derogation and subsequent adoption of deviant responses in conjunction with the *failure* to observe significant differences between *Rch SD* 1–2 scores on the part of those who continued compared to those who discontinued deviant responses following adoption suggests that increase in self-rejection is antecedent to (whether or not it is also a consequence of) the adoption of deviant responses for both groups.

In any case, the results are consistent with the conclusion that an increase in self-rejecting attitudes is an antecedent condition of the adoption of each of a range of highly independent deviant responses, regardless of whether the deviant responses are continued or discontinued.

Summary

One of the central premises of the general theory of deviant behavior outlined in Chapter 1 asserts that negative self-attitudes (stemming from adverse membership group experiences) motivate the subject to adopt deviant responses as alternatives to now disvalued normative responses, toward the goal of reducing the experience of self-rejecting attitudes. In support of this premise, data were reported that indicate that higher antecedent levels of, and greater antecedent increases in, self-rejecting attitudes anticipate subsequent adoption of a broad range of essentially uncorrelated deviant behaviors among persons who had previously denied performance of the deviant behavior. Increases in self-rejection were associated with adoption of deviant patterns, whether the pattern, once adopted, was continued or discontinued.

Further support for the premise was provided by the observation that the relationship between antecedent level of self-rejection and subsequent adoption of deviant responses was more consistently and strongly observed for those segments of the population (lower socioeconomic stratum, females) for whom it could be more easily assumed that the indicators of deviant behavior constituted contraventions of normative codes.

However, the establishment of the relationship between self-attitudes and subsequent deviant responses does not necessarily imply the hypothesized factors said to intervene between the genesis of self-attitudes and the later adoption of deviant behavior. Whether or not these factors indeed intervene is considered in the following chapter.

Chapter 6

Self-attitudes and Deviant Behavior: Intervening Variables

According to the theoretical statement outlined in Chapter 1, the need to maximize the experience of positive self-attitudes is a characteristically human motive. It is the normal outcome of infants' initial dependence on adult human beings for the satisfaction of basic biological needs. Individuals who develop characteristically intense negative self-attitudes have had a history of being unable to defend themselves against experiences in their membership groups by which they came to perceive themselves as possessing negatively valued attributes, as performing negatively valued behaviors, and as being the object of negative attitudes expressed by highly valued others.

Since their past experiences in membership groups were in fact associated with the genesis of negative self-attitudes, such individuals come to perceive an association between the membership group experiences and the personal experience of intensely distressful negative self-attitudes. By a process of association they come to associate the membership group with intrinsically distressing experiences. The negative feelings associated with those elements of the group-endorsed (that is, normative) structure that in the past were subjectively associated with the experience of negative self-attitudes are generalized to other aspects of the normative structure. Although not specifically associated with the experience of negative self-attitudes, those aspects are subjectively associated with the parts of the normative structure that *were* (in fact and subjectively) associated with negative self-attitudes. By virtue of the negative feelings associated with the normatively endorsed patterns, the individual is said to be unmotivated to conform to, and motivated to deviate from, these patterns (since to do otherwise would be to engage in intrinsically distressing activities). At the same time the person's need to experience positive (and to avoid the experience of negative) self-attitudes is exacerbated because of continuing self-devaluing membership group experiences and a decreasing tendency to use effective and acceptable self-protective mechanisms. The intensification of the self-esteem motive strengthens the person's need to become aware of and adopt alternative responses to those endorsed by membership groups (that in the past failed to permit the experience of self-acceptance and that, as a result, came to be experienced as intrinsically distressing), responses that might serve self-enhancing functions. These alternative responses constitute deviant responses, insofar as they fail to conform to the normative expectations of membership groups and stem from the person's loss of a previously existing motivation to conform or acquisition of motivation to deviate.

Earlier chapters in this volume have provided data compatible with the postulate of the self-esteem motive, in support of the assertion that self-derogation is a consequence of an inability to defend against self-devaluing implications of membership group experiences, and confirmatory of the hypothesis that antecedent self-derogation is related to subsequent adoption of deviant response patterns. This chapter considers the factors that supposedly intervene between the genesis of negative self-attitudes and the adoption of deviant behavior.

Those circumstances that are said to be the consequence of negative self-attitudes and to anticipate the adoption of deviant response patterns may be conceptualized in terms of four general factors:

1. Subjective association of the normative environment with self-devaluing experiences
2. Attitudes toward the normative environment
3. The experience of the self-esteem motive
4. The tendency to seek alternative (deviant) response patterns

The following is a test of hypotheses derived from these general propositions: (a) Changes in each of these factors are consequences of negative self-attitudes and (b) high values on these factors are antecedents of the adoption of deviant responses. But first, those propositions will be considered that concern the relationship between antecedent level of self-derogation and subsequent changes in each of the factors.

Consequences of Negative Self-attitudes

This section reports tests of nine hypotheses that were derived from four general propositions. Three of these hypotheses relate to the first proposition, two relate to the second, three relate to the third, and one relates to the fourth. The hypotheses will be stated in conjunction with a statement of the general proposition from which they were derived. Although all of the dependent variables in the hypotheses are said to be changes in a variable between two points in time, it will be recalled that a residual gain measure of change was employed (see Chapter 2). Thus, change-related terms (i.e., increase, decrease) should be understood to refer to change more or less than could have been expected on the basis of a linear prediction from the score at the earlier point in time. The common independent variable in all hypotheses is stated in terms of initial level of self-derogation, the latter being a measure of increasingly negative self-attitudes.

The three initial self-derogation groupings (low, medium, and high) were compared with each other with regard to each of the nine mean residual change variables. Each of the hypotheses took the form of asserting that increasingly greater initial levels of self-derogation would be associated with increasing (decreasing) magnitudes of subsequent change in the variable. Thus, the analysis permitted the establishment of a temporal relationship between initial self-attitudes and change in the variables. The hypotheses were tested using data from subjects who were present for both of the first two testings.

PROPOSITION I

The first general proposition states that individuals characterized by negative self-attitudes (said to be consequences of a history of being unable to defend against self-devaluing experiences in membership groups) come increasingly to perceive an association between their negative self-attitudes and their membership group experiences. Three hypotheses were tested, verification of which would be interpreted as support for the first general proposition. The hypotheses all state relationship between initial level of self-attitudes and subsequent changes in perceptions of self-devaluing experiences in membership groups that are presumed to encompass a major portion of the subjects' contemporary interpersonal experiences. It was hypothesized that persons with initially low, medium, and high levels of self-derogation, respectively, would, over the next year, manifest correspondingly greater increases (or smaller decreases) in perception of self-devaluing experiences in a peer group—for example, "the kids at school" (hypothesis 1), "in the family" (hypothesis 2), and "in the school" (hypothesis 3). The operational definitions of the three dependent variables were described in Chapter 4.

The results are summarized in Table 6.1. Negative values indicate greater than expected decreases or smaller than expected increases in the dependent variable between T_1 and T_2. Positive values indicate greater than expected increases or smaller than expected decreases in the dependent variable between T_1 and T_2.

Reference to the first three variables in the table will indicate support for the three hypotheses.

For each of the dimensions under consideration, subjects who were low, medium, and high in self-derogation, respectively, at the time of the first testing showed, as hypothesized, ever greater than expected tendencies to man-

TABLE 6.1
Mean Residual Change Scores from the First to Second Test Administrations by Self-derogation Level at the First Test Administration[a]

	Self-derogation level at T_1[c]			Analysis of variance		
	Low (1)	Medium (2)	High (3)	F	df	p
Perceptions of self-devaluing experiences in a peer group (a,b,c)	−.127 .943 1690	−.021 1.088 1489	.140 1.212 1304	27.7	2/4480	.001
Perceptions of self-devaluing experiences in the family (a,b,c)	−.088 1.166 1708	.118 1.475 1512	.328 1.683 1327	31.6	2/4544	.001
Perceptions of self-devaluing experiences in the school (a,b,c)	−.052 1.269 1652	.151 1.466 1448	.299 1.672 1272	21.3	2/4369	.001
Tendency to devalue normative structure (and to value contra-normative patterns positively) as potential sources of gratification (a,b)	−.426 1.602 1540	−.259 1.786 1348	−.174 1.898 1164	7.4	2/4049	.001
Perceptions of self-enhancing potential of normative environment (a,b)	.071 .856 1687	.020 .866 1481	−.064 .909 1296	8.8	2/4461	.001
Experience of defense-lessness/vulnerability (b,c)	−.163 2.297 1710	−.077 2.383 1497	.308 2.416 1317	16.1	2/4521	.001
Need to avoid judgment of personal responsibility for self-devaluing circumstances (a,b,c)	−.226 1.668 1699	.009 1.864 1508	.225 2.000 1321	22.6	2/4525	.001
Guilt deflection (a,b)	.400 1.843 1691	.203 1.953 1504	.204 2.098 1301	5.3	2/4493	.01
Awareness of deviant response patterns (a,b,c)	−.127 2.056 1664	.139 2.130 1439	.291 2.070 1266	8.5	2/4366	.001

[a] Part of this table, drawn from Table 1 of "Sequelae of Self-derogation: Predicting from a General Theory of Deviant Behavior," by Howard B. Kaplan, is reprinted with stylistic changes from Youth and Society, 1975, 7 (2), pp. 171–197, by permission of the publisher, Sage Publications.

[b] Parenthetical entries indicate significant ($p < .05$) difference between paired columns: a = 1 versus 2; b = 1 versus 3; c = 2 versus 3.

[c] The three entries in sequence are $\bar{X}$ Rch 1–2, standard deviation, and N.

ifest subsequent (over the next year) residual gains. Initially high self-derogation subjects showed the highest mean increase (lowest mean decrease) and initially low self-derogation subjects showed the lowest mean increase (greatest mean decrease) over the next year in the (a) perception of self-devaluing experiences in a peer group, (b) perception of self-devaluing experiences in the family, and (c) perception of self-devaluing experiences in the school.

PROPOSITION II

The second general proposition, embedded in the theoretical statement summarized previously, asserts that persons characterized by negative self-attitudes (having perceived and generalized an association between actual membership group experiences and the genesis of subjectively distressful negative self-attitudes) come increasingly to associate the membership-group-endorsed (normative) patterns with negative feelings. By virtue of these feelings the person (commensurate with the negativity of the affect) is said to lose motivation to conform to and acquire motivation to deviate from the normative structure. Verification for the fourth and fifth hypotheses would be taken as support for the second general proposition.

The fourth hypothesis states that persons with initially low, medium, and high self-derogation, respectively, will manifest correspondingly greater increases (smaller decreases) over the next year in the tendency to devalue the normative structure (and to value contranormative patterns) as potential sources of gratification. The operational definition of this dependent variable was given in Chapter 5.

The fifth hypothesis states that persons with initially low, medium, and high levels of self-derogation, respectively, will manifest correspondingly greater decreases (smaller increases) in the tendency to view the normative environment as having self-enhancing potential. This variable is measured by the following factorially derived scale. The factor loadings of the component items are indicated parenthetically.

By the time I am 25 I will probably be happily married. (.47)

I like our society pretty much the way it is. (.42)

By the time I am 30 I will probably have a good job and a good future ahead of me. (.33)

My parents always expected a lot of me. (.34)

Reference to the fourth and fifth variables in Table 6.1 again will indicate support for the hypotheses. Subjects who were low, medium, and high in self-derogation, respectively, at the time of the first testing showed ever greater than expected increases (ever smaller than expected decreases) over the next year in the tendency to devalue the normative structure and to value contranormative patterns as potential sources of gratification. They also showed ever greater than expected *decreases* (ever smaller than expected increases) in the tendency to view the normative structure as having self-enhancing potential.

These findings were consistent with the results of a number of cross-sectional survey findings, such as the observations by Rosenberg (1965, pp. 232–239) that low self-esteem subjects were more likely to indicate that they were not likely to get ahead in life as far as they would like, would not be as successful as most people seemed to be, and did not realistically think that they would enter their preferred business or profession. Also consistent with the hypotheses were the results of experimental studies in which induced self-devaluation of one sort or another was associated with subsequent measure of negative attitudes toward other group members or to the group as a whole (Baron, 1974; Frankel, 1969; M. Horowitz, 1958; Johnson, 1966; Pepitone & Wilpizeski, 1960) and, in a more general way, findings reported by Melges and associates that decreasing self-esteem is related to increasingly negative outlooks toward the future (Melges, Anderson, Kraemer, Tinklenberg, & Weisz, 1971).

PROPOSITION III

The third general proposition to be considered states that persons characterized by negative self-attitudes will experience intensification of the need to enhance their self-attitudes (by virtue of the continuing failure of the normative structure to provide motivationally acceptable response patterns that would serve this need). The intensification of the need is hypothesized to be reflected in three outcomes: an increased experience of subjective distress associated with a vulnerability to self-devaluing circumstances (that is, defenselessness); an increased predisposition to avoid personal responsibility for self-devaluing circumstances through the use of ineffective or deviant response patterns; and a decreased tendency to employ more socially approved mechanisms toward the goal of avoiding blame. Given the continuing exposure to self-devaluing experiences in the context of normative membership groups, the person would experience increased distress and sensitivity to the negative reactions of others. The failure of normative self-protective mechanisms in the presence of exacerbated self-devaluation motivates the use of even frequently self-defeating mechanisms, as if as a last resort, in order to assuage the painful self-rejecting feelings. At the same time the proven disutility of more acceptable self-protective mechanisms (as evidenced by the relatively high level of self-derogation experienced by the subject) and/or the absence of these potentially effective mechanisms in the person's repertoire would lead to relatively less use of these mechanisms by self-rejecting than by self-accepting subjects. Even where more acceptable self-protective mechanisms were episodically effective in forestalling or assuaging the experience of self-rejecting feelings, the generalized subjective association between the genesis of characteristic negative self-attitudes and the normative system might lead to the avoidance and/or rejection of these mechanisms.

Thus verification of the sixth, seventh, and eighth hypotheses would be interpretable as support for the third general proposition. Persons with initially low, medium, and high levels of self-derogation, respectively, were expected to manifest correspondingly greater increases over the next year in the experience of defenselessness/vulnerability (hypothesis 6); correspondingly greater increases over the next year in attempts to avoid personal responsibility for self-devaluing circumstances through the use of ineffective or deviant response patterns (hypothesis 7); and correspondingly greater *decreases* over the next year in guilt deflection—that is, the use of a range of socially acceptable self-protective mechanisms toward the goal of forestalling or reducing the experience of self-rejecting feelings (hypothesis 8).

The three dependent variables are described in detail in Chapter 4. The measure of defenselessness/vulnerability consists of two subsets of items—those indicative of subjective distress, and those suggesting extreme sensitivity to negative attitudes expressed by others. The avoidance of self-judgments of personal responsibility for wrongdoing or failure might be accomplished through the disavowal of personal, as opposed to external, control over one's behavior and outcomes; through emotional detachment that precludes the experience of self-blame; through interpersonal avoidance of situations characterized by risks of self-devaluation; and/or through denial of reality. The measure of guilt deflection appears to encompass a variety of socially acceptable self-protective mechanisms akin to those of rationalization and compensation as well as other mechanisms.

As reference to the sixth, seventh, and eighth sets of entries in Table 6.1 will demonstrate once more, the hypotheses were supported. Subjects who were low, medium, and high in self-derogation, respectively, at the time of the first testing showed ever greater than expected increases (smaller than expected decreases) over the next year in the experience of defenselessness/vulnerability; showed ever greater than expected increases (smaller than expected decreases) over the next year in the attempt to avoid personal responsibility for self-devaluing circumstances through the use of ineffective or deviant mechanisms; and showed ever greater than expected decreases (smaller than expected increases) over the next year on the measure of guilt deflection.

In further support of the expectation that low self-esteem subjects would be increasingly vulnerable to the distressing effects of self-devaluing circumstances are the results of experimental studies. These studies report low self-esteem subjects to be more influenced by threatening communications than by optimistic communications when a communication apparently stemmed from a source who was dissimilar in personality characteristics (Leventhal & Perloe, 1962); more influenceable following a failure manipulation (Nisbett & Gordon, 1967); relatively more concerned with the group's expectations under conditions in which they had failed and the group's expectations were high (Stotland *et al.*, 1957, p. 60); more affected by a success/failure condition with regard to subsequent negative ratings of the group (Dittes, 1959a; Frankel, 1969).

PROPOSITION IV

The fourth general proposition to be considered asserts that, in view of the inability to satisfy the self-esteem motive through the use of motivationally unacceptable normative response patterns, persons characterized by negative self-attitudes will seek and become aware of alternative deviant response patterns. Support for the ninth hypothesis would be accepted as support for this general proposition. This hypothesis states that persons with initially low, medium, and high levels of self-derogation, respectively, were expected to manifest correspondingly greater increases (smaller decreases) over the next year in awareness of deviant response patterns.

Subject awareness of deviant responses was measured by the number of "yes" responses to the following items, which indicate the perceived prevalence of behaviors selected to be representative of the more inclusive set of behaviors under investigation in the present study.

Do many of the kids at school take an active part in social protest, either at school or outside of school?

Do many of the kids at school take narcotic drugs?

Do many of the kids at school damage or destroy public or private property on purpose that does not belong to them?

Do many of the kids at school break into and enter a home, store, or building?

Do many of the kids at school carry razors, switchblades, or guns as weapons?

Do many of the kids at school take little things (worth less than $2) that do not belong to them?

Do many of the kids at school beat up on people who have not done anything to them?

Do many of the kids at school smoke marijuana?

Reference to the last set of entries in Table 6.1 will evidence support for the hypothesis. Subjects who were low, medium, and high in self-derogation, respectively, at the time of the first testing showed ever greater than expected increases (smaller than expected decreases) over the next year in awareness of alternative deviant patterns in the immediate environment.

This observed tendency for self-rejecting persons to become increasingly aware of deviant alternatives is compatible with findings from earlier research reports. Sherwood (1965), for example, reported that subjects tended not to agree with group norms when the group did not evaluate the subjects highly. Ludwig and Maehr (1967) indicated that change in preference for particular activities was associated with prior experience of approval or disapproval associated with the activities. Long and her associates (1967) observed that subjects with high originality scores tended to display significantly less self-esteem than subjects with low originality scores. Rasmussen and Zander (1954) reported that teachers who had high failure scores (discrepancy between real and ideal levels of classroom performance) were significantly less likely than those with low failure scores to indicate that they would choose teaching if they could begin their professional careers over again.

Antecedents of Deviant Behavior

In the previous section, self-derogation level was hypothesized and observed to be related to subsequent changes in each of nine variables that variously reflect the four factors or processes said to mediate between the genesis of negative self-attitudes and the adoption of deviant responses. However, a further analysis was necessary in order to establish that the factors or processes reflected in these variables do in fact mediate between antecedent negative self-attitudes and subsequent adoption of deviant responses. In addition to establishing that these processes are influenced by negative self-attitudes, it is necessary to determine that they in turn influence the adoption of deviant responses.

Thus, for each of nine variables reflecting one of the processes said to mediate between the genesis of negative self-attitudes and subsequent deviant responses, it was hypothesized that subjects who scored high relative to those who scored low on the variable at a given point in time would be significantly more (less) likely subsequently to adopt each of 28 virtually uncorrelated deviant response patterns.

The hypotheses were tested according to the following procedure. With one exception, the distributions of scores on the dependent variables were divided into high and low categories. An attempt was made to have comparable frequencies in the two categories. In the case of the devaluation of the normative structure and the positive valuation of contranormative patterns as having self-enhancing potential, the distribution of scores was divided among high, medium, and low categories.

For each of the nine independent variables, subjects who were in the high (in the case of one variable, medium) and low categories, respectively, of the independent variable in question at T_1 were compared with regard to the proportion of subjects who adopted each of the 28 deviant responses between

T_1 and T_2. Gamma was used as a measure of association between the independent variable and adoption of the deviant response.

Since only subjects who denied performance of the deviant act in question prior to T_1 were considered in the analysis, it was possible to establish a temporal relationship between score category on each independent variable at T_1 and initial report of the deviant response(s) at T_2 (referring to the period T_1-T_2).

As in the preceding analysis, all students who were present for the first two testings were considered in the analysis.

The results of the analysis are presented in Table 6.2. In general, the results provided strong support for the hypotheses. Of the 252 hypothesized relationships (9 independent variables × 28 deviant patterns), 193 (77%) were in the predicted direction and statistically significant. The relationship between some independent variables and the adoption of deviant response patterns was more consistent and stronger than in the case of other independent variables.

The relationships between each of the independent variables and the subsequent adoption of deviant response patterns will be considered in turn.

Antecedent perceived self-devaluing experiences among the kids at school was among the least consistent predictors of the later adoption of deviant response patterns. (The other poor predictor was perceived self-enhancing potential of the normative environment.) Perceived self-devaluing experiences among peers was significantly associated with adoption of deviant responses for 11 of the deviant patterns. The patterns in question tended to be expressions of both intrapunitive tendencies (thinking about or threatening to take their own lives; attempting suicide) and extrapunitive tendencies (becoming angry and breaking things). Generally, the remaining patterns that were associated with antecedent perception of self-devaluing peer experiences tended to relate to behavior directed at peers as targets, and/or to behavior carried out in a school setting (suspension or expulsion from school; carrying a weapon; receiving failing grades; using force to get money or valuables from another person; stealing things from someone else's desk or locker; and beating up someone who did nothing to them). Significant association with active participation in social protest may or may not suggest that the school environment was the target of the protest. Thus, it may be hypothesized that the modes of deviance adopted in response to perception of self-devaluing experiences among the kids at school would be those patterns that use the self-devaluing environment as the target of the deviant response. An examination of the deviant patterns that were unrelated to antecedent perception of self-devaluing experiences among the kids at school suggests that these patterns may be those that normally are carried out in peer context. Thus, the perception of self-rejection by peers precludes performance of these activities in response to the perception of self-devaluing experiences. Such activities may include minor theft (taking things worth between $2 and $50; taking things worth less than $2), substance abuse (selling narcotic drugs; using wine, beer, or liquor; using narcotic drugs; smoking marijuana), and joy riding (using a car without the owner's permission). Even cheating on an exam and starting a fistfight, both patterns not associated with antecedent perceptions of self-devaluing experiences among the kids at school, imply established peer relationships. The absence of relationships between perceived self-devaluing experiences among kids at school and subsequently coming to the attention of the authorities might similarly be accounted for by the alienation from the peer group. That is, the visibility of the deviant act would be greater if it was performed in the context of a peer group.

In short, the failure to observe a more consistent relationship between subjects' perceptions of self-devaluing experiences among the kids at school and the subsequent adoption of deviant responses might be accounted for by the alienation from the very peer group that was the occasion for, or otherwise facilitated performance of, the deviant behavior.

In any case, the relationship between antecedent self-devaluing experiences among the kids at school and subsequent adoption of deviant responses was statistically significant for 11 patterns of behavior—far more than what had been expected by chance. The data are compatible with the hypothesis that the perception of self-devaluing experiences among "the kids at school" anticipates subsequent adoption of deviant patterns, particularly where those patterns are not contingent upon integration into the peer group in question.

Antecedent perceptions of self-devaluing experiences in both the family and the school were consistently related to subsequent adoption of deviant patterns. Each of the two variables, as expected, was significantly related to subsequent adoption of each of the 28 deviant patterns under consideration.

Antecedent devaluation of the normative structure and positive evaluation of contranormative patterns as having self-enhancing potential also were consistently related to subsequent adoption of deviant response patterns. The relationship was significant in 27 of the 28 instances, and in the remaining instance it was in the hypothesized direction.

Although generally related to the adoption of deviant response patterns in the expected direction, perceived self-enhancing potential of the normative environment was one of the least consistent predictors. Antecedent perception of self-enhancing potential of the normative environment was significantly related to the subsequent adoption of nine of the deviant patterns. Subjects low in perception of self-enhancing potential of the normative environment were significantly more likely to adopt the deviant response pattern. This variable was related to deviant patterns that were more severe instances of delinquency, and/or targeted those aspects of the social system that appeared to symbolize the areas of anticipated failure. Thus, subjects with low perception of self-enhancing potential of the normative environment were significantly more

TABLE 6.2

Adoption of Deviant Responses between T_1 and T_2, by High and Low Values on Selected Variables at T
among Students Who Deny Performance of the Deviant Response during Specified Periods Prior to T_1[a]

Test item	Perceived self-devaluing experiences among kids at school[b,c]		Perceived self-devaluing experiences in family[b,c]		Perceived self-devaluing experiences in school[b,c]		Devaluation of normative str (contranormative attitudes		
	Low	High	Low	High	Low	High	Low	Medium	
3. Took things worth between $2 and $50	10 (1700)	11 (2708)	8 (2335)	14 (2086)	8 (2975)	16 (1421)	7 (1599)	12 (1473)	14
		.05		.32***		.35***		.22***	
5. Was suspended or expelled from school	5 (1669)	8 (2622)	4 (2291)	10 (2009)	4 (2888)	12 (1387)	3 (1572)	6 (1433)	12
		.24**		.49***		.52***		.46***	
7. Took things worth less than $2	22 (1520)	21 (2350)	18 (2131)	26 (1751)	19 (2697)	27 (1161)	19 (1481)	23 (1267)	24
		−.04		.21***		.22***		.11*	
10. Thought about or threatened to take own life	12 (1612)	16 (2355)	11 (2232)	19 (1747)	12 (2764)	21 (1196)	11 (1517)	15 (1320)	20
		.16**		.29***		.32***		.23***	
11. Had something to do with police, sheriff, or juvenile officers for something subject did or was thought to have done	8 (1598)	9 (2480)	6 (2207)	11 (1881)	6 (2831)	14 (1234)	5 (1543)	·9 (1337)	12
		.03		.31***		.41***		.29***	
14. Became angry and broke things	22 (1436)	28 (2148)	21 (2022)	32 (1571)	23 (2518)	32 (1055)	20 (1408)	26 (1168)	32
		.17**		.28***		.22***		.20***	
17. Carried a razor, switch-blade, or gun as a weapon	8 (1646)	11 (2607)	7 (2275)	13 (1992)	7 (2897)	16 (1346)	6 (1576)	10 (1414)	14
		.19**		.34***		.41***		.30***	
24. Sold narcotic drugs (dope, heroin)	4 (1694)	4 (2728)	2 (2317)	6 (2120)	2 (2956)	8 (1454)	2 (1584)	4 (1459)	6
		.004		.51***		.58***		.34***	
26. Received a failing grade in one or more school subjects	17 (1398)	22 (1903)	15 (1908)	27 (1403)	16 (2439)	31 (856)	12 (1366)	21 (1098)	32
		.16**		.37***		.40***		.40***	
28. Used wine, beer, or liquor more than two times	20 (1558)	22 (2490)	18 (2196)	25 (1863)	18 (2806)	29 (1232)	16 (1521)	22 (1348)	28
		.07		.21***		.29***		.22***	
29. Cheated on exams	38 (1515)	36 (2354)	34 (2117)	39 (1764)	34 (2663)	57 (1196)	36 (1469)	36 (1268)	39
		−.06		.11*		.19***		.04	
31. Attempted suicide	6 (1688)	9 (2571)	5 (2318)	11 (1952)	6 (2908)	12 (1339)	5 (1587)	7 (1417)	13
		.25**		.37***		.41***		.36***	
33. Started a fistfight	13 (1556)	13 (2417)	11 (2162)	15 (1823)	11 (2761)	18 (1205)	11 (1520)	13 (1297)	16
		.01		.17**		.25***		.17**	
38. Took narcotic drugs	11.(1671)	11 (2691)	7 (2300)	15 (2075)	8 (2940)	17 (1409)	7 (1578)	11 (1438)	15
		.01		.42***		.43***		.28***	
44. Skipped school without an excuse	16 (1657)	19 (2638)	13 (2291)	23 (2017)	13 (2907)	27 (1375)	12 (1575)	17 (1425)	25
		.09		.35***		.42***		.27***	
48. Took an active part in social protest either at school or outside of school	10 (1565)	13 (2467)	9 (2187)	15 (1856)	9 (2491)	16 (1277)	7 (1546)	11 (1338)	19
		.15*		.29***		.32***		.38***	

rceived self-...ing potential of normative vironment[b,c]		Defenselessness/ vulnerability[b,c]		Avoidance of personal responsibility for self-devaluing circumstances[b,c]		Guilt deflection[b,c]		Awareness of deviant response patterns[b,c]	
y	High	Low	High	Low	High	Low	High	Low	High
91) 9 (2918)		10 (2259)	12 (2161)	9 (2243)	12 (2180)	13 (2311)	8 (2106)	8 (2283)	14 (2078)
−.18**		.11*		.19**		−.30***		.29***	
43) 6 (2673)		5 (2187)	8 (2110)	4 (2195)	9 (2107)	8 (2252)	5 (2047)	6 (2202)	8 (2035)
−.12		.19*		.43***		−.20**		.17*	
73) 21 (2597)		20 (2041)	24 (1836)	20 (2050)	24 (1832)	25 (1951)	18 (1926)	19 (2103)	24 (1721)
−.05		.12*		.12*		−.19***		.13**	
16) 14 (2655)		10 (2157)	20 (1820)	10 (2114)	19 (1867)	16 (2027)	13 (1950)	12 (2120)	17 (1803)
−.01		.39***		.34***		−.13*		.21***	
37) 8 (2740)		8 (2093)	9 (1995)	7 (2115)	10 (1768)	10 (2101)	7 (1985)	6 (2142)	11 (1883)
−.09		.01		.23**		−.23**		.30***	
87) 26 (2398)		20 (1968)	32 (1624)	21 (1951)	31 (1643)	25 (1824)	26 (1767)	22 (1944)	30 (1596)
.004		.29***		.24***		.02		.21***	
14) 9 (2840)		9 (2164)	10 (2101)	7 (2174)	12 (2094)	12 (2222)	7 (2041)	7 (2230)	12 (1976)
−.14*		.06		.30***		−.28***		.31***	
97) 4 (2927)		4 (2215)	5 (2219)	3 (2208)	5 (2229)	5 (2334)	3 (2033)	3 (2244)	6 (2129)
−.20*		.15		.28**		−.27**		.30**	
63) 18 (2236)		18 (1750)	22 (1560)	14 (1867)	28 (1444)	21 (1671)	18 (1637)	18 (1768)	22 (1492)
−.15*		.12*		.40***		−.09		.13*	
61) 21 (2686)		20 (2097)	23 (1962)	18 (2101)	26 (1960)	23 (2083)	20 (1972)	18 (2146)	26 (1855)
−.07		.11*		.23***		−.08		.24***	
84) 36 (2588)		33 (2031)	40 (1850)	34 (2046)	40 (1836)	39 (1981)	34 (1899)	32 (2065)	41 (1762)
−.04		.15***		.11**		−.10*		.19***	
29) 7 (2831)		5 (2243)	10 (2025)	4 (2223)	11 (2050)	8 (2224)	7 (2043)	6 (2218)	10 (1992)
−.06		.36***		.49***		−.08		.24**	
30) 14 (2646)		12 (2061)	14 (1923)	11 (2078)	16 (1909)	14 (2022)	12 (1962)	11 (2112)	15 (1810)
.04***		.07		.20**		−.08		.16**	
68) 10 (2893)		9 (2224)	12 (2146)	8 (2212)	13 (2163)	13 (2290)	9 (2079)	7 (2253)	15 (2060)
−.09		.18**		.24***		−.21***		.36***	
52) 16 (2843)		16 (2192)	20 (2112)	14 (2191)	21 (2118)	21 (2249)	14 (2054)	14 (2215)	22 (2030)
−.14**		.12*		.23***		−.21***		.25**	
69) 12 (2664)		11 (2055)	12 (1986)	9 (2110)	15 (1935)	12 (2123)	11 (1918)	9 (2139)	15 (1846)
.08		.09		.22***		−.08		.26***	

(*Continued*)

TABLE 6.2—Continued

Test item	Perceived self-devaluing experiences among kids at school[b,c]		Perceived self-devaluing experiences in family[b,c]		Perceived self-devaluing experiences in school[b,c]		Devaluation of normative stru (contranormative attitudes)[d]		
	Low	High	Low	High	Low	High	Low	Medium	Hig
50. Took part in gang fights	7 (1666) .12	8 (2633)	6 (2303) .32***	10 (2009)	5 (2915) .43***	12 (1377)	4 (1601) .39***	7 (1424)	13 (
56. Was sent to a psychiatrist, psychologist, or social worker	3 (1633) .17	5 (2585)	3 (2244) .27**	5 (1986)	3 (2835) .35***	6 (1371)	3 (1515) .26**	4 (1399)	6 (
57. Used force to get money or valuables	4 (1680) .25**	6 (2658)	3 (2301) .43***	7 (2051)	3 (2920) .42***	8 (1409)	2 (1591) .43***	4 (1440)	9 (
61. Broke into and entered a home, store, or building	4 (1695) .14	5 (2730)	3 (2310) .31***	6 (2129)	3 (2938) .51***	8 (1474)	3 (1587) .27***	5 (1448)	6 (
64. Damaged or destroyed public or private property on purpose	7 (1662) .16*	9 (2630)	6 (2287) .30***	10 (2021)	6 (2915) .37***	12 (1368)	5 (1579) .31***	8 (1420)	12 (
68. Was taken to the office for punishment	20 (1345) .09	22 (2080)	17 (1939) .29***	27 (1500)	18 (2471) .37***	32 (947)	15 (1357) .31***	21 (1137)	31
69. Stole things from someone else's desk or locker	11 (1607) .12*	14 (2541)	10 (2222) .26***	16 (1941)	10 (2830) .29***	17 (1309)	8 (1538) .25***	15 (1371)	16 (
72. Used car without the owner's permission	6 (1706) .02	6 (2709)	4 (2317) .38***	8 (2111)	4 (2946) .37***	9 (1458)	3 (1597) .33***	6 (1449)	9 (
75. Beat up someone who did nothing to subject	5 (1650) .27***	8 (2590)	6 (2260) .31***	9 (1994)	5 (2871) .42***	11 (1357)	4 (1554) .32***	6 (1406)	11 (
78. Took things worth $50 or more	3 (1703) .11	4 (2757)	2 (2337) .47***	6 (2136)	2 (2965) .43***	6 (1482)	2 (1589) .35***	4 (1467)	6 (
82. Smoked marijuana	15 (1632) −.05	13 (2650)	10 (2265) .35***	18 (2032)	10 (2898) .40***	21 (1375)	10 (1559) .26***	14 (1413)	19 (
84. Took part in a strike, riot, or demonstration	5 (1643) .13	6 (2657)	4 (2257) .38***	8 (2058)	4 (2882) .42***	9 (1409)	3 (1577) .39***	5 (1408)	9 (

[a] Parts of this table, drawn from Table 1 in "Antecedents of Deviant Responses: Predicting from a General Theory of Deviant Beha by Howard B. Kaplan, are reprinted with stylistic changes from *Journal of Youth and Adolescence*, 1977, 6 (1), pp. 89–101, by permission publisher, Plenum Publishing Corporation.

[b] Initial entry indicates percentage of subjects adopting deviant response between T_1 and T_2; second entry in parentheses is cell N.

likely subsequently to adopt deviant patterns in which they stole things worth between $2 and $50, carried a weapon, sold narcotic drugs, received failing grades in one or more school subjects, skipped school without an excuse, used force to get money or valuables from another person, engaged in breaking and entering, damaged or destroyed public or private property on purpose, and stole things from someone else's desk or locker. The tendency for these patterns to be associated with property crimes and/or school-related behavior is noteworthy. These reflect the very areas associated with anticipated failure as adults. In

Perceived self-enhancing potential of normative environment[b,c]		Defenselessness/ vulnerability[b,c]		Avoidance of personal responsibility for self-devaluing circumstances[b,c]		Guilt deflection[b,c]		Awareness of deviant response patterns[b,c]	
ow	High	Low	High	Low	High	Low	High	Low	High
1449) .001	8 (2851)	7 (2199) .06	8 (2111)	5 (2211) .33***	10 (2103)	9 (2250) −.23**	6 (2060)	6 (2255) .27***	10 (1996)
1423) −.07	4 (2798)	4 (2152) .07	4 (2078)	3 (2157) .27**	5 (2074)	4 (2214) −.08	4 (2012)	3 (2166) .26**	5 (2008)
1467) −.17*	4 (2872)	4 (2207) .12	6 (2141)	3 (2217) .45***	7 (2135)	6 (2283) −.31***	3 (2064)	4 (2239) .29**	6 (2052)
1495) −.24**	4 (2932)	4 (2229) .10	5 (2208)	3 (2216) .28**	6 (2224)	6 (2341) −.33***	3 (2089)	3 (2252) .28**	6 (2124)
1435) −.14*	7 (2859)	7 (2203) .16*	9 (2100)	6 (2188) .35***	11 (2119)	10 (2245) −.25***	6 (2058)	6 (2248) .27***	10 (1997)
1115) −.10	20 (2313)	20 (1783) .06	22 (1651)	16 (1835) .31***	27 (1601)	24 (1733) −.13*	19 (1701)	18 (1852) .19***	25 (1531)
1382) −.15**	12 (2768)	10 (2147) .20**	15 (2012)	10 (2154) .23***	15 (2008)	16 (2156) −.28***	9 (2002)	10 (2192) .25***	16 (1912)
1490) −.07	6 (2928)	6 (2237) .04	6 (2189)	5 (2208) .24**	7 (2222)	7 (2336) −.23**	5 (2089)	5 (2254) .25**	7 (2112)
1432) −.10	6 (2809)	6 (2173) .15*	8 (2078)	4 (2177) .38***	9 (2076)	9 (2211) −.31***	5 (2038)	5 (2187) .27***	9 (2003)
1510) −.16	3 (2951)	3 (2257) .11	4 (2214)	2 (2237) .34***	5 (2237)	5 (2355) −.33***	2 (2115)	2 (2262) .38***	5 (2148)
1434) −.08	13 (2851)	13 (2187) .09	15 (2107)	11 (2165) .20***	16 (2134)	16 (2221) −.20***	11 (2072)	10 (2214) .33***	18 (2026)
1445) −.04	5 (2860)	5 (2188) .11	6 (2124)	4 (2177) .31***	7 (2138)	6 (2265) −.07	5 (2045)	4 (2216) .23**	7 (2041)

Centered values in second row for each variable indicate gamma. Positive gamma indicates that a high score on the independent variable is associated with a higher rate of deviant behavior. Negative gamma indicates that a low score on the independent variable is associated with a higher rate of deviant behavior. Asterisks indicate significance level for test of the null hypothesis using a conservative estimate of the z score (Goodman & Kruskal, 1963): *$p < .05$; **$p < .01$; ***$p < .001$.

contrast, the deviant patterns that were unrelated to this variable tended to be those that were relatively minor (taking things worth less than $2), reflected intrapunitive patterns (thinking about or threatening to take their own lives; attempting suicide), reflected undirected expressions of aggression (getting angry and breaking things), or reflected aggression against peers (starting a fistfight; taking part in gang fights). Although this variable may reflect emotional distancing from the normative environment, it apparently reflects also, more specifically, the targets subjectively associated with the anticipated failure in the context of the more inclusive normative environment, symbolized by economic and educational patterns.

As anticipated, individuals having relatively high levels of defenselessness/ vulnerability were significantly more likely subsequently to adopt deviant patterns in a relatively consistent fashion. Fourteen of the relationships were statistically significant. However, a number of the patterns were clearly unrelated to antecedent defenselessness/vulnerability. These patterns were either those that carried with them high risk (of physical injury or of apprehension)—such as carrying a weapon, starting a fistfight, taking part in gang fights, and using a car without the owner's permission—or those that involved interaction with authority figures—such as having something to do with police, sheriff, or juvenile officers over something the subject did or was thought to have done; being sent to a psychiatrist, psychologist, or social worker; and being taken to the office for punishment. Perhaps the lack of self-confidence implied by high defenselessness/vulnerability mitigated the predisposition to adopt high-risk deviant patterns that would otherwise have resulted from the inability to defend against self-devaluing experiences in membership groups. The failure to observe an association with the patterns reflecting coming to the attention of the authorities may result similarly from the subjects' inability to tolerate negative attitudes from others. Alternatively, the lack of association between antecedent defenselessness/vulnerability and these patterns may reflect the tenuous association between the subjects' deviant behaviors and/or the subjects' anticipation of the self-enhancing or derogating consequences of coming to the attention of the authority figures on the one hand and the responses of the authority figures (or of those bringing the subjects to the attention of the authority figures) on the other hand.

In any case, defenselessness/vulnerability does indeed generally anticipate the adoption of deviant response patterns, although the meaning of the variable has implications for the modes of deviant responses that will be adopted.

Antecedent predisposition to avoid personal responsibility for self-devaluing circumstances through the use of ineffective/deviant responses is consistently and significantly associated with the subsequent adoption of deviant patterns. In all 28 instances, individuals who scored high on this predisposition were significantly more likely subsequently to report adoption of the deviant response pattern. In addition to providing support for this variable as both a consequence of antecedent increases in self-derogation and a precursor of the adoption of deviant response patterns, these findings confirm the relationship between a variable reflecting a *predisposition* to adopt deviant response patterns as mechanisms for assuaging self-rejection on the one hand and deviant *behavioral* consequences of this predisposition on the other.

As anticipated, guilt deflection was related to subsequent adoption of deviant response patterns. For 27 of the 28 patterns, individuals who were low on guilt deflection were more likely subsequently to adopt deviant response patterns. The relationship was significant for 20 of the patterns.

Finally, the measure of *awareness* of deviant response patterns at an earlier point in time was significantly associated with subsequent adoption of each of the 28 deviant patterns.

In general, then, the anticipated relationships between antecedent factors and subsequent adoption of deviant response patterns appear to hold. At the same time, however, it is apparent that certain of these factors reflected (in part) circumstances that predisposed the person to adopt *specific* modes of deviance.

Summary

The results of the present analysis (apart from the relatively few exceptions noted) support the theoretical statements regarding factors said to mediate between the genesis of negative self-attitudes and the subsequent adoption of deviant responses. These relationships are reflected in Figure 6.1. It appears that individuals characterized by negative self-attitudes (said to be the consequence of their history of being unable to defend against self-devaluing experiences in membership groups) come increasingly to perceive an association between their negative self-attitudes and their membership group experiences. As a result of having perceived and generalized an association between actual membership group experiences and the genesis of subjectively distressful negative self-attitudes, these persons come increasingly to associate the membership

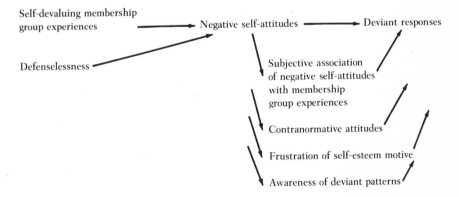

FIGURE 6.1. *Factors Influencing Adoption of Deviant Response Patterns. Adapted from Figure 1 Kaplan, Howard B., Antecedents of deviant responses: Predicting from a general theory of deviant behavior,* Journal of Youth and Adolescence, 1977, 6 (1), pp. 89–101, *with permission from the publisher, Plenum Publishing Corporation, New York.*

group patterns with negative feelings, by virtue of which they are said to lose motivation to conform to and acquire motivation to deviate from the normative structure. At the same time, persons characterized by negative self-attitudes experience intensification of the need to enhance their self-attitudes by virtue of the continuing failure of the normative structure to provide motivationally acceptable response patterns that would serve this need. In view of the inability to satisfy the self-esteem motive through the use of now motivationally unacceptable normative response patterns, persons characterized by negative self-attitudes will seek, become aware of, and adopt alternative deviant response patterns.

The analysis now turns to a consideration of the effects that deviant patterns have upon the self-attitudes that motivated them.

Chapter 7

Deviant Behavior and Self-enhancement

The theoretical model that has guided the data analyses to this point is based on the postulate of the self-esteem motive whereby, universally and characteristically, a person is said to behave in ways designed to maximize the experience of positive self-attitudes, and to minimize the experience of negative self-attitudes. Intense self-rejecting attitudes are said to be the end result of a history of membership group experiences in which the subject was unable to defend against, adapt to, or cope with circumstances having self-devaluing implications (that is, disvalued attributes and behaviors, and negative evaluations of the subject by valued others). By virtue of the actual and subjective association between past membership group experiences and the development of intensely distressful negative self-attitudes, the person loses motivation to conform to, and becomes motivated to deviate from, membership group patterns (those specifically associated with the genesis of negative self-attitudes and, by a process of generalization, other aspects of the membership groups' normative structures). Simultaneously, the unfulfilled self-esteem motive prompts the subject to seek alternative (that is, deviant) response patterns that offer hope of reducing the experience of negative (and increasing the experience of positive) self-attitudes. Thus, the person is motivated to seek and adopt deviant response patterns not only because of a loss of motivation to conform to the normative structure, which has an earlier association with the genesis of negative self-attitudes, but also because the deviant patterns represent the only motivationally acceptable alternatives that might effectively serve self-enhancing functions. Which of several deviant patterns adopted, then, would be a function of the person's history of experiences influencing the visibility and subjective evaluation of the self-enhancing or self-devaluing potential of the patterns in question.

Adoption of the deviant response has self-enhancing consequences, since it facilitates intrapsychic or interpersonal avoidance of self-devaluing experiences associated with the predeviance membership group, serves to attack (symbolically or otherwise) the perceived basis of the person's self-rejecting attitudes (that is, representations of the normative group structure), and/or offers substitute patterns with self-enhancing potential for behavior patterns associated with the genesis of self-rejecting attitudes. To the extent that the person experiences self-enhancing consequences and is able to defend against anticipated or unanticipated adverse consequences of the behavior, he or she will be confirmed in the deviant pattern. If self-devaluing consequences outweigh self-enhancing outcomes, the person is likely to experiment with alternative modes of deviance, since normative patterns would continue to be motivationally unacceptable.

The analyses up to this point have been compatible with the postulate of the self-esteem motive (Chapter 3), the hypothesized relationships concerning antecedents of self-derogation (Chapter 4), the relationship between antecedent self-derogation and subsequent adoption of deviant response patterns (Chapter 5), and the factors said to intervene between the genesis of self-rejecting attitudes and the subsequent adoption of deviant patterns (Chapter 6). The present chapter considers the hypothesized relationship between deviant response patterns and subsequent decreases in self-rejecting attitudes.

The relevant literature (that concerning the association between self-attitudes and deviant behavior) will be considered next. It is generally supportive of the expected relationship, but the studies are limited in a number of important ways, which justified the analyses to be reported subsequently.

Related Literature

Scattered throughout the literature on various modes of deviant behavior are observations regarding the association between "antecedent" deviant responses and self-enhancing attitudes, the mechanisms through which self-enhancement is said to be achieved, and the conditions under which the association is most likely to be observed.

Self-enhancing Consequences

The self-enhancing consequences of deviant patterns may be inferred from observing either temporal relationships between antecedent deviant patterns and subsequent changes in self-attitudes or cross-sectional relationships between deviant patterns and self-acceptance. Furthermore, self-enhancing functions might be inferred from the observation that deprivation of the deviant pattern is associated with increased self-rejection.

TEMPORAL RELATIONSHIPS

Temporal relationships between deviant behaviors and change toward more positive self-attitudes have been observed in a number of experimental studies. Berg (1971) investigated the effect of intoxication upon levels of self-esteem for male subjects who were psychiatrically diagnosed as alcoholic and were resident in the alcoholism unit of a psychiatric hospital for at least 2 weeks. Five days after being given the tests by which their self-attitudes were measured, the subjects submitted to the intoxication procedure during which they drank a mixture of rye whiskey and orange juice. Following the intoxication procedures the self-attitude tests were again administered. A comparison of the alcoholics' self-attitudes scores in the sober and intoxicated conditions revealed that "when intoxicated the alcoholics showed more favorable and less derogatory self-concept than when sober [Berg, 1971, p. 448]."

However, the self-enhancing effects of drinking appear to hold only for those who have a history of heavy drinking and a dependence on alcohol. When essentially the same procedures were employed on a group of social drinkers rather than alcoholics, intoxication was observed to have an adverse effect on self-attitudes.

The two sets of findings taken together are compatible with the interpretation that for alcoholic subjects intoxication represents a favored technique for enhancing self-esteem or defending against self-rejection. For nonalcoholic subjects, in contrast, intoxication does not appear to function in this way. For these subjects intoxication does not seem to be a preferred defense. Indeed, the observed decrease in self-esteem in the intoxication condition suggests that alcohol abuse either disrupts whatever favored defenses these nonalcoholic subjects characteristically employ and/or is a negatively valued activity, participation in which occasions self-devaluing responses.

In any case, not all experimental studies have demonstrated self-enhancing effects of alcohol abuse among diagnosed alcoholics. Indeed, the opposite result was observed in at least one study comparing alcoholic experimental and control groups regarding changes in self-attitudes while subjects were under the influence of alcohol (Vanderpool, 1969). Certain conclusions were not unlike those of other studies. Thus, the data suggested that alcoholics tend to have poor self-concepts when sober. Furthermore, alcoholics are prompted to drink in order to escape from feelings of loneliness, inadequacy, and low worth, and in order to gain release from psychological inhibitions toward the end of projecting a more positive self-attitude. However, in this study, far from exhibiting improved self-concepts when under the influence of alcohol, the subjects tended to manifest more negative self-attitudes. Unfortunately, this study is not strictly comparable to the study by Berg (1971). Perhaps the most meaningful differences were those relating to the drinking procedure. These differences, along with other procedural variations in the drinking sessions, suggest that Berg's alcoholic subjects attained a higher level of intoxication than did Vanderpool's subjects. This difference might account for the observation of an increase in level of self-acceptance among the former group and a decrease in self-accepting attitudes in the latter group under drinking conditions. According to this explanation, a minimum level of intoxication must be reached before alcohol will be observed to serve self-enhancing functions.

The results of a number of experimental studies are consistent with the view that aggressive behavior functions to reduce the subject's level of self-rejection insofar as they show that indices of tension associated with prior self-devaluing experience are lowered following aggressive behavior. Berkowitz (1970, pp. 5–6) cites a number of studies by Hokanson and others (Hokanson & Burgess, 1962; Hokanson, Burgess, & Cohen, 1963; Hokanson & Edelman, 1966) in which college students manifested an appreciable increase in systolic blood pressure after being insulted by the experimenter (a circumstance here interpreted as a self-devaluing experience). Following the condition in which the subjects were given a chance to behave aggressively toward the experimenter (by giving the latter personal electric shocks), the subjects displayed a quick reduction in systolic blood pressure. For the physiological tension reduction to occur, it was apparently necessary for the target of the aggressive behavior to be the person associated with the self-devaluing experience. Thus, although a rapid reduction of the subject's systolic blood pressure followed the giving of electric shocks to the person who insulted him, there was a much slower decline in blood pressure when the subject attacked some other person.

CROSS-SECTIONAL COMPARISONS

Perhaps the greater part of the literature relevant to the relationship between deviant behavior and self-attitudes involves the comparison of two groups of subjects variously characterized in terms of the presence or absence of deviant behaviors. Thus, Rathus and Siegel (1973, p. 274) report associational data "consistent with the subcultural hypothesis that self-esteem, for many delinquents, is largely dependent upon the derogation of those who serve in reciprocal role relationships—more particularly, the criminal justice personnel who participate in the process of labeling them as wrong, and/or incompetent."

Although exceptions have been noted, and consistent with the proposition that deviant patterns have self-enhancing consequences, a number of studies report either that schizophrenic subjects (generally) are not significantly different from nonpsychiatric controls or that schizophrenic patients are *less* self-rejecting than normal controls (Wylie, 1961, pp. 209–215). In one study (Rogers, 1958) the investigator reported that 30 paranoid schizophrenic patients displayed a *higher* degree of self-ideal congruence than did 30 psychiatric aides working at the hospital from which the patient subjects were drawn. Ibelle (1961) also reported results supporting the hypothesis that discrepancies between self-concept and ideal self-concept among paranoid schizophrenics would be similar to the discrepancies manifested by normal subjects. Finally, Havener and Izard (1962) reported that paranoid schizophrenics manifested smaller self-ideal discrepancies relative to other schizophrenics but were not different from normals in magnitude of self-ideal discrepancy. The authors also reported that the paranoid schizophrenics tended to be less accepting of others compared to either the normals or the other schizophrenics. These data are compatible with the interpretation that the paranoid schizophrenic style effectively enhances phenomenal self-esteem by utilization of a mechanism by which one rejects others.

Farnham-Diggory (1964) compared three groups of psychotic males with regard to level of self-evaluation. One group consisted of 21 "overt suicidals" who had made attempts to kill themselves, as evidenced by scars or witnesses. The second group consisted of 22 "covert suicidals" who talked about suicide but who were not known to have made any attempts to kill themselves. The third group consisted of 53 "nonsuicidal" patients in whose records no indication appeared that they had ever been considered suicidal by anyone at any time. The three groups were comparable on a number of characteristics, including race, education, marital status, religion, father's occupation, diagnosis, number of hospitalizations, and length of current hospitalization. Farnham-Diggory reported that the nonsuicidal subjects tended to display the most positive self-evaluations, followed closely by the overt suicidal subjects. The covert suicidal subjects were the least positive in their self-evaluations. The difference in self-evaluation between the nonsuicidal and overt suicidal subjects was not significant. However, the difference in level of self-evaluation between the covert suicidals and nonsuicidal subjects was statistically significant at the .05 level. That is, the self-evaluations of the overt suicidals more closely approximated the relatively positive self-evaluations of the nonsuicidal patients than did the self-evaluations of the coverts. Thus, although the data do not permit determination of whether or not the attempted suicide evoked positive environmental responses and/or was in some measure cathartic, the results are consonant with the thesis that the active attempt to commit suicide exerted a self-enhancing influence on the subjects' self-attitudes.

Also consistent with this thesis is the report by Farberow (1950) that subjects who *threatened* suicide manifested significantly more negative feelings on the Hildreth Feeling and Attitude Scale than did *attempted* suicides and nonsuicidal patients, a result that would be expected if active suicidal behavior was indeed functional in increasing one's level of self-acceptance.

DEPRIVATION OF THE DEVIANT PATTERN

The self-enhancing function of alcohol abuse may be inferred by noting the apparent effects of withdrawal from this pattern upon self-evaluation. Illustrative data that permit such an inference are provided by White and Gaier (1965). These data concern the relationship between self-concept and length of time sober. The subjects were 104 male members of Alcoholics Anonymous. The results revealed a gradual decrease in self-cathexis scores, ranging from a mean score of 3.54 for subjects reporting sobriety periods between 0 to 3.0 months to a mean score of 3.03 for subjects reporting sobriety periods of 12.1 to 36.0 months. Thereafter, self-concept scale "mean scores gradually vacillated to 3.08 for those Ss with 60 months or more of sobriety maintenance [White & Gaier, 1965, p. 375]."

The data of White and Porter (1966) are similarly interpretable as supporting the view that when alcoholics enter into periods of sobriety they deprive themselves (or are deprived) of previously preferred mechanisms for maintaining acceptable levels of self-esteem. The subjects for this study were 35 hospitalized male alcoholics who were actively participating in the Alcoholics Anonymous program at a state hospital. The subjects' sobriety intervals ranged from 8 to 94 days. Self-concept data were derived from responses to the McKinney Sentence Completion Blank. The investigators reported a negative correlation between length of time sober and what was taken to be an index of favorability of self-concept, and a positive correlation between sobriety interval and responses interpreted as indicating self-defeat, guilt, and fear. White and Porter concluded that these findings may be accounted for in any of a number of ways. For example, the increased negativity toward self with increased intervals of sobriety might be explained in terms of group (Alcoholics Anonymous) pressure on the subject to admit personal weakness and culpability with regard to the craving for alcohol. However, again, the finding is also consistent with the position that alcoholism constitutes a preferred defense against self-rejecting attitudes, and the deprivation of this defensive pattern increases the probability of developing increasingly negative self-attitudes.

The self-devaluing consequences of being deprived of favored defenses are also suggested by the evaluation of a halfway house approach to the rehabilitation of narcotic addicts (H. B. Kaplan & Meyerowitz, 1969). A pre–post comparison of subjects who passed through the halfway house program and subjects released directly into the community suggests that the main effect of the Southmore House experience related to the preexisting ego defense system of the subjects. The experience appeared to be successful in curbing the residents' impulsivity and their emotional attachment to the neighborhood, which for them was presumed to be symbolic of the deviant subculture. However, in order to accomplish this it was necessary to break through the defenses put up against self-devaluing attitudes (such as rigidity and withdrawal defenses), which had functioned well in the past. When deprived of the opportunity to resume the psychological defenses, apparently through the effects of the halfway house program, they indeed appeared to be defenseless, as reflected in their increased self-estrangement and decreased ego-strength relative to the comparison group. At this point the ex-residents appeared to be most vulnerable, because they had learned what to reject but not yet what goals to strive for. There was a gap between the rejection of deviant modes and acceptance of and by conventional modes. Such stress might account for the failure of the halfway house experience to curb drug use and additcion in the face of its success in maintaining addicts in functional roles within conventional society. The results implied that the treatment programs need to provide defenses that are adaptive within the context of the conventional structure to replace the defenses that, in their own way, were adaptive within the context of a deviant structure. The program was relatively successful in keeping addicts in the community and in fostering a normative orientation toward society. There was a higher employment rate and a lower rearrest rate for the halfway house group. However, the program was unsuccessful in decreasing addiction or drug use relative to the level of a comparison addict group. The analysis of specific psychosocial changes suggests that the program successfully fostered the rejection of the addicts' environment and the destruction of what might be considered undesirable defenses. However, there was no evidence of an increased positive attitude toward socially approved goals, with the result that the addicts experienced an increase in feelings of self-estrangement. They were deprived of their former defenses but had no newer purposes or equally effective socially acceptable defenses with which to replace them. The removal of the undesirable adaptations, although a necessary step in the rehabilitation of the addict, will be futile if the second stage is not reached—the provision of purpose and socially acceptable adaptive mechanisms that will permit the addict to achieve and maintain positive self-evaluation.

Self-enhancing Mechanisms

Deviant behavior may serve self-enhancing functions in any number of ways. It has been convenient to classify the mechanisms through which self-enhancement is achieved into three categories:

1. Intrapsychic or interpersonal avoidance of those aspects of the normative structure that are subjectively associated with the genesis of negative self-attitudes
2. Symbolic or physical attacks upon the normative structure, its representations, or its representatives

3. Substitution of new experiences with self-enhancing potential for experiences within the normative structure

With regard to avoidance functions, the adoption of socially disvalued deviant behavior patterns might serve to assert the person's separation from a world in which he or she is not valued. Alternatively, deviant behavior might permit individuals to avoid recognizing their own objectionable characteristics or self-devaluing experiences. Or, the negative reactions of others to the individuals' deviant acts may lead to their exclusion from active group participation and membership and, hence, from the very self-devaluing experiences associated with the genesis of the characteristic self-rejection. The effect, as well as the conscious or unconscious intent of the deviant behavior, thus might serve avoidance functions.

With regard to the attack functions of deviant response patterns, if the attitudes of society (or parents, peers, or particular social institutions) toward subjects are perceived by the subjects as derogatory and at the root of their own self-rejection, then deviant behavior directed against society (or parents, peers, or social institutions) might serve as symbolic rejection of the standards associated with these targets by which the subjects have come to devalue themselves. By attacking and perhaps "destroying" these standards, such persons attack the basis of their own self-devaluation.

In addition to permitting subjects to avoid or attack the normative structure associated with the genesis of self-rejecting attitudes (and thereby to reduce the level of self-rejection), the deviant response patterns might provide substitute self-enhancing experiences in any of a number of ways. Such behavior might signify to the subjects the presence in themselves of other personally valued traits. Thus, successful aggression might symbolize not only the nullification of the standards by which the subjects have failed but at the same time their own supremacy over those standards. Not only do the subjects destroy the basis for their self-devaluation, but they provide evidence of their own potency that belies their previously felt impotence. Or, individuals frequently highly value and identify with groups in which they are not yet members but in which they desire membership. To the extent that such groups are perceived as valuing a deviant behavior for its own sake, these individuals might adopt such behavior as personally valued, or in the expectation of evoking positive responses from the members of these reference groups. In either case their self-attitudes might be enhanced.

Although the presumed self-enhancing functions of various deviant patterns frequently have been described in the literature in different terms, they all may be thought of as falling within one or more of these three general categories.

The deviant pattern may serve self-enhancing functions by enhancing a person's position within a social system. Thus, Feldman (1968) points to the significance of the social definitions of the slum environment with regard to how prestige may be won or lost. According to the slum neighborhood ideology, high-status reputations are earned by conforming to behavior patterns that are represented in the ideal type of the "stand-up cat." In order for a candidate to achieve this kind of reputation, situations must arise or be sought out in which he "can prove his daring, strength, predilection for excitement, and ultimate toughness [p. 133]." The introduction of drug use into the neighborhood is said to offer such an opportunity. Thus, it is asserted that in the slum environment initial experimentation with drugs is a way of achieving prestige "within a social system where the highest prizes go to persons who demonstrate attributes of toughness, daring, and adventure. Within the life style of the stand-up cat, movement into heroin use is one route to becoming a 'somebody' in the eyes of the important people who comprise the slum social network [Feldman, 1968, p. 138]."

However, although drug abuse patterns may function to enhance self-attitudes in an environment where such behavior is admired, more to the point is the relationship between the adoption of deviant patterns and self-enhancing consequences when the predeviance environment more clearly defines the act as inappropriate. For example, Sharoff (1969) argues that individuals who tend to use narcotic drugs or hallucinogens try, through the use of these substances, to resolve problems related to unacceptable levels of self-esteem. Individuals who tend to use narcotic drugs, whether because of objective life changes or subjective feelings of inadequacy, are said to be unable to develop feelings of self-esteem. The abuse of narcotics in part depresses the intensity of the demands for achievement made by the individual's superego. The need for achievement simply seems relatively unimportant under the influence of drugs. The individual is permitted "to withdraw from his conflicts without struggle or self-condemnation [p. 189]." Furthermore, to the extent that adoption of drug abuse patterns is accompanied by rejecting attitudes on the part of society, individuals are enabled to justify their own failure by blaming it on such unfair societal attitudes. In the face of the obstacles imposed by these attitudes, addicts can justifiably (in their own eyes) give up any further struggle for achievement. Concomitantly, subjects are said to achieve a measure of satisfaction from perceiving the trouble they have caused for the society that has rejected them.

Although narcotic drugs presumably resolve problems related to lack of self-esteem through their impact on the subject's superego and drives, the hallucinogens tend to effect resolution of these problems through their impact on the sensory and perceptual functions. The hallucinogen substances permit the distortion of reality toward the goal of achieving self-enhancing attributes. These drugs allow the users to "feel through perceptual distortions that they have become in reality what they believe they are in imagination [Sharoff,

1969, p. 192]." Similarly, according to Hoffman (1964) the drug addict is said to be characterized by a history of failures in interpersonal transactions that results in extremely low self-esteem. Because of an inability to maintain an acceptable level of self-esteem through such symbolic modes of functioning as gratifying interpersonal experiences or vocational achievements, the addict returns to a physiological mode of self-esteem maintenance. Perhaps the effectiveness of the drug in elevating self-esteem is accounted for by its ability to evoke a mood reminiscent of the euphoric mood experienced by the feeding baby: "This stirs up unconscious memories of the warmth and security felt when the infant was held by its mother and attended to. It therefore implies being wanted, being loved, being important—all in relation to the crucially significant mothering figure [Hoffman, 1964, p. 264]."

The many functions of crime and delinquency for coping with, adapting to, or defending against distressful or disvalued circumstances have been considered in numerous contexts. Within delinquent subcultures and criminal gangs, the deviant response may be the route to status, positive peer responses, and enhanced self-esteem, and property crimes per se may permit the achievement of material and success goals (DeLamater, 1968).

Delinquent behavior has been conceptualized as a form of ego restriction, "as a way of avoiding situations which endanger self-esteem and of engaging in experiences that promise a form of self-enhancement [Gold, 1978, p. 292]." Gold and Mann (1972, p. 464) argue that "delinquent behavior is a mechanism whereby a derogated self-image may be reclaimed for more positive conscious apperception." The delinquent role is a clearly defined role. Although it is negatively regarded, it consists of such positively valued features as potency and daring, and it is available as an alternative role on the occasion of self-devaluation due to failure to fulfill other salient roles. "In the process of refurbishing the self-image by adopting the delinquent role, the adolescent anesthetizes himself from the anxiety generated by realization of an ineffective and unworthy self [Gold & Mann, 1978, p. 464]."

Leon (1969), discussing excessively cruel crimes, suggests that the person perceives aggressive behavior as a vehicle for self-enhancement and indeed, through this behavior, may evoke self-gratifying responses from others. In this connection he notes that the criminals were frequently boastful about their aggressive ability and occasionally enjoyed great prestige. The criminal's atrocities may function "as a form of self-assertion and achieving distinction. The criminal in this way gains notoriety and steps out of the limbo of mediocrity and anonymity in which he feels immersed. This amounts to achieving self-assertion through outdoing others in cruelty [Leon, 1969, p. 1572]."

It has been suggested that civil disorder or urban revolt is one of many forms of acting-out behavior (other forms include hippiedom, civil rights actions, and fanatical patriotism) that for many people constitute ways of maintaining "psychological equilibrium [Usdin, 1969, p. 92]." Many of the people who engage in civil disorder in the name of a moral cause are said to do so to satisfy any of a variety of psychodynamic frustrations: "Their needs may be to destroy, to rebel, to get caught and punished, to be one of the group, to secure attention, or to be martyred by injury or imprisonment [p. 92]."

The satisfaction of such needs is clearly interpretable as fulfilling self-enhancing functions: By being punished, the subject may relieve himself of guilt regarding a more profound basis of self-rejection; by "destroying" or rebelling against society, the person destroys or denies the relevance of the source of his self-rejection; the gaining of a group identity and attention attests to the subject's becoming a person of note; by being "martyred" the person evidences a strong identification with a highly worthy cause, thus demonstrating personal worth as well.

Maris (1971, p. 123) argued that the majority of self-destructive women are engaging in modes of "ego-defensive risk-taking." They attempt to cope

> through a kind of psychic surgery: cutting themselves off from pathological families of origin, evolving a narcissistic personality to fend off labels of "worthless" and "inadequate," deviating from prescribed sexual behavior in a manner to find warmth and affection, withdrawing from time to time into a subcommunity of drug users, even attempting suicide—a dramatic *communique* and plea to a public that has stigmatized and ostracized them.

Also with regard to self-destructive behavior, a study of adolescent girls indicated that self-destructive acts related to felt lack of control over one's life and to low self-esteem. It was argued that self-destructive acts provide "a temporary feeling of self-control, prevent the ego from being overwhelmed by anxiety, and defend against psychotic decompensation [Coghlan & Gold, 1974, p. 252]."

The self-enhancing functions of a variety of patterns of psychiatric disorder have been noted. For example, Arieti asserts that many psychological defenses are ways of protecting the self, and provides several examples:

> The detached or schizoid person decreases his emotional or actual participation in life in order not to feel inadequate and injure his self-image. The hypochondriacal person protects his self by blaming only his body for his difficulties. A women leads a promiscuous life; she feels she is unacceptable as a person, but as a sexual partner she feels appreciated [Arieti, 1967, p. 732].

Obsessions and phobias have been interpreted as avoidance methods that arise by way of defending against threats to self-esteem (Salzman, 1965). Paranoid hostility has been interpreted as serving self-enhancing functions: "By avoiding others responsible for one's fate and accusing them of plotting and hatred, the paranoiac salvages a sense of self-value. He is at least worth hating, and his life takes on positive meaning, if only in relation to the malevolence of others [E. Becker, 1962, p. 149]."

With regard to psychopathic behavior, La Barba (1965) argues that the psychopath does experience anxiety, contrary to popular belief. The lack of manifest anxiety during the clinical interview is said to derive from feelings of inadequacy and inferiority. By focusing on emotionally neutral and externalized aspects of behavior during the interview, by admitting to and describing his socially undesirable behavior, he becomes able to maintain his distorted sense of superiority and keep any felt anxiety covert.

In like manner, homosexual behavior has been interpreted in terms of attempts to enhance devalued self-images (E. A. Kaplan, 1967). A central feature of the relationship is said to be the search for an ego ideal. In brief, admiration for individuals who have highly valued characteristics may be sexualized and immediate identification vicariously achieved in the context of the homosexual relationship.

A Conditional Relationship

Numerous studies in the literature suggest that the relationship between deviant behavior and self-enhancement is a conditional one. Among the conditions noted are those related to commitment to or fixity in the deviant pattern, and ability to forestall self-devaluing consequences of the deviant pattern itself.

COMMITMENT/PATTERN FIXITY

If the adoption of deviant patterns does indeed have consequences for improving self-attitudes, it is to be expected that persons who are more committed to the deviant pattern, and/or have been fixed in the delinquent response pattern for longer periods of time, would have more self-accepting attitudes than persons who are less committed to, or established in, the delinquent response pattern.

Some support for this thesis is provided by Hall's (1966) observation that, among self-defined and adjudicated delinquents, increasing delinquency orientation is associated with increasing level of positive self-evaluation. It is argued that the delinquent subculture provides the delinquent with the opportunity to gain more positive self-attitudes by engaging in behavior that is rewarded. As individuals increasingly come to identify with the delinquent subculture, they exchange the standards of the conventional culture that provided the basis for previously low self-evaluation for delinquent group standards of self-evaluation. To the extent that they conform to these standards they will judge themselves more positively than they did prior to identifying with the delinquent subculture. Totally committed delinquents, completely involved in only the delinquent subculture, thus would be expected to manifest relatively high levels of self-evaluation. However, marginal delinquents have not completely detached themselves from the conventional standards by which they have failed. Although they have some delinquent identity, they have not yet made the delinquent group the primary reference for purposes of self-evaluation. Consequently, such marginal delinquents would be expected to manifest lower self-evaluation, relative to that of totally committed delinquents.

In testing the hypothesis that delinquency orientation is positively related to level of self-evaluation among juvenile delinquents, three categories of delinquent males were considered: self-reported delinquent boys from public schools who admitted to having committed delinquent acts and to having friendships with delinquents; delinquents on probation; and delinquents placed in a county institution. The selected adjudicated delinquent boys were working-class whites between the ages of 14 and 16 who had appeared before juvenile court for theft. Delinquency identification was measured in terms of responses to questions indicating delinquent self-conceptions, negative attitudes toward parents, delinquent peer group orientation, and rejection of middle-class values and other attributes understood to be characteristic of the ideal type "totally committed delinquent." Self-evaluation was measured in terms of responses to a checklist of self-descriptive words or phrases. The boys who committed delinquent acts and who strongly identified with the delinquent subculture were significantly more likely to manifest more positive self-evaluations than boys who similarly committed delinquent acts but were less strongly identified with the delinquent subculture. If it is assumed that identification with the delinquent subculture represents a later stage in the delinquent's career, then the observed association is highly consistent with the view that the adoption of delinquent patterns (presumably in part a response to initial self-rejection) is associated with an increase in positive self-attitudes.

Data possibly indicative of a relationship between degree of fixity in a delinquent response pattern and self-acceptance are provided by a study of black and white boys attending an urban school in an area characterized by high social disorganization and a lower-class population (Schwartz & Stryker, 1970). Among the findings was the observation that, among boys nominated by their teachers as likely to come into contact with the police or juvenile courts at some future time, older subjects (16 and above) were significantly more positive in self-evaluation than younger subjects (12 to 15). If it is assumed that older boys are more likely than younger boys to be entrenched in, or committed to, delinquent patterns because of a longer experience with these patterns, these data may be interpreted as supporting the hypothesis that the adoption of delinquent patterns functions to increase level of self-acceptance. However, as Schwartz and Stryker (1970, p. 79) point out, caution should be exercised in interpreting data regarding the older students in this lower-class school, in view of possible circumstances attendant upon keeping them in school beyond the age of compulsory attendance.

Greater degrees of commitment to, or fixity in, aggressive behavior patterns also appear to be more closely associated with more positive self-attitudes than are lesser degrees of commitment to such patterns. Operationally, "degree of fixity in the pattern" might be indicated by low perceived probability that the subject will change his pattern of aggressive behavior. Schwartz, Fearn, and Stryker (1966) studied children who were being treated as inpatients in two Canadian psychiatric institutions. The children were all said to be engaged in highly aggressive acting-out behavior. Apparently none of the subjects was seriously psychotic or autistic. The children were administered an instrument by which they rated "How you feel about yourself" (as well as other stimuli) on an evaluative index.

The children, whose average age was 12.5 years, were distributed by the therapists among four prognostic categories: very good, good, poor, and very poor. The various groupings were quite similar in terms of a number of variables, including length of time in therapy, age, and sex. The results revealed that the children in the "poor" and "very poor" categories rated themselves appreciably higher and were less variable in their self-rating than the children in the "good" or "very good" prognosis categories. That is, children who were (according to their therapists) least likely to recover were most likely to offer consistent and positive self-evaluations.

Alternative interpretations are consistent with the view that the adoption of patterns of aggressive behavior is functionally related to the reduction of self-rejecting feelings. The observed association between poor prognosis and positive self-evaluation might reflect either or both of two processes that would necessarily be operative in the establishment of such a functional relationship. First, the observed association might reflect the process by which the adoption of aggressive behavior patterns leads to more positive self-feelings. Second, the observed association might reflect the process by which those children (from among a more inclusive grouping of children who tentatively perform aggressive acting-out behavior) who experience aggressive behavior as self-enhancing and anxiety-reducing become confirmed in the aggressive behavior pattern. In the former case, the aggressive behavior pattern is understood to be temporally prior to change in self-attitudes. In the latter case, the establishment of the aggressive behavior pattern is understood to be a consequence of the prior experience of improved self-attitudes as a concomitant of experimentation with aggressive behavior. In either case, the explanation rests upon the interpretation of therapists' prognostic evaluations as an index of pattern fixity.

Also consistent with the expectation that commitment to a deviant identity facilitates self-enhancement are data observed to support either of two models

(Hammersmith & Weinberg, 1973, p. 78). "Both of these models propose that, for homosexuals, commitment—i.e., having 'settled into' a homosexual identity—leads to better psychological adjustment as indicated by a more stable, positive self-image, fewer anxiety symptoms, and less depression." One model asserts that support of the homosexual identity by significant others positively influences the homosexual's commitment to that identity. The other model suggests that the homosexual's commitment influences selective evaluation of the importance attached to others' opinions of him.

ADVERSE CONSEQUENCES

The expectation that alcohol abuse or other deviant patterns function to enhance self-attitudes is based on the assumption that the adoption of this pattern, as a provisional attempt to deal with preexisting self-rejecting attitudes, will not evoke new experiences that would exacerbate negative self-attitudes. To the extent that such experiences are evoked, the pattern should not be expected to result in improved self-attitudes. On the contrary, it might be associated with increased self-rejection. Congruent with this reasoning are certain of the findings reported by Nocks and Bradley (1969) for diagnosed alcoholic male patients admitted to the acute alcoholic wards of a state hospital. Among the results was the observation that those patients who denied having a drinking problem received significantly higher scores on a measure of self-esteem than did the other patients. This finding is interpretable in a number of ways. For example, the denial of a drinking problem might reflect the continuity of relatively intact defenses that serve to shield the subject from self-rejecting attitudes. On the other hand, and not inconsistent with the previous interpretation, admitting to a drinking problem might reflect the occurrence of a number of self-devaluing experiences consequent upon adoption of the drinking pattern, such as being the object of rejecting attitudes by one's family, friends, and employer. Such experiences not only might have neutralized an otherwise self-enhancing effect of alcohol abuse but might even have intensified self-rejecting attitudes.

Also congruent with the position that alcohol abuse is functional in increasing self-acceptance under conditions in which this pattern does not induce new self-devaluing experiences are certain findings resulting from a comparison of three categories of nonpsychotic patients committed to either of two state hospitals for treatment of alcoholism (Mindlin, 1964): patients who previously had psychotherapy (5 or more sessions), patients who had previous experience (10 or more meetings) with Alcoholics Anonymous but had never been in psychotherapy, and patients (the "no-help" group) who had not reported previous therapy for alcoholism or Alcoholics Anonymous experience. Among the findings was the observation that self-esteem was highest in the no-help group and lowest in the therapy group. Although, again, alternative interpretations are possible, this finding also suggests that the nature of the processes characteristic of therapy and the Alcoholics Anonymous experience might serve to call into question the acceptability of the alcohol abuse pattern, thus, to a degree, negating what might otherwise have been the self-enhancing effects of alcoholism.

Similarly, if it is argued that chronic schizophrenia is functional in enhancing self-attitudes, then it is to be expected that the functional value of the illness will be decreased if the setting in which the subject operates provides him with devaluing experiences—for example, by reminding him of his inadequacy through the imposition upon him of less than minimal demands (Manasse, 1965). In this connection, Kaplan and his associates, observing male patients on an open psychiatric ward of a Veterans Administration hospital, noted two sets of circumstances that might arise in response to the adoption of psychopathological patterns and might have adverse effects upon patient's self-evaluation (H. B. Kaplan, Boyd, & Bloom, 1964). The first set of circumstances relates to the nature of the therapeutic process, entry into which is certainly one possible consequence of adopting psychopathological patterns. The process of treating the patient might have consequences that, at least on a short-term basis, could adversely affect the patient's self-attitudes. For example, traditional psychotherapeutic techniques might involve the uncovering and interpretation of the patient's characteristic modes of defense through which he maintains an acceptable self-image. The disruption of these defenses might well make the subject vulnerable to self-devaluing experiences and tend to lower his level of self-esteem. The second set of circumstances relates to public and institutional attitudes toward mental illness. Such is the nature of public attitudes toward mental illness that the adoption of psychopathological patterns is likely to evoke negative attitudes from significant others, which in turn could be expected to increase levels of self-rejection among the mentally ill.

The investigators describe a number of patterned responses evolved by the patient groups in response to these two sets of circumstances that were said to function to maintain acceptable levels of self-esteem. Clearly, the effectiveness of psychopathological patterns in reducing self-rejection would be a function both of the tendency to evoke circumstances having adverse consequences for self-attitudes and of the ability to evolve such patterns of response as would contain the potentially negative consequences of these circumstances upon self-attitudes. In any case the self-esteem motive would lead the person to make strenuous attempts to evolve such self-protective responses as a defense against the potentially adverse consequences of adopting instrumental patterns of mental illness.

The literature that has been reviewed is generally consistent with the expected relationship between deviant responses and decreased self-rejection. These studies further suggest the conditions under which the relationship was observed and the mechanisms through which various deviant patterns effect

reductions in self-rejecting attitudes. However, as was the case with the literature reviewed in Chapter 6, these studies are characterized by one or more
limitations: small, unrepresentative samples; failure to consider multiple modes
of deviance simultaneously; research designs that preclude conclusions regarding antecedent–consequence relationships; and absence of appropriate control
groups.

In the present context, one of the more severe limitations of these studies is
that they frequently involve consideration of subjects who have come into
treatment or otherwise to the attention of the authorities. Thus, they may have
been preselected for having failed to achieve self-enhancing consequences
where they have voluntarily sought help. Or, by virtue of being involuntarily
incarcerated, they may have been subjected to self-devaluing circumstances
such as the stigma associated with the institutionalization process itself or with
the reactions of others to the fact of institutionalization (Ageton & Elliott, 1974;
Fishman, 1976; Kitsuse, 1975; Mahoney, 1974; Waldo, Chiricos, & Dobrin,
1973) or deprivation of the self-enhancing deviant pattern (e.g., alcohol,
drugs). Alternatively, self-esteem may be occasioned by the adverse reactions of
normative agents (Rathus & Siegel, 1973). In short, the process of formal
institutional response, where it is not systematically controlled, does not permit
clear interpretation of the relationship between deviant behavior and self-
enhancement. It is not possible to separate out the differential effects of deviant
behavior and the formal institutional responses.

Although the consideration of a noninstitutionalized population does not
preclude informal and interim formal sanctions having occurred, the subjects'
availability for interview at least implies that their current responses are not
influenced by the fact of institutionalization and its correlates.

Because the population under consideration in the present study was not
institutionalized and the research design permitted consideration of the association between antecedent multiple modes of deviance and subsequent decreases
in self-rejecting attitudes, testing the hypothesis was facilitated.

Analysis

In order to understand the mode of analysis selected to test the hypothesized
relationship between deviant responses and subsequent decreases in self-
rejecting attitudes, theoretical and methodological issues must be considered.

Theoretical Issues

According to the theoretical statement guiding the present analysis, those
persons who develop intensely distressful negative self-attitudes in the course
of their membership group experiences come to associate the genesis of negative

self-attitudes with the normative patterns characterizing the group. Consequently, they lose motivation to conform to and acquire motivation to deviate from the now intrinsically disvalued normative expectations. At the same time, they seek and adopt alternative *deviant* patterns that promise to reduce the still unsatisfied (and, indeed, intensified) self-esteem motive in the absence of effective normative patterns. Thus, one condition for observing the hypothesized relationship is that self-rejecting persons are *unable to defend* against, and are therefore vulnerable to, the experiences in their membership groups that have in the past produced, and continue to generate, negative self-attitudes. Therefore, in testing the hypothesis, it should be determined that the subjects under consideration fulfill the condition. If they do not fulfill the condition uniformly, then the distinction should be made between those who do and those who do not, and the relationship should be observed only for those who do fulfill the condition.

The theory also asserts that the adoption of deviant response patterns by self-rejecting persons will have self-enhancing consequences by virtue of facilitating avoidance of self-devaluing membership group experiences, serving to attack the perceived basis of self-rejecting attitudes, and/or offering substitute patterns with self-enhancing potential, and to the extent that the patterns do not have unanticipated self-devaluing circumstances as consequences of adopting the deviant response pattern. Thus, a second condition for observing the hypothesized relationship is the *absence of self-devaluing consequences* of adopting the deviant response patterns. Therefore, in testing the hypothesis, it should be determined that the subjects fulfill this condition as well. If they do not fulfill the condition uniformly, then again the distinction should be made between those who do and those who do not fulfill the condition, and the hypothesis should be tested only for those who do fulfill the condition.

In fact, circumstances do lead to the suspicion that these theoretical conditions did not apply uniformly to self-rejecting subjects. One circumstance relates to the *measure of self-rejection* itself. Although the highly self-rejecting subjects in the present study manifested more negative self-attitudes than the remainder of the subjects, the absolute level of intensity of self-rejection was problematic. Without certainty about the severity of self-rejecting attitudes, it cannot be assumed that subjects will lose motivation to conform to, and become motivated to deviate from, normative patterns. The *relatively* high, but by some absolute standard *moderate,* level of self-rejection is less likely to be the consequence of pervasive self-devaluation in the course of membership group experiences. Therefore, self-rejection might not lead to a generalized disaffection with the normative structure, but to dissatisfaction with a more specific (if any) aspect of the normative structure. This narrower response might lead to the attempt to assuage self-rejecting feelings through alternative normative patterns or through deviant patterns particularly related to the blameworthy aspect of the normative structure rather than to the generalized normative structure. In any case, the availability of alternative normative patterns in these circumstances would mitigate the subjects' total state of defenselessness/vulnerability (the first condition) and they would not necessarily be entirely dependent on deviant patterns for the reduction of self-rejecting attitudes. Furthermore, to the extent that subjects have not rejected the total normative structure of their membership groups, they remain amenable to self-reproach and negative sanctions by other group members as a consequence of the adoption of deviant patterns. Thus, the second condition (freedom from self-devaluing consequences of deviant behavior) would not have been uniformly applicable to those manifesting high scores on the self-derogation scale.

A second circumstance concerns the characteristics of the subjects who continued or discontinued participating in the study. The research design required that the hypothesis be tested using students who remained in school during the junior high school years. The continued presence in school of relatively highly self-rejecting individuals (many of whom were beyond the age of legal constraint to attend school) suggests that some of the subjects did not associate the normative structure (or at least its educational aspect) with the genesis of self-rejecting feelings, and did anticipate future self-enhancement in the context of the normative structure. Although they may have associated aspects of the normative structure with the development of negative self-attitudes, these students experienced positive emotional ties or feared anticipated negative sanctions, so that they were unwilling or unable to become totally disaffected from the normative structure (and from adverse consequences of adopting deviant patterns). This further implies (a) that these students were *not* necessarily in a total state of defenselessness/vulnerability (the first condition) in the sense that no normative patterns were available to them that might effectively forestall or reduce the experience of self-rejecting attitudes and only deviant patterns might serve this end and (b) that these students were not necessarily totally independent of membership group experiences for emotional gratification, and therefore were likely to experience distress in association to negative responses by group members to their deviant behavior.

These two theoretical conditions for observing the hypothesized relationship were suggested also by the preceding literature review. It was noted that the self-enhancing functions of deviant patterns in general (*a fortiori*, in particular) are conditional on a number of factors. Among these factors are the lack of availability of alternative patterns (inferred from the observation that self-enhancing outcomes are not as clearly seen where the person is not as committed to or fixed in the pattern) and the absence of *new* self-devaluing consequences of the pattern. Such consequences mitigate the self-enhancing consequences of the deviant pattern, a condition inferred from observations that the self-devaluation and other-devaluation of the pattern, indicated by self-description or by the fact of entering into treatment, are occasions for lower levels of self-acceptance by those who have adopted deviant response patterns. In fact, these two factors may be mutually influential. That is, self-devaluing consequences of deviant responses may impede full (voluntary) commitment to a deviant pattern if exclusion from normative membership groups is not total, and commitment to a deviant pattern may forestall awareness of devaluing responses from others as the occasion for self-devaluation. In any case where persons have been unable to defend against self-devaluing circumstances, given the range of normative opportunities at their disposal, they are most likely to receive self-enhancing consequences from alternative deviant response patterns. Where they are best able to defend against any self-devaluing implications of the deviant pattern, they are even more likely to receive such benefits.

A third theoretical condition for observing a relationship between deviant response patterns and self-enhancing outcomes presumes that the so-called deviant behaviors are in fact deviant from the viewpoint of the subjects and their predeviant membership groups. If the patterns in question were not deviant but rather a part of the same environment that was previously ineffective in forestalling or reducing self-rejecting feelings, then there would be no reason for anticipating self-enhancing consequences. Insofar as the subjects may not have been uniform in identifying with the normative membership groups that were likely to define the response patterns as deviant, then, once again, a distinction should be drawn between those who do and do not fulfill the condition, and the hypothesized relationship should be anticipated only for the former group.

Of course such a possibility does exist. Although the subjects who continued to participate in the study have by implication continued to participate in the normative environment, many of these may already have adopted or become subject to group or subcultural influences that define the "deviant" acts as acceptable. These subjects may have continued to participate in the normative structure only because of the threat of undesirable (even from the viewpoint of deviant reference groups) formal negative sanctions.

In view of the problematic fulfillment of the aforementioned theoretical conditions, it was necessary to distinguish operationally between those who were more and less likely to fulfill each of them.

DEFENSELESSNESS/VULNERABILITY

The first theoretical condition was operationalized in terms of the measure of defenselessness/vulnerability first introduced in Chapter 4. Subjects who scored high on this measure while displaying relatively high levels of self-derogation were taken to be unable to forestall or reduce the experience of negative self-attitudes in the context of normative membership groups. By implication, they were dependent on deviant alternatives for increasing their level of self-acceptance. Individuals who were low in defenselessness/vulnerability (while displaying high levels of self-rejection) presumably had available to them normative self-protective patterns that might function to enhance self-attitudes. These patterns might also obviate the need for (and, insofar as the subject continued to maintain positive attitudes toward the membership groups, the effectiveness of) deviant response patterns.

The measure of defenselessness/vulnerability, as an index of the person's inability to employ *normative* patterns to forestall or reduce the experience of self-rejecting attitudes, may also imply the inability to forestall adverse consequences of *deviant* patterns as well. Thus, in order to enjoy the self-enhancing consequences of deviant patterns, a person frequently must be able to forestall adverse responses from other deviant group members, justify inability to conform to deviant group norms, and in general display many of the self-protective capabilities that are necessary for the maintenance of self-accepting attitudes in the normative context of predeviance membership groups. The dual implications of the measure might be expected to mitigate its conditional significance for facilitating the observed relationship between deviant behavior and self-enhancing consequences. Where the first implication (total dependence on *deviant* patterns for self-enhancing experiences) would facilitate observation of the relationship, the second (inability to forestall or reduce self-devaluing experiences associated with deviant patterns) would impede the observation of self-enhancing consequences of deviant responses. It is also recognized, however, that this second implication is more relevant for certain deviant patterns than for others, perhaps those involving group participation, special skills, or high visibility.

SELF-DEVALUING CONSEQUENCES

In order to test the hypothesis that the absence of self-devaluing consequences is a condition for the observation of a relationship between deviant responses and subsequent self-enhancement, the analyses were carried out separately for males and females. That is, gender was taken to be an operational measure of likelihood of self-devaluing consequences of deviant responses. The behavioral science literature is quite consistent about the conclusion that deviant behavior is less likely to have self-enhancing consequences for females than for males, presumably because of the adverse effects of personally internalized standards and the positive emotional significance of the responses to the deviant behaviors on the part of other group members.

Thus, Gold and Mann (1972, p. 469) regarded data related to the hypothesized function of self-reported delinquent behavior of American adolescents (as a defense against a negative self-image) and concluded that the boys' data fit the defensive model better than the girls' data, since delinquency is a predominantly masculine defense and therefore does not function as well to raise girls' self-esteem. The emotional significance of others' responses was suggested by the observation of Tittle and Rowe (1973) that in a study of the relative effects of a moral appeal and a sanction threat on college classroom cheating, females were influenced far more by the sanction threat than were the males. Consistent with these studies are reports that girls were more likely (a) to show emotional upset when they believed that they had deviated from adult expectations (Sears, Ray, & Alpert, 1965), (b) to manifest fantasy confession to deviance (Rebelsky, Alinsmith, & Grinder, 1963), (c) to show more highly developed and influential consciences (Rempel & Signoi, 1964; Sears, Maccoby, & Levin, 1957), (d) to score lower on lie and defensiveness scales (Maccoby & Jacklin, 1974), (e) to display a need for affiliation (Exline, 1962; Lansky, Crandall, Kagan, & Baker, 1961; Spangler & Thomas, 1962), and (f) to show greater interest in and positive feeling for others (Maccoby, 1966). Furthermore, nondelinquent females scored significantly higher than non-delinquent males on a measure of vindication said to involve "an attempt to avoid blame and maintain the appearance of conformity to approved social norms [Washburn, 1963]."

Although it was anticipated that, in general, deviant resonses would be more likely to evoke adverse responses from self and others among females than among males, it was also expected that these differences would be more likely to be displayed for certain modes of deviant response rather than for others. This would depend upon such factors as approval by self and others of attributes of the act as consistent with gender-related roles to which the subject feels a commitment, although the act itself might be defined as deviant (as when the successful exercise of power, risk-taking behavior, and active manipulation of the environment associated with certain forms of delinquency are viewed as compatible with the masculine role). However, where the act is judged by valued others and self as incompatible with the requirements of the roles to which the person feels a commitment, self-enhancement is less likely to follow adoption of the deviant pattern. This assumes that the gender-related roles are not themselves the basis of the person's self-rejection. If this were the case then deviant patterns compatible with these roles might evoke self-devaluing circumstances, and role-incompatible patterns might be self-enhancing.

Numerous studies have offered observations suggesting that specific deviant patterns are more likely to be associated with one or the other gender and are more or less likely to evoke adverse responses from subjects of a particular gender. Morris (1964) cites reports by Grosser (1951) indicating that the types of offenses committed by members of each sex are expressions of their own sex roles. Boys are said to destroy property or steal because they are mainly concerned with "status" goals (i.e., power, prestige, and wealth). Girls become involved in illegitimate sexual relationships or in aggravated family relationships as an expression of their primary concern with "relational" goals. The concern of boys with power is suggested also by the greater tendency of males than females to use alcohol (Jessor, Carman, & Grossman, 1970; Smart & Whitehead, 1974), a pattern that has been said to increase power fantasies (McClelland, 1972). Washburn (1963) also cites a report (Fine, 1955) of gender-related tendencies to adopt specific deviant patterns—with girls tending toward running away from home, truancy, and sex-related offenses, and males tending toward stealing, auto theft, injury to others, property damage, and burglary. Such observations might lead to the hypothesis that such preferences reflect compatibility with gender-related roles and are therefore more likely to be associated with self-enhancing, and less likely to be associated with self-devaluing, consequences. (Again, these observations assume that the basis of self-rejecting feelings is not gender-related.) That choice of pattern may be related to compatibility with desirable gender-prescribed characteristics may again be illustrated with reference to the use of alcohol, which has frequently been viewed as implying masculine virtues (McCord & McCord, 1960; Zucker, 1968). That alcohol use is more an extension of the masculine than of the feminine role is also suggested by a longitudinal study (Jones, 1968, 1971) of problem drinkers. It was found that females who were to become problem drinkers were more unlike females who were to become normal drinkers than their male counterparts were unlike males who were to become normal drinkers.

On the basis of the frequency with which such responses were observed, as well as the behavior of others evoked by such responses, aggressive modes of deviant response might also be expected to be more likely to eventuate in self-enhancing consequences and less likely to eventuate in self-devaluing outcomes when performed by males than when performed by females. Numerous studies (reviewed in greater detail by H. B. Kaplan, 1977b) have reported that males were more likely than females to display aggression. For example, McCandless, Bilous, and Bennett (1961) observed that boys initiated more conflicts than girls, and that girls were more likely to change the activity in which they were engaged following conflict. S. G. Moore (1964) reported that boys, following frustration, were more likely to display direct aggression, with less displacement of aggression. T. Moore and Ucko (1961) reported that anxious boys were more likely to give aggressive responses, whereas anxious girls were more likely to give passive responses or no response (that is, to avoid the problem). In the relatively few instances in which females were observed to be higher on some index of aggression or hostility, they tended to be higher on prosocial aggression but lower on antisocial aggression (Sears, 1961), or higher on covert hostility but lower on overt hostility than males (Bennett & Cohen, 1959). Consistent with these observations are reports that males were more likely to manifest "turning against object" defenses or projection defenses, whereas females were more likely to display "turning against self" defenses (Bogo, Winget, & Gleser, 1970; De Fundia, Draguns, & Phillips, 1971; Gleser & Ihilevich, 1969). Among children brought to a clinic, males were more likely to manifest hyperaggression (among other symptoms), whereas females were reported to have more problems related to overdependence and emotional over-control (Beller & Neubauer, 1963).

That aggression was less likely to be compatible with the female role and more likely to be associated with adverse consequences was congruent with observations of a tendency for females to experience greater anxiety or guilt over aggression (Buss & Brock, 1963; Rothaus & Worchel, 1964; Sears, 1961; Wyer, Weatherley, & Terrell, 1965), an association among subjects of each gender between feminine sex-role identity and anxiety about aggression cues (Consentino & Heilbrun, 1964), a tendency for boys' mothers to be more permissive of aggression toward parents and peers (Sears *et al.*, 1957), and a tendency for teachers to express greater liking for dependent girls than for aggressive girls (Levitin & Chananie, 1972).

The tendency for patterns of deviance to be associated with gender has been noted even within a narrow range of deviant patterns such as those related to substance abuse, as in the report by Smart and Whitehead (1974) that males consistently were more frequent users of alcohol, tobacco, marijuana, and hallucinogens, whereas tranquilizer use was more characteristic of females. The differential use of response patterns by subjects of each gender, however, should not obscure the observations that the same pattern may be congruent with each gender's tendency to respond to stress, and that the adoption of the same pattern may have different consequences. Thus, Jessor, Jessor, and Finney (1973, p. 12) reported that the use of marijuana among females is associated with a relative increase in alienation (e.g., a sense of isolation from others, concern about identity), but among males marijuana use was associated with social criticism (a conviction about the inadequacy of policies, mores, and institutions of the larger American society). And Burke and Eichberg (1972) have reported that among drug-taking samples males indicated lower self-esteem than did females.

Thus, it was hypothesized that the very category (females) that was most likely to adopt "deviant" responses in response to high levels of self-derogation (see Chapter 5), presumably because for this category the acts were most likely to be defined as deviant, would be least likely to enjoy the fruits of the deviant acts (in the form of self-enhancement), presumably because they were most emotionally dependent upon and therefore most vulnerable to the criticism of group members in response to their deviant behavior. This paradox reflects the dual implications of the measure of defenselessness/vulnerability, suggested earlier. In fact, among both subjects of lower- and higher-socioeconomic status, females were significantly more likely than males to score higher on the measure of defenselessness/vulnerability. Among subjects of lower-socioeconomic status, 61% of the females ($N = 694$) compared with 46% of the males ($N = 630$) scored high (6 or more) on this measure. The corresponding figures for subjects of higher-socioeconomic status were 52% ($N = 2635$) and 44% ($N = 2522$). Insofar as the measure reflected the absence of available normative self-protective patterns that might forestall or reduce the experience of negative self-attitudes and, by implication, subjectively perceived dependence upon deviant patterns for future self-enhancement, it was to be expected that females would more consistently adopt deviant responses as a consequence of antecedent self-rejection (as was observed in Chapter 5). Also, insofar as the measure reflected continued needs for positive responses from others and/or personal conformity to internalized standards, the deviant behaviors would be less likely to eventuate in increased self-acceptance for females than for males.

DEVIANT DEFINITIONS

The distinction between those who were and were not likely to define the acts as deviant was drawn in terms of the previously introduced (Chapter 6) measure of perceived self-enhancing potential of the normative environment. It was assumed that those who scored high on this measure by tying their hopes of beneficent outcomes to the normative contexts reflected in the measure would share definition of what constitutes deviance with other group members.

It is recognized, however, that (as in the case of defenselessness/vulnerability) the measure of perceived self-enhancing potential of the normative environment is an imperfect one for defining the condition of accepting deviant definitions of the responses. Although these patterns are more likely to be defined as deviant where the individual views his future self-enhancing outcomes as associated with continued participation in the normative membership groups, and thus are likely to eventuate in self-enhancing consequences for subjects who developed highly self-derogating attitudes in the course of the same membership group experiences, at least two possibly confounding circumstances associated with this variable must be considered. First, a high score on this variable implies being vulnerable to adverse responses to the subject's deviant behavior, a circumstance that might mitigate otherwise self-enhancing consequences of deviant responses. Although this issue might be obviated by controlling on the subject's gender—presumed to be associated with vulnerability to adverse responses by others in the person's membership group—a second issue remains. This issue relates to the possibility that anticipation of future self-enhancing outcomes might imply the availability of normative self-protective patterns and hence the lack of complete dependence on deviant behavior for self-enhancing outcomes, another circumstance that might mitigate otherwise self-enhancing consequences of the deviant responses. Thus, this variable as a control must be seen as a very conservative device in the analysis of the relationship between the adoption of deviant responses and changes in self-attitudes.

Methodological Requirements

In order to test the hypothesized relationship between the antecedent deviant responses by self-derogating subjects and subsequent self-enhancement, it was necessary to determine (a) that the person was relatively high in self-derogation at the time prior to the performance of the deviant act and (b) that the change in self-attitudes was subsequent to the performance of the deviant behavior. In order to determine that the person was relatively high in self-derogation at the time of the deviant performance (a theoretical requirement), it was not possible to use T_1 reports of deviant behavior. Apart from issues of the small number of affirmative reports and the relatively brief and nonuniform time reference employed, the major problem arose from the fact that the *performance* of the deviant acts reported at T_1 antedated the earliest report of self-derogation (determined at T_1). Thus, the nature of the self-attitudes at the time the act was performed could not be determined. Althouth the high self-derogation at T_1 might have reflected the level of self-attitudes prior to the adoption of the deviant act, it might also have been the consequence of the deviant act.

The earliest report of deviant behavior for which prior self-attitude data were available was that made at T_2 for the period $T_1 - T_2$. Thus, by considering only those subjects who were highly self-derogating at T_1, by comparing those among them who had and had not reported performance of a given deviant act between T_1 and T_2 with regard to residual gains in self-derogation $T_2 - T_3$, it was apparently possible to test the hypothesized relationship between antecedent performance of deviant behavior by highly self-rejecting subjects and subsequent increases in self-enhancing attitudes. However, since the deviant act could have been performed at any time during the year interval between T_1 and T_2, self-attitudes might have changed sufficiently over the period so that the subjects at the time of the deviant acts might not still have been highly self-derogating. The only way to ensure this was to preselect for consideration relatively highly self-derogating subjects at T_1 who maintained or increased their level of self-derogation during the period $T_1 - T_2$. This was the decision that was ultimately made. The distribution of self-derogation scores at T_1 was divided into relatively high and relatively low self-derogation categories. Independently, the distribution of absolute change in self-derogation scores between T_1 and T_2 was divided into those who decreased on the one hand and those who either stayed the same (zero change) or showed increases in self-derogation on the other hand.

Only those subjects who were relatively high in self-derogation at T_1 and who remained at that level or who increased their self-derogation over the

T_1–T_2 interval were considered in testing the hypothesis. Among these subjects, those who reported adopting a particular deviant act between T_1 and T_2 (the reports were made at T_2) were compared with those who denied performance of the act over the same period with regard to subsequent *residual gains* in self-derogation between T_2 and T_3. The reasons for employing residual (rather than absolute) gains in self-derogation were considered in Chapters 2 and 3.

This decision to include only subjects who maintained or increased their initially (T_1) high level of self-derogation between T_1 and T_2 had at least one important consequence for the observation of self-enhancing outcomes. Although it permitted the establishment of a clear temporal relationship between deviant behavior performed by highly self-rejecting persons and subsequent decreases in self-rejection, this decision also precluded the observation of short-term self-enhancing consequences of deviant behavior. Some self-enhancing consequences of deviant responses are more immediate than others—the gratifying sense of power that might follow directly on substance abuse or winning a fistfight versus the enjoyment derived from the reputation of being a "tough guy" or a sense of belonging associated with being an accepted gang member. By excluding those who decreased their level of self-rejection in the period in which the deviant behavior was performed, the observer necessarily excludes observation of the more immediate self-gratifying consequences. Of course, insofar as certain deviant patterns tend to be associated with more immediate consequences, a relationship between the former deviant patterns and beneficent changes in self-attitudes would be less likely to be observed.

There is at least one circumstance, however, in which a deviant pattern would evoke immediate self-enhancing consequences yet would be associated with a decrease in self-rejection over the year following that during which the deviant response occurred. The deviant pattern may have both long- and short-term consequences, as when aggressive responses are associated with a short-term increase in felt power and with a long-term (delayed) attenuation of the person's identification with the normative environment (the source of continuing self-devaluing experiences).

It might be argued that a deviant pattern with short-term self-enhancing consequences would have a greater probability of those consequences being observed if that pattern and its near-term consequences were evoked episodically in response to self-devaluing circumstances, as when the pharmacologically induced sense of power resulting from alcohol abuse is stimulated by self-devaluing experiences. To the extent that high levels of self-derogation are associated with the likelihood of self-devaluing experiences, there would be a good probability that during the following year self-enhancing consequences (decreased self-rejection) might occur if the deviant pattern became part of the person's way of life, being performed regularly (and not necessarily *only* in response to self-devaluing circumstances), as in habitual use of alcohol. However, by excluding subjects whose level of self-rejection decreased less than expected (or increased more than expected) no such short-term self-enhancement was permitted to be observed (because of the requirements discussed earlier). Indeed a corollary consequence of the exclusion of these subjects from the analysis was the increased likelihood that if the deviant pattern had any short-term implications for change in self-attitudes at all, only short-term self-devaluing consequences could be observed. Thus, in effect, the analysis only permitted conclusions that were highly conservative with regard to self-enhancing consequences of deviant behavior, excluding as it did short-term self-enhancing consequences and giving extra weight to any self-devaluing consequences of the deviant pattern over the short term.

No distinction was made among those who reported performing the deviant act T_1–T_2 between those who had and had not reported performing the act prior to T_1 (by report at T_1). On the one hand, some argument could be made for this distinction. Those who affirmed the act at both T_1 and T_2, it could be argued, were more likely to have defined the act as deviant, since the acts were likely to be more inappropriate for younger than for older children. That is, those who initially reported the act at T_2 might include those who were coming to adopt a pattern that by the older age was more acceptable. This argued for exclusion from the analyses of those who initially reported the act between T_1 and T_2, since only self- and other-defined deviant acts were theoretically expected to eventuate in decreased self-rejection.

In further support of this position, it could be asserted that the initial report of a deviant act between T_1 and T_2 may reflect a single experimental occasion that is not subjectively defined as a deviant response and is not likely to be continued. As such, the act could have no necessary theoretical relationship with subsequent change in self-attitudes (according to the theory under consideration). However, the affirmation of deviant behavior at both T_1 and T_2 increases the probability that the act is patterned deviance rather than experimental behavior, and that it is the absence of adverse consequences and/or the absence of more motivationally acceptable alternative responses (theoretical conditions for self-enhancing consequences of the deviant behavior) that permit continuity of the response.

On the other hand, it might be argued that the hypothesis of self-enhancing consequences of deviant behavior could be tested better by *excluding* those who reported the behavior at T_1, since the early (T_1) manifestation of deviant behavior, by virtue of its early adoption, could be seen as an expression of a normative, or at least acceptable, response among the individual's membership groups. Hence it could not constitute a legitimate test of the general theory of deviant behavior under consideration. A contraindication of this argument is the observed tendency of the dropouts from the study to engage in early deviant behavior, which suggests that the subjects who remained in the study and manifested early adoption of the pattern were more closely tied to the normative structure and were more likely to define the acts as deviant. Therefore, it would be appropriate in the current theoretical context to anticipate that the early adoption of the pattern by highly self-derogating subjects would tend to eventuate in reduction of self-rejecting attitudes.

Although the weight of the arguments perhaps favors drawing the distinction between those who initially adopted the deviant act between T_1 and T_2 and those who affirmed the act at both T_1 and T_2, and including only the latter subjects in the analysis, the arguments are not sufficiently compelling to do so when this decision would have the effect of so diminishing the deviant actors available for the analysis that the *conditional* relationships between deviant behavior and subsequent self-enhancement could not be tested. An earlier provisional test of the hypothesis (H. B. Kaplan, 1978a), without stating the conditions related to defenselessness and self-enhancing potential of the normative environment, clearly indicated the paucity of cases that would be available to test the conditional relationship if only subjects who affirmed the deviant response at both T_1 and T_2 were included. For this reason, along with the less than compelling reasons for drawing the distinction and excluding one or the other groupings from analysis, the decision was made to consider all subjects who reported deviant acts between T_1 and T_2 without consideration of whether they had reported the deviant occurrence prior to T_1.

The basic test of the hypothesis then involved a comparison of subjects who reported a given deviant act between T_1 and T_2 with those who did not report the act with regard to subsequent change in self-derogation scores (residual gains) between T_2 and T_3 considering *only* subjects who were relatively high in self-derogation at T_1 and who remained at that level or increased in self-derogation between T_1 and T_2. This comparison was carried out for each of the 28 deviant acts separately.

These analyses were carried out separately within each of several subject groupings variously defined in terms of the three conditional variables considered: defenselessness/vulnerability, gender, and self-enhancing potential of the normative environment. The analyses were carried out independently for defenselessness/vulnerability and self-enhancing potential of the normative environment, since these two variables were uncorrelated ($r = .00$) and, in any case, simultaneous consideration of the two values (high/low, male/female) of the three variables would have resulted in eight groupings of eligible subjects, which would have so depleted the frequency of deviant acts in many of the groupings that the hypothesis could not have been tested.

However, as was indicated earlier, defenselessness/vulnerability and self-enhancing potential of the normative environment, in addition to implying the absence of self-enhancing mechanisms in the normative environment and deviant definitions of the acts under consideration, respectively, which they were selected to reflect, also imply vulnerability to self-devaluing consequences of deviant acts. Therefore, each of these two variables was considered simultaneously with gender in defining the categories of subjects for which the comparisons would be made, since gender was taken to be an indicator of likelihood of self-devaluing consequences of deviant responses. For the first analysis, comparisons between those reporting and not reporting deviant behavior with regard to subsequent changes in self-derogation were made separately for each of the four subject groupings resulting from simultaneous consideration of gender and defenselessness/vulnerability: male, low defenselessness; male, high defenselessness; female, low defenselessness; female, high defenselessness. For the second analysis, similar comparisons were made for the following: male, low self-enhancing potential of the normative environment; male, high self-enhancing potential of the normative environment; female, low self-enhancing potential of the normative environment; female, high self-enhancing potential of the normative environment.

The "high" and "low" categories of defenselessness/vulnerability and self-enhancing potential of the normative environment were determined by dividing the distribution of scores on these scales at T_2 into two as closely equivalent categories as possible ("low" and "high"). These scales were first introduced in Chapters 4 and 6. The T_2 scores, rather than the T_1 scores, were employed in defining the conditional variables, in order to determine that the condition had not changed as a result of the contemporary ($T_1 - T_2$) deviant response and that it was still antecedent to the anticipated change in self-attitudes.

In each of the four categories (in each analysis), then, among subjects who scored high in self-derogation at T_1 and who maintained or increased that high level over the $T_1 - T_2$ period, those who reported each of the 28 deviant occurrences for the period $T_1 - T_2$ were compared with those who denied the occurrence with regard to subsequent residual gains in self-derogation over the period $T_2 - T_3$. Significance of difference between means was determined by a t test (one-tailed) assuming unequal variances (Welch, 1947).

These procedures permitted the establishment of a temporal relationship between deviant response patterns (defined as prior to T_1 and/or between T_1 and T_2) and subsequent decreases in self-derogation (between T_2 and T_3) among initially high self-derogation subjects that could not be accounted for by the subjects' levels of self-derogation at T_2.

Results

The results of each of the two major analyses will be presented in turn.

Gender by Defenselessness/Vulnerability

The results of the analysis of the relationship between antecedent deviant responses and subsequent decreases in self-derogation for each of the four gender by defenselessness/vulnerability combinations are summarized in Table 7.1. Under the theoretical conditions stated, the relationship was expected to be observed under conditions of high rather than low defenselessness and was considered to be more likely to be observed for boys than for girls. These expectations were met. Considering the range of 28 modes of deviant occurrence, for high-defenselessness male subjects (relative to the other three categories) it was more likely to be the case that highly self-derogating subjects who reported the deviant occurrence T_1-T_2 (relative to those who did not so report) showed greater than expected (on the basis of T_2 scores) decreases or smaller than expected increases in self-derogation between T_2 and T_3.

Among high-defenselessness males, in 22 of the 28 deviant occurrences, highly self-derogating subjects who affirmed the deviant occurrence over the period T_1-T_2 manifested appreciably greater than expected decreases or smaller than expected increases (indicated by increasingly negative or decreasingly positive scores) in self-derogation for the period T_2-T_3 than similarly highly self-derogating subjects who denied occurrence of the deviant acts over the T_1-T_2 period. (Although residual gain scores are to be interpreted as greater than expected increases or lower than expected decreases, for purposes of simplicity in presentation changes in self-derogation scores will be referred to as increases or decreases henceforth.)

For six of the items the differences were significant at the $p < .05$ level. For three deviant occurrences, the differences were significant at the $p < .10$ level. At the $p < .05$ level, high-defenselessness male subjects who affirmed that between T_1 and T_2 they took things worth between \$2 and \$50; took things worth less than \$2; participated in gang fights; used force to get money or valuables from another person; broke into and entered a home, store, or building; or beat up someone who did nothing to them displayed, on the average, significantly greater decreases in self-rejecting attitudes over the subsequent period T_2-T_3 than high-defenselessness males who denied occurrence of the deviant acts during the T_1-T_2 period. At the $p < .10$ level, high-defenselessness males who indicated that over the period T_1-T_2 they sold narcotic drugs, damaged or destroyed public or private property on purpose, or stole things from someone else's desk or locker showed on the average significantly greater decreases in self-rejecting attitudes over the subsequent T_2-T_3 period than similarly high-defenselessness males who denied performance of these acts over the T_1-T_2 period. Appreciably greater decreases in self-rejecting attitutdes were also observed for those who affirmed antecedent performance of 13 other deviant acts as well, although these differences were not particularly significant.

In only six instances were deviant acts associated with subsequent increases in self-rejection, although in none of these instances were the differences statistically significant. Three possible explanations suggest themselves. First, these items may reflect the intensity of the self-devaluing experiences as much

TABLE 7.1

Residual Gains in Self-derogation T_2–T_3 by Sex, Levels of Defenselessness, and Report of Deviant Response Patterns $(T_1–T_2)$ among Subjects Who Were Both Initially High in Self-Derogation at T_1 and Maintained or Increased Level of Self-Derogation T_1-T_2

Test item	Males[a]				Females[a]			
	Low defenselessness		High defenselessness		Low defenselessness		High defenselessness	
	Yes	No	Yes	No	Yes	No	Yes	No
Took things worth between $2 and $50	0.42 *	−7.19	−4.75 *	5.32	7.93	−0.77	3.95	2.24
	21.25	24.11	25.14	27.81	12.46	25.79	21.00	25.27
	14	59	27	102	4	86	27	196
Was suspended or expelled from school	17.93 *	−5.88	−4.14	3.41	14.14 *	−0.89	−0.73	2.61
	9.67	23.85	20.46	27.84	7.83	25.63	26.16	24.75
	2	72	7	121	3	87	19	203
Took things worth less than $2	−3.75	−6.14	−0.62 *	7.62	0.24	−0.52	4.09	1.52
	27.26	21.81	25.10	29.60	23.68	25.87	23.56	25.33
	28	46	69	60	16	74	69	154
Thought about or threatened suicide	1.06	−6.48	5.48	1.96	4.66	−2.43	3.72	1.11
	26.80	23.26	29.21	26.58	22.81	26.23	26.06	23.67
	14	59	46	83	26	64	99	124
Contact with police, sheriff, or juvenile officer	−1.14	−5.88	−1.60	4.31	−7.97	−0.12	0.95	2.34
	25.64	23.73	26.49	27.71	29.81	25.36	26.73	24.68
	10	64	24	105	3	87	15	208
Became angry and broke things	−4.30	−5.81	5.48	−0.27	8.27 *	−2.70	2.65	2.38
	25.19	23.29	27.77	27.04	22.63	25.71	21.66	27.05
	28	46	81	47	19	71	99	125
Carried a razor, switchblade, or gun as a weapon	−5.13	−6.54	0.81	4.02	2.03	−0.76	7.57	2.28
	26.81	22.52	24.40	28.90	5.54	25.80	18.36	25.07

	34.07	23.40	20.12	28.14		23.??	35.??	24.15
	4	69	9	117	1	88	11	207
Received a failing grade in one or more school subjects	3.25 * / 23.78 / 32	−13.10 / 20.38 / 41	2.78 / 27.40 / 57	3.88 / 27.80 / 71	3.62 / 22.66 / 24	−1.84 / 26.30 / 66	0.26 / 23.22 / 63	3.36 / 25.33 / 160
Used wine, beer, or liquor more than two times	−4.10 / 23.35 / 23	−5.75 / 24.30 / 51	0.07 / 22.15 / 39	4.97 / 29.43 / 89	−7.38 + / 26.11 / 19	1.48 / 25.02 / 71	2.62 / 24.07 / 55	2.38 / 25.05 / 168
Cheated on exams	−7.09 / 26.60 / 35	−3.57 / 21.33 / 39	4.76 / 24.98 / 68	1.49 / 30.16 / 61	−1.39 / 25.55 / 41	1.39 / 24.86 / 48	4.31 + / 25.15 / 120	−0.08 / 24.12 / 104
Attempted suicide	9.77 * / 12.98 / 6	−7.02 / 24.09 / 67	10.05 / 29.81 / 22	1.71 / 27.15 / 105	3.46 / 27.53 / 16	−1.22 / 25.00 / 74	2.17 / 25.96 / 50	2.43 / 24.45 / 173
Started a fistfight	−12.28 + / 23.57 / 15	−3.01 / 24.33 / 55	7.07 / 25.63 / 42	1.36 / 28.29 / 87	8.35 / 31.60 / 5	−0.24 / 24.49 / 84	−0.63 / 24.52 / 30	2.80 / 24.80 / 194
Took narcotic drugs	−4.47 / 38.64 / 6	−5.30 / 22.56 / 68	−2.01 / 25.48 / 25	4.32 / 28.01 / 103	4.90 / 15.38 / 6	−0.76 / 25.96 / 84	5.24 / 25.25 / 39	1.88 / 24.66 / 184
Skipped school without an excuse	−5.18 / 27.73 / 16	−5.97 / 23.04 / 56	0.69 / 28.35 / 40	4.35 / 27.17 / 89	2.43 / 26.76 / 11	−0.99 / 25.42 / 78	4.66 / 23.46 / 51	1.69 / 25.12 / 173
Participated in social protest	8.38 + / 25.50 / 8	−6.44 / 23.38 / 62	−4.29 / 29.34 / 10	4.52 / 26.92 / 116	−3.87 / 34.87 / 5	−0.18 / 24.97 / 85	−5.74 * / 25.19 / 37	3.97 / 24.38 / 186
Took part in gang fights	−0.11 / 33.53 / 8	−5.43 / 22.60 / 65	−6.18 * / 24.50 / 28	5.82 / 27.81 / 101	−3.97 / 37.62 / 4	−0.22 / 24.97 / 86	2.17 / 22.14 / 14	2.33 / 25.05 / 207

(Continued)

TABLE 7.1—*Continued*

Test item	Males[a]				Females[a]			
	Low defenselessness		High defenselessness		Low defenselessness		High defenselessness	
	Yes	No	Yes	No	Yes	No	Yes	No
Was sent to a psychiatrist, psychologist, or social worker	−0.25 20.22 6	−6.47 24.14 65	5.08 20.54 12	3.08 28.23 115	12.93 10.29 2	−0.69 25.55 88	6.00 27.92 9	2.66 24.64 211
Used force to get money or valuables	11.53 * 23.30 7	−6.99 23.40 67	−6.74 * 27.96 20	5.37 27.04 108	17.77 37.53 3	−0.46 24.54 86	−0.03 20.28 11	2.49 24.97 213
Broke into and entered a home, store, or building	26.50 * 10.23 9	−10.03 21.73 64	−14.57 * 23.54 17	6.08 27.09 110	−3.46 1 1	−0.64 25.51 88	9.58 27.29 7	2.34 24.53 213
Damaged or destroyed public or private property on purpose	3.64 + 22.65 12	−7.62 23.49 61	−1.46 + 24.70 38	5.47 28.48 90	−1.18 28.75 4	−0.35 25.39 86	3.27 27.37 17	2.18 24.61 206
Was taken to office for punishment	2.76 * 25.26 26	−8.16 21.80 45	2.43 28.54 63	3.96 27.10 62	5.09 24.53 12	−0.95 25.60 77	3.89 23.67 62	2.22 25.46 156
Stole things from someone else's desk or locker	−1.26 28.08 22	−6.92 21.92 52	−2.44 + 26.77 43	5.83 27.65 85	−8.36 22.07 7	0.29 25.63 83	3.26 25.76 34	2.30 24.73 186
Used a car without owner's permission	20.39 * 16.53	−6.92 23.44	−2.75 24.27	3.53 27.85	36.54	−0.30 25.??	7.08	2.25

	18.81	24.16	27.13	26.??	4	84	19	201
	7	66	22	104				
Took things worth $50 or more	5.03	-5.22	-6.93	3.98	5.95	-0.05	6.35	2.41
	20.78	24.09	25.36	27.59	9.56	25.37	8.09	24.94
	4	68	9	120	3	86	4	219
Smoked marijuana	-20.83 +	-5.23	0.76	3.99	10.39 *	-1.73	-0.96	2.87
	24.06	22.98	23.51	28.70	14.68	26.15	27.97	23.81
	6	64	31	98	10	80	42	179
Participated in strike, riot, or demonstrations	9.60 *	-8.14	-2.29	3.94	34.36	-0.58	-5.32	2.57
	20.71	22.96	27.89	27.52	0	24.93	34.35	24.31
	6	65	14	112	1	87	10	211

+ $p < .10$

* $p < .05$

** $p < .01$

[a] First entry indicates mean residual gain in self-derogation, $T_2 - T_3$, second entry indicates standard deviation, and third entry indicates cell N.

as they reflect more or less adaptive responses to the self-devaluation. This explanation might account for the increase in self-rejection associated with antecedent reports of at least three of the items (thinking about or threatening suicide; attempting suicide; being sent to a psychiatrist, psychologist, or social worker) and possibly one other of the six items (becoming angry and breaking things). A second possible explanation suggests that all of these patterns or their consequences may or may not have eventuated in short-term self-enhancing gratification, but they were in any case ineffectual over the long term in reducing self-rejecting attitudes. Following suicidal behavior or a temper tantrum, the individual might feel momentarily good, but might not have effected any long-term reduction in self-devaluing feelings. A third explanation, not mutually exclusive of the other two, suggests that whatever the short-term gratifications involved in these behaviors or their correlates, the behaviors may evoke intensely self-devaluing experiences. This might be particularly the case with regard to "started a fistfight." Thus, although this item was associated with a subsequent increase in self-rejecting attitudes, "beating up someone who did nothing to them" was associated with a subsequent decrease in self-rejection, as has been noted. This suggests that more often than not interpersonal aggression by high-defenselessness males has immediate self-devaluing consequences (presumably, losing the fight). However, when the successful confirmation of the aggression is stipulated, the act tends to be associated with subsequent self-enhancement. Thus, highly self-rejecting males, in the absence of alternative self-protective or self-enhancing mechanisms, apparently can use deviant responses to advantage in that performance of any of a wide range of deviant acts is associated with subsequent self-enhancing consequences.

In contrast, although 22 of the 28 deviant acts were associated with subsequent decreases in self-derogation among the high-defenselessness males, among low-defenselessness males 25 of the deviant acts were associated with subsequent *increases* in self-rejection. In all but three deviant responses, low-defenselessness males who affirmed the response for the period T_1-T_2 manifested appreciably greater increases or smaller decreases in self-derogation for the period T_2-T_3 than did low-defenselessness males who denied the deviant responses over the T_1-T_2 period. The differences were significant at the $p < .05$ level for eight of the deviant patterns (being suspended or expelled from school; receiving a failing grade in one or more school subjects; attempting suicide; using force to get money or valuables from another person; breaking and entering; being taken to the office for punishment; using a car without the owner's permission; and participating in a strike, riot, or demonstration) and were significant at the $p < .10$ level for an additional three items (participating in a social protest; damaging or destroying public or private property on purpose; beating up someone who did nothing to them). Apparently, then, where the self-derogating person has some resources available to him (as indicated by his low state of defenselessness) the performance of deviant acts is likely to have self-devaluing consequences, whether because of his own self-reproach or the adverse responses of others in the normative environment (to which he remains tied) in response to the deviant acts.

Low-defenselessness males manifested greater subsequent decreases in self-rejection (or smaller increases) if they reported antecedent performance of each of three deviant patterns than if they denied antecedent performance of those patterns. These three patterns included cheating on examinations (not significant), starting a fistfight ($p < .10$), and smoking marijuana ($p < .10$). These three deviant patterns, compared to the remainder, suggest relatively minor infractions within the context of the broader peer group. It is possible that these low-defenselessness males—that is, males who are not completely without resources—have chosen participation in peer groups as the primary vehicle for self-enhancing adaptations to preexisting high levels of self-rejection.

Among female subjects, as anticipated, the relationship between deviant responses and subsequent decreases in self-rejection was much less consistent. Among high-defenselessness females, only 12 of the patterns were associated with subsequent decreases in self-rejection (approximately twice the number of patterns that were so associated among low-defenselessness females). However, only 2 of the items were significantly associated with subsequent reduction in self-rejection. High-defenselessness females who indicated that they participated in social protests during the period $T_1 - T_2$ manifested significantly greater subsequent reductions in self-derogation between T_2 and T_3 than did high-defenselessness females who denied participating in social protests between T_1 and T_2. Consistent with this was the observation made earlier regarding the relationship between gender and aggression/hostility: In the relatively few studies in which females were observed to be higher on some index of aggression or hostility than males, they tended to be higher on prosocial aggression but lower on antisocial aggression (Sears, 1961) or higher on covert hostility than males (Bennett & Cohen, 1959).

Inconsistent with this literature, however, is the further observation that high-defenselessness females who indicated that they beat up someone who did nothing to them during the period $T_1 - T_2$ manifested significantly ($p < .10$) greater subsequent decreases in self-rejection over the period $T_2 - T_3$ than did high-defenselessness females who denied performance of this act between T_1 and T_2. Along with this pattern, other antisocial aggressive patterns showed a nonsignificant association with subsequent decreases in self-rejection over the period $T_2 - T_3$. These included starting a fistfight, taking part in gang fights, and using force to get money or valuables from another person. Although antisocial aggression might be antithetical to the feminine role, and therefore might evoke self-reproach and adverse attitudinal responses from others in the subjects' membership groups over the short term, it is possible that over the long term (particularly where the source of the self-devaluation is associated with gender-related role differentiations) the awareness of the high-defenselessness females that they can actively influence the environment may provide the self-confidence to achieve in other areas. All of this, of course, is highly speculative at this juncture.

Another vehicle through which deviant activity might effect self-enhancing consequences is suggested by the observation of nonsignificant relationships between being suspended or expelled from school and coming into contact with police, sheriff, or juvenile officers on the one hand and subsequent decreases in self-rejection on the other. Since the numerous studies cited suggested that females are more closely tied to the normative environment than males, and they are more highly dependent upon the attitudes of others for their self-evaluation, deviant patterns may function to evoke adverse responses from authorities, label the violators, and thereby attenuate the relationship between the female and the source of her self-devaluation.

It is interesting to note that the one instance in which a deviant pattern was significantly ($p < .10$) related to an *increase* in self-rejection was anticipated by another study previously cited. The pattern in question was cheating on examinations. High-defenselessness females who reported this pattern relative to those who denied the pattern over the T_1-T_2 period manifested significantly greater increases in self-rejection over the period T_2-T_3. This was foreshadowed by the report of Tittle and Rowe (1973) that in a study of the relative effects of a moral appeal and a sanction threat on college classroom cheating, females were influenced far more by the sanction threat than were the males.

In any event, perhaps the most striking finding from an analysis of the relationship between gender and self-enhancing effects of deviant patterns (under a condition of high defenselessness) is the observation that, for the most part, these effects tend to be observed for males rather than females, consistent with derivations from the theoretical framework under consideration. This observation is also consistent with the conclusions of others (Gold & Mann, 1972) to the effect that the model of delinquent behavior as a defense against a negative self-image fits better for the boys' data than for the girls' data, since delinquency is a predominantly masculine defense and does not function as well to raise girls' self-esteem.

Gender and Self-enhancing Potential of the Normative Environment

The results concerning the relationship between deviant patterns and self-enhancing consequences by gender and perceived level of self-enhancing poten-

tial of the normative environment are summarized in Table 7.2. It was anticipated that highly self-rejecting subjects who perceived a relatively high self-
enhancing potential of the normative environment at the same time would be
most likely to define the acts under consideration as deviant. Therefore, these
acts, since they represent the true alternatives to the normative patterns by
which subjects had failed to gain self-accepting attitudes, would permit
avoidance of the subjects' self-devaluing environment, as well as attacks upon
the normative basis of their self-rejection; the acts would also provide substitute
sources of gratification. It was anticipated that males would be less vulnerable
than females to self-reproach and rejecting attitudes by significant others as a
consequence of adopting deviant response patterns. These expectations again
were met. Among males who perceived a relatively high self-enhancing potential of the normative environment, for 20 of the 28 deviant patterns those who
reported the deviant occurrence for the period $T_1 - T_2$ manifested greater decreases in self-rejection over the period $T_2 - T_3$ than did subjects who denied
occurrence of the deviant act over the period $T_1 - T_2$. At the $p < .10$ level or
better, the comparisons were significant for 10 of the deviant items. At the $p
< .01$ level, highly rejecting subjects who indicated that they stole things from
someone else's desk or locker during the period $T_1 - T_2$ manifested significantly
greater decreases in self-rejection between T_2 and T_3 than did subjects who
indicated they did not perform this act over a comparable period. At the $p < .05$
level, subjects who indicated that they used wine, beer, or liquor more than two
times during the preceding week, took part in gang fights, or took things worth
$50 or more showed significantly greater decreases in self-rejection over the
following year than subjects who denied performing these acts during the
earlier period. At the $p < .10$ level, subjects who took things worth less than
$2, had contact with police, sold narcotic drugs, cheated on exams, engaged in
breaking and entering, or smoked marijuana during the period $T_1 - T_2$ manifested significantly greater decreases in self-rejection over the subsequent
period ($T_2 - T_3$) than did subjects who denied performing these acts during the
period $T_1 - T_2$. In addition, several other deviant patterns were associated with
subsequent decreases in self-rejection, albeit not at a statistically significant
level. Among these patterns were taking things worth between $2 and $50,
carrying a weapon, using narcotic drugs, engaging in vandalism, and beating up
someone who did nothing to them. Thus, highly self-rejecting males who were
high in perceived self-enhancing potential of the normative environment tended
to enjoy self-enhancing consequences of a wide variety of deviant patterns. It is
interesting to note that one of the patterns that was associated with self-
rejecting consequences in the discussion of defenselessness had self-enhancing
consequences here. This item (cheating on exams) may reflect one of the
alternative implications of perceived self-enhancing potential of the normative
environment. If the subjects did anticipate that they would be an integral part

TABLE 7.2

Residual Gains in Self-derogation $T_2 - T_3$ by Sex, Level of Perceived Self-enhancing Potential of Normative Environment, and Report of Deviant Response Patterns $(T_1 - T_2)$ among Subjects Who Were Both Initially High in Self-derogation at T_1 and Maintained or Increased Level of Self-derogation $T_1 - T_2$

	Males[a]				Females[a]			
	Low self-enhancing potential of normative environment		High self-enhancing potential of normative environment		Low self-enhancing potential of normative environment		High self-enhancing potential of normative environment	
Test item	Yes	No	Yes	No	Yes	No	Yes	No
Took things worth between $2 and $50	-0.00 / 24.21 / 23	0.03 / 27.69 / 77	-6.18 / 22.74 / 19	1.07 / 26.49 / 81	5.95 / 24.70 / 10	3.39 / 25.21 / 109	3.75 / 17.98 / 21	0.02 / 25.60 / 172
Was suspended or expelled from school	1.29 / 20.86 / 9	-0.27 / 27.28 / 91	11.10 / 0.0 / 1	-0.11 / 26.04 / 100	11.26 / 23.82 / 7	3.14 / 25.29 / 111	-3.36 / 24.77 / 15	0.71 / 24.95 / 177
Took things worth less than $2	1.31 / 26.80 / 49	-0.88 / 26.87 / 52	-4.48 + / 23.33 / 47	3.90 / 27.62 / 54	8.38 + / 17.87 / 27	2.20 / 26.75 / 92	1.03 / 25.49 / 58	-0.05 / 24.70 / 135
Thought about or threatened suicide	0.32 / 29.89 / 40	0.42 / 24.77 / 60	10.67 * / 22.87 / 20	-2.63 / 26.09 / 81	6.30 / 21.34 / 55	1.28 + / 27.85 / 64	1.87 / 28.37 / 69	-0.70 / 22.70 / 124
Contact with police, sheriff, or juvenile officer	3.76 / 26.20 / 22	-0.82 / 26.95 / 79	-8.00 + / 22.85 / 14	1.29 / 26.28 / 87	13.59 + / 16.39 / 7	2.90 / 25.34 / 113	-9.53 / 28.42 / 11	0.82 / 24.67 / 181
Became angry and broke things	1.70	-2.59	3.72 +	-3.12	2.97	3.85	4.15 *	-1.57

	24.94 32	27.63 66	24.93 27	26.16 73	[illegible] 8	[illegible] 110	[illegible] 7	[illegible] 185
Sold narcotic drugs (dope, heroin)	2.81 21.51 7	−0.50 27.43 91	−15.40 + 23.99 6	1.17 26.02 93	6.44 29.57 6	3.51 24.62 112	−19.32 + 30.02 6	0.83 24.57 183
Received a failing grade in one or more school subjects	6.52 ** 25.70 52	−6.74 26.69 47	−1.71 26.12 35	0.91 25.98 66	4.49 21.69 36	3.10 26.39 84	−1.28 24.02 50	1.03 25.23 143
Used wine, beer, or liquor more than two times	2.96 22.03 36	−1.45 29.27 64	−7.61 * 22.10 26	2.64 26.76 75	2.25 22.31 28	3.91 25.85 92	−1.73 26.27 47	1.05 24.50 146
Cheated on exams	5.35 * 25.79 54	−5.99 27.07 46	−4.43 + 24.68 48	4.01 26.60 53	6.86 + 24.80 60	−0.08 25.06 59	0.78 25.67 98	0.37 23.77 95
Attempted suicide	7.25 27.21 18	−1.88 26.83 80	14.93 * 26.94 10	−1.64 25.44 91	6.18 22.91 27	2.75 25.63 93	−0.08 28.17 39	0.48 24.10 153
Started a fistfight	3.53 29.01 25	−0.70 26.39 73	0.76 24.46 32	−0.08 26.86 68	9.35 25.13 13	3.39 24.56 105	−4.48 24.53 22	0.97 24.88 172
Took narcotic drugs	0.83 28.57 19	−0.22 26.53 81	−7.74 26.70 12	1.05 25.80 89	9.80 22.49 15	2.92 25.43 103	2.89 24.81 30	−0.12 24.89 164
Skipped school without an excuse	0.66 26.78 33	−0.50 27.18 66	−1.33 29.88 23	0.40 24.85 78	5.48 21.18 20	3.20 25.88 99	3.63 25.57 41	−0.64 24.70 152

(Continued)

TABLE 7.2—Continued

Test item	Males[a]				Females[a]			
	Low self-enhancing potential of normative environment		High self-enhancing potential of normative environment		Low self-enhancing potential of normative environment		High self-enhancing potential of normative environment	
	Yes	No	Yes	No	Yes	No	Yes	No
Participated in social protest	-4.90	1.93	1.96	-0.19	-3.20	4.48	-6.80 *	1.52
	29.69	26.17	23.89	26.24	31.17	24.01	23.20	25.03
	8	85	9	92	15	105	27	165
Took part in gang fights	-0.18	0.28	-9.64 *	2.24	-2.68	4.00	3.02	0.09
	30.07	25.99	19.71	26.52	32.47	24.68	20.67	25.23
	21	80	16	84	7	112	11	180
Was sent to a psychiatrist, psychologist, or social worker	6.14	-0.72	-0.25	0.02	14.08 *	3.26	0.61	0.77
	20.26	27.46	20.44	26.44	7.85	25.40	31.06	24.72
	10	87	8	93	5	114	7	183
Used force to get money or valuables	-4.49	1.00	-2.94	0.36	11.51	3.03	-3.95	0.80
	28.34	26.53	24.96	26.16	27.70	24.86	19.30	24.92
	15	86	11	90	7	113	7	185
Broke into and entered a home, store, or building	7.90	-1.76	-9.99 +	1.35	6.13	3.63	3.38	0.26
	30.80	26.18	21.82	26.25	23.74	25.15	30.48	24.66
	14	84	12	89	4	115	5	184
Damaged or destroyed public or private property on purpose	3.45	-1.96	-5.76	1.72	16.58 *	2.85	-3.24	0.54
	23.89	27.88	23.93	26.38	17.57	25.30	28.41	24.61
	30	69	20	80	6	113	15	178
Was taken to office for punishment	1.77	0.30	2.83	-1.95	8.86	2.80	1.71	0.15
	27.93	25.06	25.96	26.??				

	37	63	29	72	13	104	28	165
Used a car without owner's permission	8.40	−0.34	−2.68	0.16	19.33 **	3.20	4.92	0.33
	16.01	27.30	26.67	26.14	7.08	25.21	27.29	24.98
	6	93	6	93	4	115	9	178
Beat up someone who did nothing to subject	−1.59	−0.50	−6.59	0.68	0.18	4.10	−3.22	1.23
	30.34	26.22	21.31	26.39	29.36	24.81	26.09	24.63
	14	83	15	85	9	108	14	176
Took things worth $50 or more	7.16	−0.60	−19.91 *	1.62	5.21	3.49	6.57 +	0.52
	20.22	27.31	20.73	25.78	12.26	25.17	7.52	24.98
	8	92	5	94	2	118	5	187
Smoked marijuana	0.95	−0.60	−8.14 +	1.42	11.15 *	1.87	−4.98	1.10
	24.76	27.82	24.21	26.09	20.81	25.75	27.61	23.97
	22	75	15	86	20	98	32	161
Participated in strike, riot, or demonstration	0.21	0.14	2.34	−0.54	18.65 +	2.17	−26.14 *	1.35
	23.31	27.25	29.69	25.65	27.56	24.82	26.38	24.42
	10	88	10	90	6	111	5	186

+$p < .10$
*$p < .05$
**$p < .01$
[a] First entry indicates mean residual gain in self-derogation, $T_2 - T_3$, second entry indicates standard deviation, and third entry indicates cell N.

of the normative environment, cheating on exams may be perceived as a means to these ends.

For the remaining seven items that were related to self-rejecting consequences for these subjects (one of the deviant items was reported by only one subject in this subgroup and will not be considered), three of the items were interpretable as expressions of intense self-rejection as well as functional adaptations to subjective distress associated with self-rejecting attitudes. Thus, subjects who reported suicidal ideation or gestures ($p < .05$), becoming angry and breaking things ($p < .10$), or attempting suicide ($p < .05$) were significantly more likely to display subsequent increases in self-rejection than subjects who did not report these antecedent occurrences. Presumably, the increase in self-rejecting attitudes was a result of the manifest inability to cope with adverse circumstances in combination with the felt dependence upon the very normative environment that deprived them of ultimate gratification. The nonsignificant relationship between being taken to the office for punishment and subsequent increases in self-rejection may be accounted for by the individual's apparent need to conform to the norms of the membership groups, since future gratification is dependent upon these groups.

In contrast, among males who perceived the self-enhancing potential of the normative environment as low, highly self-derogating subjects were unlikely to experience a reduction in negative self-attitudes as a result of adopting deviant responses. In only six instances was even a minor reduction in self-rejection noted and none of these was statistically significant. Conversely, for 22 of the deviant patterns, antecedent reports of the deviant response were associated with subsequent increases in self-rejection. This is exactly what would be expected on the basis of the theoretical model if low self-enhancing potential of the normative environment can be assumed to reflect a lesser tendency to define these acts as deviant. If these acts were more acceptable for individuals who were low on these measures, yet in the social environment that defined these acts as acceptable the individuals still were unable to reduce their relatively high levels of self-rejection, it is to be expected that continuity in these patterns would exacerbate their existing self-rejecting attitudes or at least prevent them from lowering them relative to the ability of others to do so. This interpretation seems warranted when it is noted that among the six deviant patterns that were associated with a reduction in self-rejecting attitudes the greatest decrease was noted for *prosocial* acting out (that is, participating in social protests). The implication is that in an environment where the other "deviant" patterns are more acceptable, prosocial acting out may be defined as deviant and hence (again, according to the theory under consideration) as having self-enhancing potential.

Paralleling the results of the earlier analysis, among females the relationship between antecedent deviant patterns and subsequent reduction in self-rejecting attitudes was much less consistent than among males. As anticipated, the relationship was much more likely to be observed among highly self-derogating females who perceived the self-enhancing potential of the normative environment as high rather than among those who perceived the self-enhancing potential of the normative environment as low.

Among highly self-derogating females who perceived the self-enhancing potential of the normative environment as high, for 15 of the deviant patterns those who affirmed antecedent occurrence of the deviant pattern displayed greater subsequent decreases in self-rejection than subjects who denied antecedent performance of the deviant responses. However, only three of the comparisons were statistically significant. Consistent with earlier findings and the results of other studies cited earlier, two of the statistically significant comparisons involved prosocial acting out. Subjects reporting participation in social protests or participation in a strike, riot, or demonstration manifested appreciably greater subsequent decreases in self-rejection than subjects denying antecedent performance of these acts. Subjects were also observed to manifest significantly greater subsequent decreases in self-rejection ($p < .10$) if they reported selling narcotic drugs during the preceding period than if they denied selling narcotic drugs. A consideration of the nature of these patterns along with the other deviant patterns that were associated (albeit at a nonsignificant level) with subsequent decreases in self-rejection is instructive in suggesting the mechanisms through which these patterns may operate. Thus, for these subjects the relationship between antecedent suspension or expulsion from the school and contact with the police or other authorities, on the one hand, and subsequent decrease in self-rejection, on the other hand, suggests that the deviant patterns may attenuate the girls' emotional dependence on the very groups in which participation leads to severe self-devaluation. Consistent with this is the observation of a relationship (again, nonsignificant) between marijuana use and subsequent decrease in self-rejection. Thus, Jessor and his associates (1973) reported that the use of marijuana among females is associated with a relative increase in alienation (for example, a sense of isolation from others).

As in the earlier analysis, another cluster of deviant patterns that showed a nonsignificant association with subsequent decrease in self-rejection involved physical aggression. Subjects who reported antecedent instances of starting a fistfight, using force to get money or valuables from another person, damaging or destroying public or private property on purpose, and beating up someone who did nothing to them manifested greater subsequent reductions in self-rejection than subjects who denied antecedent instances of these patterns. Again, although such patterns are antithetical to the feminine role and are likely to evoke adverse responses from other members of their groups, it is possible that, along with the attenuation of group ties resulting from other deviant patterns, the exercise of physical power may have to a degree negated the traditionally passive and acquiescent female role that might have been associated with the genesis of their self-rejecting attitudes. Consistent with this interpretation, in view of the association of alcohol use with increased power fantasies (McClelland, 1972), is the further observation of a slight tendency for females who reported alcohol abuse to manifest greater subsequent reductions in self-rejecting attitudes than females who denied antecedent alcohol abuse.

In contrast to the females who perceive a high self-enhancing potential in the normative environment, those who perceive that the self-enhancing potential of the normative environment is low are quite unlikely to experience self-enhancing consequences associated with antecedent deviant occurrences. In only five instances was even a weak association along these lines observed, and none of these was significant. On the other hand, for 23 of the deviant patterns, antecedent performance of the deviant responses was associated with subsequent increase in self-rejection. The relationship was significant in eight of these instances. Thus, highly self-rejecting females who reported antecedent theft of things worth less than $2, contact with the police or other authorities, cheating on exams, being sent to a psychiatrist or other therapist, vandalism, using a car without the owner's permission, smoking marijuana, and participating in a strike, riot, or demonstration manifested significantly greater increases in self-rejection than subjects denying antecedent occurrence of these events. Similar but nonsignificant relationships were observed for such patterns as antecedent suspension or expulsion from school, suicidal ideation, carrying a weapon, selling narcotic drugs, attempting suicide, starting a fistfight, using narcotic drugs, using force to get money or valuables from another person, breaking and entering, being taken to the office for punishment, and stealing things from someone else's desk or locker. Again, if perception of a low potential for self-enhancement in the normative environment is associated with a sociocultural context that finds such patterns more acceptable, and if these patterns were associated with the genesis of the subjects' devaluing attitudes, then continued performance of these patterns by the subjects would be likely to result in maintenance or increase in their level of self-rejection. This, of course, is what was observed.

Again, the results were consistent with the theoretical derivation. Among highly self-derogating subjects, males who perceived the self-enhancing potential of the normative environment were most likely to experience appreciable decreases in self-rejecting attitudes over the period T_2-T_3 associated with antecedent reports of deviant occurrences for the period T_1-T_2. This was consistent with the guiding theoretical framework, insofar as the perception of a high potential for self-enhancement in the normative environment reflected an increased likelihood that the patterns in question were indeed deviant from the subjects' point of view, and insofar as males reflected a decreased likelihood of vulnerability to self-reproach or adverse attitudinal responses from significant others in the subjects' membership groups in response to performance of the deviant patterns.

Summary

According to the theory under consideration, subjects who develop severe and pervasive self-rejecting attitudes in the course of their membership group experiences come to associate these experiences with the source of their self-devaluation, and generalize this association to other aspects of the normative environment not necessarily related to the genesis of self-rejecting attitudes. As a consequence they come to lose motivation to conform to and acquire motivation to deviate from the normative expectations associated with their membership groups, and they seek alternative deviant patterns that offer (consciously or unconsciously) promise of fulfilling the yet unsatisfied self-esteem motive. The adoption of such deviant responses is said to work in the service of the self-esteem motive by facilitating avoidance of self-devaluing experiences in the context of membership groups, attacking the normative structures that constituted the basis for the person's self-rejection, and offering substitute sources of self-enhancement for those patterns that in the past had led to severe self-rejecting attitudes.

The questions addressed in this chapter related to whether or not the adoption of deviant responses indeed was associated with subsequent reduction in self-derogation. Highly self-rejecting subjects who reported each of 28 deviant occurrences over the period $T_1 - T_2$ were compared with highly self-rejecting subjects who denied the occurrence of each of the deviant acts over the same period with regard to subsequent $(T_2 - T_3)$ decreases in self-derogation beyond those that could have been predicted linearly from knowledge of the self-derogation score at T_2. However, the prediction of this relationship is based on certain theoretical premises, and a number of circumstances suggested that these premises did not uniformly hold for all highly self-derogating subjects. Therefore a number of conditions were set forth for observation of the relationship that was said to be roughly reflected in specified variables. One premise was that the presence of severely self-rejecting attitudes was a reflection of the inability of individuals to satisfy the self-esteem motive in the context of their normative membership groups. To reflect the presence or absence of this condition, highly self-rejecting subjects were divided into those who were more or less "high" on a measure of defenselessness/vulnerability. Another premise stated that the acts under investigation were in fact subjectively defined as deviant by the subjects prior to the adoption of the deviant pattern. This condition was said to be reflected in the high or low values displayed by the self-rejecting subjects on a measure of perceived self-enhancing potential of the normative environment, on the assumption that subjects who perceived the self-enhancing potential of the normative environment to be high would be more likely to define the acts under consideration as deviant. A third premise asserted that the subjects, as a result of the association of membership group experiences with the genesis of subjectively distressful self-rejecting attitudes, came to be sufficiently disassociated from their membership groups that they were not emotionally vulnerable to self-reproach or to the reproach of other group members as a result of their performing the deviant acts. In view of the large literature suggesting that females are least likely to be able to divorce themselves emotionally from their membership group experiences to permit themselves to perform deviant acts with impunity, gender was taken to be a rough reflection of the degree of emotional dependence upon the group and, by implication, of vulnerability to self-devaluing consequences of deviant responses. Thus, two analyses were carried out. In the first analysis the relationship between antecedent deviant responses and subsequent reduction in self-rejecting attitudes was examined for each of the four groups formed by the possible combinations of male and female gender on the one hand and low and high levels of defenselessness on the other. In the second analysis the relationship between antecedent deviant occurrences and subsequent reduction in self-rejection was examined for each of the four groups formed by the possible combinations of male and female gender on the one hand and low and high levels of subjective perceptions of self-enhancing potential of the normative environment on the other hand.

In each case, the predictions based on theoretical expectations were fulfilled. Highly self-rejecting subjects who were unable to utilize normative patterns to reduce feelings of self-rejection and who were least likely to be vulnerable to adverse consequences of adopting alternative deviant patterns in the service of the self-esteem motive (that is, high-defenselessness males) were reasonably consistent in displaying an association between antecedent performance of deviant responses and subsequent reduction in self-rejecting attitudes. In like manner, highly self-rejecting subjects who could be expected to define the acts under consideration as deviant and who, again, were less likely to be vulnerable to negative sanctions from self and others because they had adopted deviant patterns in the service of the self-esteem motive (that is, males who perceived the self-enhancing potential of the normative environment as high) were reasonably consistent in displaying an association between antecedent deviant responses and subsequent reduction in self-derogation.

The findings are thus highly compatible with the theoretical formulation that guided the plan of analysis. However, it is recognized that the measures taken to reflect the theoretical condition could be interpreted only as rough indicators of these conditions. Finer specifications must be made in the future. The data, by the absence of uniformity, also indicated the need for further specification of the conditions under which the relationship between deviant behavior and subsequent reduction in self-rejecting attitudes might occur. The absence of uniformity in the findings, however, did provide clues to the nature of the mechanisms through which various deviant patterns effected reductions in self-derogation.

Chapter 8

Retrospect and Prospect

In this chapter the theory guiding the research that has been reported will be placed in historical perspective. The research findings will be reviewed and evaluated in relationship to the theoretical expectations, and the implications of these findings for future theoretical development and empirical research will be considered.

Historical Context

The use of self-related concepts in theories of deviance has a long history. The theoretical structure under consideration was of course influenced by earlier considerations of the relationship between these concepts and deviance-relevant concepts. However, it is perhaps more difficult for those attempting to articulate the relationship between self and deviance to specify the precise nature of these influences than it is for someone who is reviewing theoretical patterns in the use of self-concept in the study of deviance. Therefore the placement of the theoretical statement that guided the research reported in this book within its historical context has been facilitated greatly by Wells' review (1978) of theories of deviance in which the self-concept has been used. He notes that the early deviance literature separated the psychological and sociological levels of analysis, thereby effectively precluding the use of the self-concept as an explanatory construct; this construct is most useful in the middle ground between the two levels "where one focuses on the interpersonal processes by which socially distributed contingencies coordinate with individual motivations to produce situated behavior [p. 189]." However, in the 1950s, contemporary with the emergent influence of interactionist social psychology in sociological thinking, the self-concept began to be more widely used in theoretically based analyses of deviance. Wells cites works by Cohen (1955),

Reckless, Dinitz, and Murray (1956), and Lemert (1951) as signaling the emergence of three theoretical viewpoints, which in the 1960s were to become "dominant perspectives on the use of the self-concept in the study of deviance [Wells, 1978, p. 190]." Each of these three viewpoints—structural interactionism, socialization-control analyses, and labeling analyses—will be discussed in turn.

Generally, *structural interactionism*, both in its beginnings (Cohen, 1955) and in its later development (Chapman, 1966; Hall, 1966; Short & Strodtbeck, 1965), focused on deviance in subcultural terms as a collective response to social variables. For Cohen (1955), gang delinquency emerged as a collective response to status-frustration that resulted "from the intersection of social dysfunction and the fundamental motivation of people to enhance or validate their self-identities through social interaction [Wells, 1978, p. 190]." This work was an attempt, then, to articulate motivational, interpersonal, and situational considerations, on the one hand, with social structural theories (notably, anomie theory). Further attempts to link social structural conditions (differentially distributed resources, experiences, and values) with the interpersonal events by which they are produced took the form of self-role theory. Within this perspective, a self-identity is said to arise within ongoing social interactions that in turn are influenced by social structures of available or appropriate identities. The socially organized sense of self guides the construction of new actions and is influenced by others' responses to past actions. Wells cites, as examples of this approach in the study of deviance, motivational models of deviance adoption (Cohen, 1965, 1966; Cohen & Short, 1966), and differential identification theory emphasizing the selective influence of significant others or valued reference groups upon reflected appraisal.

From the second perspective, *socialization-control analyses*—and particularly in the early (Reckless, 1967; Reckless *et al.*, 1956) and later development (Schwartz & Tangri, 1965; Voss, 1969) of containment theory—self-concept was treated as a developing personality variable rather than as an interactional process intervening between individual- and group-level events. A favorable self-concept, as a mechanism of inner containment, as an insulator against deviance, was introduced to explain deviance along with the previously propounded social control factors (that is, socially institutionalized structures of inducements and constraints). In the course of the socialization process the development of a favorable self-concept functioned to inhibit dispositions toward deviance.

The *labeling perspective*, for present purposes, was significant for focusing on the influence of deviance on self-conception, as well as on the influence of self-processes on deviance (Becker, 1963; Kitsuse, 1962; Lemert, 1951; Scheff, 1966). The labeling hypothesis, an integral part of several statements of this perspective, argues that social control responses (particularly those that are in effect stigmatizing) to deviance serve to define the social identity and self-concept of the deviant actor and thereby stabilize deviant patterns. Thus, initial deviance influences change in self-concept, and self-concept change influences deviance.

Wells (1978) notes that, although the arbitrary division of viewpoints on the theoretical relationship between self-concept and deviance into structural interactionist, socialization-control, and labeling perspectives appeared reasonable with regard to prior work, new developments in the 1970s suggest the need to modify the descriptive structure somewhat. Two such major developments are described: (a) the testing and restatement of the division between labeling theory and other theoretical viewpoints, and (b) the blurring of a distinction between structural interactionist analyses and socialization-control analyses. For the purpose of placing the present theoretical structure into historical perspective, the second development is significant. The theoretical perspective guiding the research reported in this volume (H. B. Kaplan, 1975b) is cited as one of two major examples (the other mentioned being Hewitt's 1970 statement) of this rapprochement.

The synthesis between structural interactionist and socialization-control analyses would appear to be the outgrowth of the recognition

> that social structural differences are produced through the distribution of socialization experiences and role-learning opportunities, as well as through the distribution of resources. It reemphasizes that socialization is a social process consisting essentially of interpersonal associations and patterns which connect individuals interactively to larger social contexts [Wells, 1978, p. 194].

Thus the synthesis both grounds socialization in broader social processes and enables social structural influences to explain more than subcultural forms of deviance.

Both exemplars (Hewitt, 1970; H. B. Kaplan, 1975b) are said to relate self-concept and deviance to the social structure by the following proposals:

1. Commitment to the normative order is influenced by adequacy of level of self-esteem.
2. Level of self-esteem is a cumulative product of socialization experiences variously distributed across different social sectors or interpersonal associations.

When the situational structure is unable to maintain an acceptable level of self-esteem, the person will be disposed to seek individual or collective deviant alternatives that might provide more positive experiences. The actual adoption of the alternative activities will also be a function of the external structure of rewards, opportunities, and resources.

Although Wells does not suggest this, it is indeed the case that the implications of the labeling perspectives are also represented in the theoretical structure under consideration, although these implications are not as fully developed. Labeling theory is implicit in the theoretical structure under consideration in terms of the following:

1. The subject's anticipation of the reactions of others (including labeling) to proposed deviant adaptations in the service of the self-esteem motive, which (depending on the personal meaning of these anticipated responses by others) will influence the subject's expectations regarding net self-enhancing or self-devaluing consequences and will thereby influence the subject's adoption of the deviant response
2. The effects of the labeling phenomenon in terms of facilitating avoidance of self-devaluing membership group experiences, attacks upon the basis of self-evaluation, and substitute self-enhancing opportunities (as when labeling results in attenuation of the subject's relationship with the very membership groups that induced pervasive self-devaluing attitudes, symbolizes his opposition to the normative expectations that were the basis of failure, or provided a deviant identity that was self-enhancing insofar as it evoked positive responses from selected others)
3. The continuity of the deviant pattern insofar as labeling influences the net self-enhancing or self-devaluing consequences of the deviant pattern, the costs of reentry into normative membership groups, and thereby the opportunities to take advantage of newly available self-protective or self-enhancing mechanisms

However, the implications of the labeling perspective have not been incorporated beyond these levels of abstraction and have not been formulated as testable propositions.

In any case, the theoretical structure that guided the study reported in this volume would appear to reflect aspects of all three of the perspectives considering the relationship between self-concept and deviance—structural interactionism, the socialization-control perspectives, and the labeling perspectives—whether or not the process of developing this synthesis was consciously influenced by an awareness of these perspectives.

Having established what may well be the historic roots of the guiding theoretical framework, the discussion turns now to a summary of the research findings reported in Chapters 3–7, and an evaluation of the compatibility of the findings with the statement of the general theory of deviant behavior outlined in Chapter 1.

Review and Evaluation

A basic premise of the theory guiding this investigation asserts that, universally, a characteristic motive of the person is to achieve, maintain, or restore a subjectively acceptable level of self-esteem. A number of specific hypotheses based on implications of the postulated self-esteem motive were tested and supported. Consistent with the postulate, it was observed that the mean self-derogation score among subjects present for all three testings decreased from the first to the second, and from the second to the third testings. Collateral evidence suggested that the decrease in self-rejection over time was to be accounted for by the subjects' own behaviors (presumably stimulated by the self-esteem motive), rather than by increasingly benign effects of the environment, or by maturation over the same time span. It was also observed that persons having initially more negative self-attitudes manifested significantly greater subsequent decreases in self-rejecting attitudes than subjects having initially less negative self-attitudes. This finding is in conformity with the expectation that subjects who are more highly motivated to restore or attain self-esteem would be more likely to behave in ways calculated to achieve acceptable levels of self-esteem. Analyses using residual gain scores and stability coefficients over variable time intervals suggested that the relatively greater decreases in self-derogation on the part of the initially more self-rejecting subjects could not be accounted for solely in terms of consequences of the measurement process. Rather, they reflected true changes presumably influenced by the greater intensity of the self-esteem motive among those subjects. Arguing that initially more self-rejecting individuals, insofar as they are more motivated to achieve greater self-esteem, would be quicker to respond with self-protective responses to self-devaluing circumstances and would be more sensitive to the self-devaluing implications of life events, it was anticipated and observed that antecedent level of self-rejection was related to subsequent instability of self-attitudes. The observed tendency for subjects to endorse socially desirable self-descriptions and to deny socially disvalued self-descriptions was consistent with the postulated prevalence of the self-esteem motive, whether the observed tendencies were taken to reflect successful striving for qualities and behaviors that would earn self-approval, unconscious perceptual distortion toward the goal of avoiding self-rejection, or conscious dissimulation toward the end of presenting a favorable image to others, thereby evoking positive attitudinal responses from them. Since, according to the postulate of the self-esteem motive, an unacceptable level of self-esteem would constitute a subjectively distressful state, it was hypothesized that self-rejecting attitudes would be associated with subsequent experience of each of 16 indicators of subjective distress. As anticipated, increasingly greater antecedent levels of self-rejection were related to subsequent reports of symptoms among subjects who had denied the symptoms earlier. Finally, also compatible with the implication of the postulated prevalence of the self-esteem motive that people who are more highly motivated to reduce feelings of self-rejection would be most likely to adopt self-protective responses calculated to forestall or reduce the adverse effects of self-devaluing experiences, antecedent level of self-rejection was observed to be related to the subsequent adoption of each of several apparently self-protective responses. Among persons who had denied performing the responses in question earlier, initially more self-derogating persons were significantly more likely subsequently to affirm items indicative of revised self-expectations, justification of disvalued attributes and behaviors, dissemblance, devaluation of the basis for self-rejection, avoidance of the basis for self-rejection, and substitution of new relationships and values offering greater promise than earlier ones of self-enhancing experiences. Thus, these findings together lend a good deal of support to the conclusion that people tend to need acceptable levels of self-esteem. This is not to say, however, that they will ultimately gain an acceptable level of self-esteem. So long as the same conditions that led to self-rejecting attitudes continue to hold, limits will be placed on the extent to which the subjects will be able to gain self-acceptance within the context of the normative environment. Although all of the hypotheses were supported, the magnitudes of association observed were less than optimal. To be sure, part of the explanation for less than perfect associations relate to measurement error. In addition, the circumstance reflects the need for further specification of the conditions under which the relationship will be observed. Thus, although the data are quite compatible with the postulated prevalence of the self-esteem motive, its unconditional prevalence has yet to be demonstrated. At the present time, it may be asserted that empirical support for the range of hypotheses implied by the postulate is *compatible* with the assertaion that, universally, people ordinarily seek to attain, maintain, or restore feelings of self-acceptance and seek to avoid the experience of self-rejecting attitudes.

According to the general theory of deviant behavior outlined in Chapter 1, the inability to satisfy the self-esteem motive is attributable to three analytically distinguishable but mutually influential sets of membership group experiences: self-perceptions of failure to possess personally valued attributes or to perform personally valued behaviors; self-perceptions of failure to be the object of positive attitudes by personally valued others; and failure to possess and employ self-protective response mechanisms that preclude the experience, or mitigate the effects, of the first two sets of experiences.

The findings in the present study were consistent with the theoretical formulation. With regard to the first set of factors, it was observed that among subjects who judged a set of qualities or behaviors to be important, those who described themselves at T_1 as not possessing the important quality or not performing the personally valued behavior tended to be more self-rejecting 1 year and 2 years later, and to display relatively greater residual increases in self-derogation between T_1 and T_2, than subjects who described themselves as possessing the quality or behavior in question. With reference to the second set of experiences, subjects who were "high" on measures of perceived devaluation by peers, family, school, and membership groups in general, and on perceived devaluation by others because of specified ascribed characteristics at an earlier point in time, compared to subjects who were "low" on these measures, manifested higher self-derogation scores both 1 and 2 years later (at T_2 and T_3, respectively), and showed greater residual gains between T_1 and T_2 in self-derogation. Thus the data provided clear support for the expectation that the subjectively perceived expression of negative attitudes toward the subject by others would be related to higher future levels of, and greater future increases in, self-derogation. With regard to the third set of determinants of self-rejecting attitudes (that is, failure to set aside the self-esteem motive), the findings again supported the expectation that self-protective attitudes would influence level of self-acceptance. Interpreting the index of defenselessness/vulnerability as reflecting the absence of effective/socially acceptable patterns for the avoidance or mitigation of self-rejecting feelings, the index of avoidance of personal responsibility as reflecting the adoption of ineffective/deviant attempts to forestall or mitigate self-rejecting feelings, and the index of guilt deflection as reflecting the adoption of effective/socially acceptable patterns in order to forestall or assuage the experience of self-rejecting feelings, it was hypothesized that high scores on the first two variables and low scores on the third variable at T_1 would be related to significantly higher self-derogation scores 1 and 2 years later (at T_2 and T_3, respectively) and to significantly greater residual increases in self-derogation between T_1 and T_2. All hypotheses were supported. The results, then, were consistent with the theoretical formulation regarding determinants of self-attitudes. The ability to demonstrate these relationships is somewhat surprising. By the time subjects have reached the early adolescent years, one might have thought that the independent variables under consideration would already have influenced self-attitudes as much as they were able. Again, the results must be interpreted with caution. Although the findings with regard to subsequent residual gains in self-attitudes are more compelling, the relationship between antecedent influences on self-attitudes and subsequent levels of self-derogation may have been confounded by the implications of the relationship between earlier levels of self-attitudes and later levels of self-attitudes with regard to the temporal ordering of the relationship between self-attitudes and the presumed determinants of the self-attitudes. In any case, the total pattern of results is highly consistent with the theoretical formulation regarding the bases of self-devaluation.

The theoretical formulation specifies that, given the self-esteem motive in conjunction with the development of negative self-attitudes in the course of membership group experiences, individuals will be disposed to seek deviant alternatives to newly disvalued normative patterns in order to satisfy the self-esteem motive. In support of this formulation, data were reported that indicated that higher antecedent levels of, and greater antecedent increases in, self-rejecting attitudes anticipate subsequent adoption of a broad range of essentially uncorrelated deviant behaviors among persons who had previously denied performance of the deviant behaviors. The antecedent increases in self-rejection were associated with adoption of deviant patterns, whether the pattern once adopted was continued or discontinued. Further support for the premise was provided by the observation that the relationship between earlier level of self-rejection and subsequent adoption of deviant responses was more consistently and strongly observed for those segments of the population (higher socioeconomic stratum, females) for whom it could be more easily assumed that the indicators of deviant behavior constituted violations of normative codes.

The theoretical formulation, furthermore, specifies the factors that mediate the relationship between antecedent self-derogation and subsequent adoption of deviant patterns. Persons characterized by negative self-attitudes (said to be the consequence of their history of being unable to defend against self-devaluing experiences in their membership groups) come increasingly to perceive an association between their negative self-attitudes and their membership group experiences. As a result of having perceived and generalized an association between actual membership group experiences and the genesis of subjectively distressful negative self-attitudes, these persons come increasingly to associate the membership group patterns with negative feelings, by virtue of which these people are said to lose motivation to conform to and acquire motivation to deviate from the normative structure. At the same time, persons characterized by negative self-attitudes experience intensification of the need to enhance their self-attitudes by virtue of the continuing failure of the normative structure to provide motivationally acceptable response patterns that would serve this need. In view of the inability to satisfy the self-esteem motive by the use of now motivationally unacceptable normative response patterns, persons characterized by negative self-attitudes will seek, become aware of, and adopt alternative deviant response patterns. Implicit in this formulation are four general intervening factors: subjective association of the normative environment with self-devaluing experiences, attitudes toward the normative environment, the experience of the self-esteem motive, and a tendency to seek alternative deviant response patterns. To test this formulation, it was hypothesized that initial level of self-derogation would be associated with subsequent residual gains in one or more of the indicators of each of the four intervening factors. It was further hypothesized that, among subjects who denied performance of the deviant acts prior to T_1, the score on each of the indicators of the four general factors would be related to subsequent reports of each of the range of deviant acts. Although exceptions were noted, the results were consistent with the expectations. Subjects with initially low, medium, and high levels of self-derogation showed, over the next year, correspondingly greater residual increases in (a) perception of self-devaluing experiences in a peer group, (b)

perception of self-devaluing experiences in the family, and (c) perception of self-devaluing experiences in the school. They also showed similar increases in the tendency to devalue the normative structure and to value contranormative patterns positively as potential sources of gratification; decreases in the tendency to view the normative structure as having self-enhancing potential; increases in the experience of defenselessness/vulnerability; increases in attempts to avoid personal responsibility for self-devaluing experiences through the use of ineffective or deviant response patterns; decreases in guilt deflection—that is, the use of a range of socially acceptable self-protective mechanisms toward the goal of forestalling or reducing the experience of self-rejecting feelings; and increases in awareness of deviant alternatives in the environment. In like manner, the anticipated relationships between scores on each of these indicators and subsequent adoption of deviant response patterns was generally observed, although some of these indicators reflected circumstances that predisposed the person to adopt specific modes of deviance as well as reflecting the general factors said to intervene between negative self-attitudes and adoption of deviant response patterns.

Given the adoption of deviant response patterns by highly self-rejecting persons, and given the emotional rejection of the normative membership groups associated with the genesis of negative self-attitudes, which in the past had been unable to provide the subject with self-enhancing or self-protective mechanisms, it was expected that the adopted deviant patterns would function as alternative sources of self-enhancement. Generally, these expectations were met. Highly self-rejecting subjects who reported each of 28 deviant occurrences over the period T_1-T_2 were compared with similar highly self-rejecting subjects who denied the occurrence of each of the deviant acts over the same period, with regard to subsequent (T_2-T_3) decreases in self-derogation beyond those that could have been predicted linearly from knowledge of the self-derogation score at T_2. Since there was reason to suspect that theoretical preconditions for testing the hypothesis were not uniformly present among the highly self-rejecting subjects, the hypothesis was tested for different subgroups variously defined in terms of indicators of the theoretical preconditions. One such precondition was the inability of individuals to satisfy the self-esteem motive in the context of their normative membership groups. A second precondition was the subjective definition of the acts under consideration as deviant. A third precondition was the emotional rejection of the normative membership groups by the highly self-rejecting subjects, which would have as a consequence (among others), decreased vulnerability to membership group sanctions consequent upon adoption of deviant response patterns. Where the analyses were carried out for subgroups of the highly self-rejecting subjects who appeared to fulfill these conditions, the adoption of any of several of the deviant patterns was associated with subsequent decreases in self-rejecting attitudes.

Highly self-rejecting subjects who were unable to utilize normative patterns to reduce feelings of self-rejection and who were less likely to be vulnerable to adverse consequences of adopting alternative deviant patterns in the service of the self-esteem motive (that is, high-defenselessness males) were reasonably consistent in displaying an association between antecedent performance of deviant responses and subsequent reduction in self-rejecting attitudes. Similarly, highly self-rejecting subjects who could be expected to define the act under consideration as deviant and who, again, were less likely to be vulnerable to negative sanctions from self and others as a result of adopting the deviant patterns (that is, males who perceived the self-enhancing potential of the normative environment as high) were reasonably consistent in displaying an association between antecedent deviant responses and subsequent reduction in self-derogation. However, even within the categories of subjects defined as fulfilling the theoretical preconditions, several deviant patterns were not associated with subsequent reduction in self-rejecting attitudes. The absence of uniformity suggests either that all theoretical preconditions were not empirically fulfilled for the subjects for whom the hypothesis was tested, or that all of the theoretical preconditions were not specified. In any case, the degree of consistency that was observed in the groups defined in terms of the theoretical preconditions suggests support for the basic theoretical structure.

As a whole, although the results of the analyses are highly compatible with central features of the theoretical structure, much of the variance in self-attitudes and deviant behavior remains to be explained. This does not gainsay the value of the observed results in validating the outline of the general theory of deviant behavior that guided the analyses. Indeed the consistency of the results with the theoretical structure is in many ways quite remarkable. However, the relatively small portion of the variance accounted for does indicate the need for further specification of the theoretical conditions under which the mutual influences of self-attitudes and deviant behavior will be observed and for research processes that are appropriate to the testing of these specifications.

Implications for Future Research and Theoretical Development

Although the results that have been reported confirm in a significant but limited way the usefulness of the general theory of deviant behavior, these results also have clear implications for future research and theoretical development. Further research is necessary to confirm these results on the same population, to determine the generalizability of the theory to other populations, and to test yet untested propositions that represent components of the theoretical structure. The results of this study also made clear the need for theoretical developments in other areas and, where some development has occurred, amplification of theoretical conditions.

The research described was limited in a number of ways. The subjects were selected from a narrow age-range and from an in-school population. The degree to which the results may appropriately be generalized to other ages and to subjects who dropped out of school is problematic. Similarly, we can only speculate about how other sources of sample attrition may have affected the nature of the observed relationships. These issues must await resolution by the results of other research on more inclusive and stable populations.

Another limitation relates to the determination that theoretically specified conditions that are presumed to hold in the population under investigation do in fact hold. In future research attention must be paid to the threshold of self-derogation that is presumably antecedent to deviant responses in absolute as well as relative terms. Future research must more consciously establish the personal meaning of acts with regard to their deviant or nondeviant character. If the theoretical basis for anticipating a relationship between antecedent self-attitudes and subsequent adoption of deviant responses requires establishment of the subjects' conscious or unconscious perception of the deviant or non-deviant nature of the act, then this should be more clearly established than it was in the present study. In like manner, the satisfaction of other theoretical conditions must be more clearly established. The indicators of absence of normative self-protective or self-enhancing mechanisms and of vulnerability to adverse consequences of adopting deviant responses used in this study were ambiguous.

Although the project permitted the evaluation of a number of segments of the theoretical structure, other segments remain untested. Does the experience of self-enhancing consequences of deviance in fact confirm a person in the deviant pattern? Will a person who experiences self-devaluing consequences of one mode of deviance adopt alternate *deviant* patterns? These questions and others implicit in the theoretical formulation also await future consideration.

Although the theoretical structure guiding this research was explicit with regard to a number of relationships, other relationships were stated at such an abstract level that they could not be tested. Self-rejecting attitudes might be expected to increase the likelihood of subsequent adoption of any of a range of deviant behaviors, but what are the precise personal and social structural conditions that increase the probability of one rather than another mode of deviant responses? The specific answers to this question were barely hinted at in this volume. Although the adoption of deviant responses by self-rejecting subjects might generally be expected to evoke self-enhancing consequences, what specific deviant patterns in interaction with what personal and social structural conditions are more likely to evoke such consequences? In this connection, where deviant patterns may be expected to eventuate in the reduction

229

of negative self-attitudes, through what specific *mechanisms* may particular modes of deviance in combination with specified personal qualities and situational contingencies be expected to have this consequence? What are the characteristics of the deviant act itself with regard to visibility, periodicity, whether or not it is normally performed in the company of others, and other dimensions that influence the likelihood of self-enhancing or self-devaluing outcomes?

In need of theoretical development are specifications regarding the social structural, interpersonal situational, and personal factors influencing the probability of self-perceptions of positively or negatively valued attributes and behaviors, self-perceptions of evoking positive or negative attitudinal responses from significant others, and the development of variably efficient self-protective mechanisms—those variables that most clearly impinge on the genesis of characteristically positive or negative self-attitudes. Also required are specifications regarding the factors influencing the visibility and net self-enhancing or self-devaluing outcomes of deviant responses.

These questions also require theoretical amplification. Under what conditions will confirmation occur and under what conditions will deviant respones be self-limiting? Will the experience of increased self-acceptance associated with the adoption of deviant patterns under certain circumstances so increase the deviant actor's feelings of competence that he is now willing to attempt to gain self-acceptance by the achievement of normatively defined goals through socially acceptable instrumental patterns? Or, as Hewitt (1970) suggested, will the continuity of deviant patterns that render the person vulnerable to continuing self-devaluing experiences be interrupted by the arrival, with maturity, of new opportunities to gain personal satisfactions by entering into new roles in heterosexual, familial, and occupational spheres?

In short, although the theoretical statement, as it has been developed up to this point, has been supported in many of its aspects by the research findings reported in this volume, many of the testable propositions comprising the theory remain to be evaluated against empirical observation, and strong indications for further theoretical amplification are apparent. However, the theoretical structure that guided this research, centering as it does around the reciprocal relationship between self-attitudes and deviant behavior, continues to show promise as a device for integrating existing research, providing a framework for incorporating systematically related tested and testable propositions, defining lacunae in research programs and the theoretical structure itself, and permitting a rapprochement between social structural, interpersonally situated, and personal levels of analysis in accounting for the disposition toward, adoption of, and continuity in diverse modes of deviant behavior.

References

Ageton, S. S., & Elliott, D. S. The effects of legal processing on delinquent orientations. *Social Problems*, 1974, 22, 87–100.

Archer, D. Power in groups: Self-concept changes of powerful and powerless group members. *Journal of Applied Behavioral Science*, 1974, 10(2), 208–220.

Arieti, S. Some elements of cognitive psychiatry. *American Journal of Psychotherapy*, 1967, 124, 723–736.

Aronson, E., & Mettee, D. R. Dishonest behavior as a function of differential levels of induced self-esteem. *Journal of Personality and Social Psychology*, 1968, 9, 121–127.

Bachman, J. G. *Youth in transition, Vol. 2: The impact of family background and intelligence on tenth-grade boys.* Ann Arbor, Mich.: Institute for Social Research, 1970.

Bachman, J. G., Green, S., & Wirtanen, I. *Youth in transition, Vol. 3: Dropping out—Problem or symptom?* Ann Arbor, Mich.: Institute for Social Research, 1971.

Bachman, J. G., Kahn, R. L., Mednick, M. T., Davidson, T. N., & Johnston, L. D. *Youth in transition, Vol. 1: Blueprint for a longitudinal study of adolescent boys.* Ann Arbor, Mich.: Institute for Social Research, 1967.

Bachman, J. G., & O'Malley, P. M. Self-esteem in young men: A longitudinal analysis of the impact of educational and occupational attainment. *Personality and Social Psychology*, 1977, 35 (6), 365–380.

Baron, P. H. Self-esteem, ingratiation, and evaluation of unknown others. *Journal of Personality and Social Psychology*, 1974, 30, 104–109.

Becker, E. *The birth and death of meaning: A perspective in psychiatry and anthropology.* New York: Free Press, 1962.

Becker, H. S. *Outsiders: Studies in the sociology of deviance.* New York: Free Press, 1963.

Beller, E. K., & Neubauer, P. B. Sex differences and symptom patterns in early childhood. *Journal of the American Academy of Child Psychiatry*, 1963, 2, 414–433.

Bennett, E. M., & Cohen, L. R. Men and women: Personality patterns and contrast. *Genetic Psychology Monographs*, 1959, 59, 101–155.

Berg, N. L. Effects of alcohol intoxication on self-concept. *Quarterly Journal of Studies on Alcohol*, 1971, 32, 442–453.

Berkowitz, L. Experimental investigations of hostility catharsis. *Journal of Consulting and Clinical Psychology*, 1970, 35, 1–7.

References

Bogo, N., Winget, C., & Gleser, G. Ego defenses and perceptual styles. *Perceptual and Motor Skills*, 1970, *30*, 599–604.

Bohrnstedt, G. W. Observations on the measurement of change. In E. F. Borgatta & G. W. Bohrnstedt (Eds.), *Sociological methodology 1969*. San Francisco: Jossey-Bass, 1969.

Braaten, L. J., & Darling, C. D. Suicidal tendencies among college students. *Psychiatric Quarterly*, 1962, *36*, 665–692.

Brownfain, J. Stability of the self-concept as a dimension of personality. *Journal of Abnormal Psychology*, 1952, *47*, 597–606.

Burke, E. L., & Eichberg, R. H. Personality characteristics of adolescent users of dangerous drugs as indicated by the Minnesota Multiphasic Personality Inventory. *Journal of Nervous and Mental Disease*, 1972, *154*, 291–298.

Buss, A. H., Brock, T. C. Repression and guilt in relation to aggression. *Journal of Abnormal and Social Psychology*, 1963, *66*, 345–350.

Chamblis, W. The negative self: An empirical assessment of a theoretical assumption. *Sociological Inquiry*, 1964, *34*, 108–112.

Chapman, I. Role and self-concept assessments of delinquents and nondelinquents. *Sociological Quarterly*, 1966, *7*, 373–379.

Clark, J. P., & Tifft, L.L. Polygraph and interview validation of self-reported deviant behavior. *American Sociological Review*, 1966, *31*, 516–523.

Clifford, E., & Clifford, M. Self-concepts before and after survival training. *British Journal of Social and Clinical Psychology*, 1967, *6*, 241–248.

Coelho, G. V., Hamburg, D. A., & Adams, J. E. (Eds.). *Coping and adaptation*. New York: Basic Books, 1974.

Coghlan, A. J., & Gold, S. R. Self-destructive behavior in female adolescent addicts. *American Journal of Orthopsychiatry*, 1974, *44*, 252–253.·

Cohen, A. K. *Delinquent boys*. Glencoe, Ill.: Free Press, 1955.

Cohen, A. K. The sociology of the deviant act: Anomie theory and beyond. *American Sociological Review*, 1965, *30*, 5–14.

Cohen, A. K. *Deviance and control*. Englewood Cliffs, N.J.: Prentice-Hall, 1966.

Cohen, A. K., & Short, J. Juvenile delinquency. In R. K. Merton & R. A. Nisbet (Eds.), *Contemporary social problems* (2nd ed.). New York: Harcourt, Brace and World, 1966.

Consentino, F., & Heilbrun, A. B. Anxiety correlates of sex-role identity in college students. *Psychological Reports*, 1964, *14*, 729–730.

Coopersmith, S. *The antecedents of self-esteem*. San Francisco: W. H. Freeman, 1967.

Cronbach, L. J., & Furby, L. How we should measure "change"—Or should we? *Psychological Bulletin*, 1970, *74*, 68–80.

Crowne, D. P., & Stephens, M. W. Self-acceptance and self-evaluative behavior: A critique of methodology. *Psychological Bulletin*, 1961, *58*, 104–121.

Davidson, H. H., & Gottlieb, L. The emotional maturity of pre- and post-menarcheal girls. *Journal of Genetic Psychology*, 1955, *86*, 261–266.

Davidson, H. H., & Lang, G. Children's perceptions of teachers' feelings toward them related to self-perception, scholastic achievement, and behavior. *Journal of Experimental Education*, 1960, *29*, 107–118.

Davidson, T. N. *Youth in transition*, Vol. 4: *Evolution of a strategy for longitudinal analysis of survey panel data*. Ann Arbor, Mich.: Institute for Social Research, 1972.

De Fundia, T. A., Draguns, J. G., & Phillips, L. Culture and psychiatric symptomatology: A comparison of Argentine and United States patients. *Social Psychiatry*, 1971, *6*, 11–20.

Deitz, G. E. A comparison of delinquents with nondelinquents on self-concept, self-acceptance, and parental identification. *Journal of Genetic Psychology*, 1969, *115*, 285–295.

DeLamater, J. On the nature of deviance. *Social Forces*, 1968, *46*, 445–455.

References

Diller, L. Conscious and unconscious self-attitudes after success and failure. *Journal of Personality*, 1954, *23*, 1-12.

Dittes, J. E. Attractiveness of group as a function of self-esteem and acceptance by group. *Journal of Abnormal and Social Psychology*, 1959, *59*, 77-82. (a)

Dittes, J. E. Effect of changes in self-esteem upon impulsiveness and deliberation in making judgments. *Journal of Abnormal and Social Psychology*, 1959, *58*, 348-356. (b)

Douvan, E., & Adelson, J. The psychodynamics of social mobility in adolescent boys. *Journal of Abnormal and Social Psychology*, 1958, *56*, 31-44.

Douvan, E., & Adelson, J. *The adolescent experience*. New York: Wiley, 1966.

Eisen, M. Characteristic self-esteem, sex and resistance to temptation. *Journal of Personality and Social Psychology*, 1972, *24*, 68-72.

Engel, M. The stability of the self-concept in adolescence. *Journal of Abnormal Psychology*, 1959, *58*, 211-215.

Erickson, M. L., & Empey, L. T. Court records, undetected delinquency and decision-making. *Journal of Criminal Law, Criminology and Police Science*, 1963, *54*, 458-459.

Exline, R. V. Effects of need for affiliation, sex, and the sight of others upon initial communications in problem-solving groups. *Journal of Personality*, 1962, *30*, 541-556.

Farberow, N. L. Personality patterns of suicidal mental hospital patients. *Genetic Psychology Monographs*, 1950, *42*.

Farnham-Diggory, S. Self-evaluation and subjective life expectancy among suicidal and nonsuicidal psychotic males. *Journal of Abnormal and Social Psychology*, 1964, *69*, 628-634.

Farrington, D. P. Self-reports of deviant behavior: Predictive and stable? *Journal of Criminal Law and Criminology*, 1973, *64*, 99-110.

Feldman, H. W. Ideological supports to becoming and remaining a heroin addict. *Journal of Health and Social Behavior*, 1968, *9*, 131-139.

Fine, B. *1,000,000 delinquents*. New York: World, 1955.

Fisher, S., & Mirin, S. Further validation of the special favorable responses occurring during unconscious self-evaluation. *Perceptual and Motor Skills*, 1966, *23*, 1097-1098.

Fishman, G. The paradoxical effect of labeling. *International Journal of Criminology and Penology*, 1976, *4*, 1-7.

Frankel, A. S. Attitudes toward a group as a function of self-esteem, group achievement level, and success or failure on a group-relevant task. *Proceedings of the 77th Annual Convention of the American Psychological Association*, 1969, *4*, 351-352.

Freemesser, G. F., & Kaplan, H. B. Self-attitudes and deviant behavior: The case of the charismatic religious movement. *Journal of Youth and Adolescence*, 1976, *5*, 1-9.

French, J. R. P. The conceptualization and measurement of mental health in terms of self-identity. In S. B. Sells (Ed.), *The definition and measurement of mental health*. Washington, D.C.: DHEW, Public Health Service, Health Services and Mental Health Administration, National Center for Health Statistics, 1968.

Gibby, R. G., Sr., & Gibby, R. G., Jr. The effects of stress resulting from academic failure. *Journal of Clinical Psychology*, 1967, *23* (January), 35-37.

Gibson, H. B., Morrison, S., & West D. J. The confession of known offenses in response to a self-reported delinquency schedule. *British Journal of Criminology*, 1970, *10*, 278.

Glaser, K. Attempted suicide in children and adolescents: Psychodynamic observations. *American Journal of Psychotherapy*, 1965, *19*, 220-227.

Gleser, G. C., & Ihilevich, D. An objective instrument for measuring defense mechanisms. *Journal of Consulting and Clinical Psychology*, 1969, *33*, 51-60.

Gold, M. Undetected delinquent behavior. *Journal of Research in Crime and Delinquency*, 1966, *3*, 30.

Gold, M. *Delinquent behavior in an American city*. Belmont, Calif.: Brooks/Cole, 1970.

Gold, M. Scholastic experiences, self-esteem and delinquent behavior: A theory for alternative schools. *Crime and Delinquency*, 1978, *24* (July), 290–308.

Gold, M., & Mann, D. Delinquency as defense. *American Journal of Orthopsychiatry*, 1972, *42*, 463–479.

Goldfried, M. R. Feelings of inferiority and the depreciation of others: A research review and theoretical reformulation. *Journal of Individual Psychology*, 1963, *19*, 27–48.

Goodman, L., & Kruskal, W. Measures of association for cross-classifications, I. *Journal of the American Statistical Association*, 1954, *49*, 732–764.

Goodman, L., & Kruskal, W. Measures of association for cross-classifications, III: Approximate sampling theory. *Journal of the American Statistical Association*, 1963, *58*, (302), 322ff.

Gordon, R. A., Short, J. F., Cartwright, D. S., & Strodtbeck, F. L. Values and gang delinquency: A study of street-corner groups. *American Journal of Sociology*, 1963, *69*, 109–128.

Gough, H. G., & Peterson, D. R. The identification and measurement of predispositional factors in crime and delinquency. *Journal of Consulting Psychology*, 1952, *15*, 207–212.

Gould, R. E. Suicide problems in children and adolescents. *American Journal of Psychotherapy*, 1965, *19*, 228–246.

Graf, R. G. Induced self-esteem as a determinant of behavior. *Journal of Social Psychology*, 1971, *85*, 213–217.

Grosser, G. H. *Juvenile delinquency and contemporary American sex roles*. Unpublished doctoral dissertation, Harvard University, 1951.

Gunderson, E. K. Body size, self-evaluation, and military effectiveness. *Journal of Personality and Social Psychology*, 1965, *2* (December), 902–906.

Gunderson, E. K., & Johnson, L. C. Past experience, self-evaluation, and present adjustment. *Journal of Social Psychology*, 1965, *66*, 311–321.

Hall, P. M. Identification with the delinquent subculture and level of self-evaluation. *Sociometry*, 1966, *29*, 146–158.

Hammersmith, S. K., & Weinberg, M. S. Homosexual identity: Commitment, adjustment, and significant others. *Sociometry*, 1973, *36*(1), 56–79.

Harrow, M., Fox, D. A., Markhus, K. I., Stillman, R., & Hallowell, C. B. Changes in adolescents' self-concepts and their parents' perceptions during psychiatric hospitalization. *Journal of Nervous and Mental Disease*, 1968, *147*, 252–259.

Hattem, J. V. Precipitating role of discordant interpersonal relationships in suicidal behavior. *Dissertation Abstracts*, 1964, *25*, 1335–1336.

Havener, P. H., & Izard, C. E. Unrealistic self-enhancement in paranoid schizophrenics. *Journal of Consulting Psychology*, 1962, *26*, 65–68.

Hess, A. L., & Bradshaw, H. L. Positiveness of self-concept and ideal self as a function of age. *Journal of Genetic Psychology*, 1970, *117*, 57–67.

Hewitt, J. P. *Social stratification and deviant behavior*. New York: Random House, 1970.

Hirschi, T. *Causes of delinquency*. Berkeley: University of California Press, 1969.

Hoffman, M. Drug addiction and "hypersexuality" related modes of mastery. *Comprehensive Psychiatry*, 1964, *5*, 262–270.

Hokanson, J. E., & Burgess, M. The effects of three types of aggression on vascular processes. *Journal of Abnormal and Social Psychology*, 1962, *64*, 446–449.

Hokanson, J. E., Burgess, M., & Cohen, F. Effects of displaced aggression on systolic blood pressure. *Journal of Abnormal and Social Psychology*, 1963, *67*, 214–218.

Hokanson, J. E., & Edelman, R. Effects of three social responses on vascular processes. *Journal of Personality and Social Psychology*, 1966, *3*, 442–447.

Horney, K. *Neurosis and human growth*. New York: Norton, 1950.

Horowitz, F. D. The relationship of anxiety, self-concept and sociometric status among fourth, fifth and sixth grade children. *Journal of Abnormal and Social Psychology*, 1962, *65*, 212–214.

References

Horowitz, M. The veridicality of liking and disliking. In R. Tagiuri & L. Petrullo (Eds.), *Person perception and interpersonal behavior.* Stanford, Calif.: Stanford University Press, 1958. Pp. 191–209.

Hulbary, W. E. Race, deprivation, and adolescent self-images. *Social Science Quarterly,* 1975, 56(1), 105–114.

Hunt, J. G., & Hunt, L. L. Racial inequality and self-image: Identity maintenance as identity diffusion. *Sociology and Social Research,* 1977, 61(4), 539–559.

Ibelle, B. P. Discrepancies between self-concepts in paranoid schizophrenics and normals. *Dissertation Abstracts,* 1961, 21, 2004–2005.

Isenberg, P., Schnitzer, R., & Rothman, S. Psychological variables in student activism: The radical triad and some religious differences. *Journal of Youth and Adolescence,* 1977, 6, 11–24.

Jacques, J. M., & Chason, K. J. Self-esteem and low status groups: A changing scene? *Sociological Quarterly,* 1977, 18, 399–412.

Jensen, G. F. Inner containment and delinquency. *Journal of Criminal Law and Criminology,* 1973, 64, 464–470.

Jessor, R., Carman, R. S., Grossman, P. H. Expectations for need satisfaction and patterns of alcohol use in college. In G. Maddox (Ed.), *Domesticated drug: Drinking among collegians.* New Haven, Conn.: New Haven College and University Press, 1970.

Jessor, R., Graves, R. D., Hanson, R. C., & Jessor, S. L. *Society, personality and deviant behavior.* New York: Holt, Rinehart and Winston, 1968.

Jessor, R., Jessor, S. L., & Finney, J. A social psychology of marijuana use: Longitudinal studies of high school and college youth. *Journal of Personality and Social Psychology,* 1973, 26, 1–15.

Johnson, H. H. Some effects of discrepancy level on responses to negative information about one's self. *Sociometry,* 1966, 29 (March), 52–66.

Jones, M. D. The later careers of boys who were early- or late-maturing. *Child Development,* 1965, 36, 899–911.

Jones, M. D. Personality correlates and antecedents of drinking patterns in adult males. *Journal of Consulting and Clinical Psychology,* 1968, 32, 2–12.

Jones, M. D. Personality antecedents and correlates of drinking patterns in women. *Journal of Consulting and Clinical Psychology,* 1971, 36, 61–69.

Jorgensen, E. C., & Howell, R. J. Changes in self, ideal-self correlations from ages 3 through 18. *Journal of Social Psychology,* 1969, 79, 63–67.

Kaplan, E. A. Homosexuality—A search for the ego-ideal. *Archives of General Psychiatry,* 1967, 16, 355–358.

Kaplan, H. B. Self-derogation and adjustment to recent life experiences. *Archives of General Psychiatry,* 1970, 22, 324–331. (a)

Kaplan, H. B. Self-derogation and childhood family structure. *Journal of Nervous and Mental Disease,* 1970, 151, 13–23. (b)

Kaplan, H. B. Age-related correlates of self-derogation: Contemporary life space characteristics. *Aging and Human Development,* 1971, 2, 305–313. (a)

Kaplan, H. B. Social class and self-derogation: A conditional relationship. *Sociometry,* 1971, 34, 41–65. (b)

Kaplan, H. B. *The sociology of mental illness.* New Haven, Conn.: New Haven College and University Press, 1972. (a)

Kaplan, H. B. Toward a general theory of psychosocial deviance: The case of aggressive behavior. *Social Science and Medicine,* 1972, 6, 593–617. (b)

Kaplan, H. B. Self-derogation and social position: Interaction effects of sex, race, education, and age. *Social Psychiatry,* 1973, 8, 92–99.

Kaplan, H. B. Increase in self-rejection as an antecedent of deviant responses. *Journal of Youth and Adolescence,* 1975, 4, 281–292. (a)

References

Kaplan, H. B. *Self-attitudes and deviant behavior.* Pacific Palisades, Calif.: Goodyear, 1975. (b)

Kaplan, H. B. The self-esteem motive and change in self-attitudes. *Journal of Nervous and Mental Disease,* 1975, *161,* 265–275. (c)

Kaplan, H. B. Sequelae of self-derogation: Predicting from a general theory of deviant behavior. *Youth and Society,* 1975, 7(2), 171–197. (d)

Kaplan, H. B. Antecedents of negative self-attitudes: Membership group devaluation and defenselessness. *Social Psychiatry,* 1976, *11*(2), 15–25. (a)

Kaplan, H. B. Self-attitudes and deviant response. *Social Forces,* 1976, *54,* 788–801. (b)

Kaplan, H. B. Antecedents of deviant responses: Predicting from a general theory of deviant behavior. *Journal of Youth and Adolescence,* 1977, 6(1), 89–101. (a)

Kaplan, H. B. Gender and depression: A sociological analysis of a conditional relationship. In W. E. Fann, A. D. Pokorny, I. Karacan, & R. L. Williams (Eds.), *Phenomenology and treatment of depression.* New York: Spectrum, 1977. (b) Pp. 81–113.

Kaplan, H. B. Increase in self-rejection and continuing/discontinued deviant response. *Journal of Youth and Adolescence,* 1977, 6(1), 77–87. (c)

Kaplan, H. B. Deviant behavior and self-enhancement in adolescence. *Journal of Youth and Adolescence,* 1978: 7(3), 253–277. (a)

Kaplan, H. B. Self-attitudes and schizophrenia. In W. E. Fann, I. Karacan, A. D. Pokorny, & R. L. Williams (Eds.), *Phenomenology and treatment of schizophrenia.* New York: Spectrum, 1978. (b) Pp. 241–287.

Kaplan, H. B. Social class, self-derogation, and deviant response. *Social Psychiatry,* 1978, *13,* 19–28. (c)

Kaplan, H. B., Boyd, I., & Bloom, S. W. Patient culture and the evaluation of self. *Psychiatry,* 1964, 7, 116–126.

Kaplan, H. B., & Meyerowitz, J. H. The community's response to substance misuse: Integrated community approach in the rehabilitation of narcotic addicts. *The International Journal of Addictions,* 1969, 4(1), 65–76.

Kaplan, H. B., & Meyerowitz, J. H. Social and psychological correlates of drug abuse: A comparison of addict and non-addict populations from the perspective of self-theory. *Social Science and Medicine,* 1970, *4,* 203–225.

Kaplan, H. B., & Pokorny, A. D. Self-derogation and psychosocial adjustment. *Journal of Nervous and Mental Disease,* 1969, *149*(5), 421–434.

Kaplan, H. B., & Pokorny, A. D. Age-related correlates of self-derogation: Report of childhood experiences. *British Journal of Psychiatry,* 1970, *117,* 533. (a)

Kaplan, H. B., & Pokorny, A. D. Aging and self-attitude: A conditional relationship. *Aging and Human Development,* 1970, *1,* 241–250. (b)

Kaplan, H. B., & Pokorny, A. D. Self-derogation and childhood broken home. *Journal of Marriage and Family,* 1971, *33,* 328–338.

Kaplan, H. B., & Pokorny, A. D. Sex-related correlates of adult self-derogation: Reports of childhood experiences. *Developmental Psychology,* 1972, *6,* 536.

Katz, P. A., Zigler, E., & Zalk, S. R. Children's self-image disparity: The effects of age, maladjustment, and action–thought orientation. *Developmental Psychology,* 1975, *11*(5), 546–550.

Kitsuse, J. I. Societal reaction to deviant behavior: Problems of theory and method. *Social Problems,* 1962, *9,* 247–257.

Kitsuse, J. I. The new conception of deviance and its critics. In W. Gove (Ed.), *The labeling of deviance.* New York: Halsted, 1975. Pp. 273–284.

La Barba, R. C. The psychopath and anxiety—A reformulation. *Journal of Individual Psychology,* 1965, *21,* 167–170.

Landis, J. R., Dinitz, S., & Reckless, W. C. Implementing two theories of delinquency: Value orientation and awareness of limited opportunity. *Sociology and Social Research,* 1963, *47,* 408–416.

References

Lansky, L. M., Crandall, V. J., Kagan, J., & Baker, C. T. Sex differences in aggression and its correlates in middle-class adolescents. *Child Development,* 1961, *32,* 45–58.

Lemert, E. *Social pathology.* New York: McGraw-Hill, 1951.

Leon, C. A. Unusual patterns of criminals during La Violencia in Colombia. *American Journal of Psychiatry,* 1969, *125,* 1564–1575.

Leventhal, H., & Perloe, S. I. A relationship between self-esteem and persuasibility. *Journal of Abnormal and Social Psychology,* 1962, *64,* 385–388.

Levitin, T. A., & Chananie, J. D. Responses of female primary school teachers to sex-typed behaviors in male and female children. *Child Development,* 1972, *43,* 1309–1316.

Livson, N., & Peskin, H. Prediction of adult psychological health in a longitudinal study. *Journal of Abnormal Psychology,* 1967, *72,* 509–518.

Long, B. H., Henderson, E. H., & Ziller, R. C. Self-social correlates of originality in children. *Journal of Genetic Psychology,* 1967, *111,* 47–57.

Long, B. H., Ziller, R. C., & Bankes, J. Self–other orientations of institutionalized behavior-problem adolescents. *Journal of Consulting and Clinical Psychology,* 1970, *34,* 43–47.

Luck, P. W., & Heiss, J. Social determinants of self-esteem in adult males. *Sociology and Social Research,* 1972, *57,* 69–84.

Ludwig, D. J., & Maehr, M. L. Changes in self-concept and stated behavioral preferences. *Child Development,* 1967, *38,* 453–467.

Maccoby, E. E. (Ed.). *The development of sex differences.* Stanford, Calif.: Stanford University Press, 1966.

Maccoby, E. E., & Jacklin, C. N. *The psychology of sex differences.* Stanford, Calif.: Stanford University Press, 1974.

Maddox, G. L. Drinking among Negroes: Inference from the drinking patterns of selected Negro male collegians. *Journal of Health and Social Behavior,* 1968, *9,* 114–120.

Maehr, M. L., Mensing, J., & Nafzger, S. Concept of self and the reaction of others. *Sociometry,* 1962, *25,* 353–357.

Mahoney, A. R. The effect of labeling upon youths in the juvenile justice system: A review of the evidence. *Law and Society Review,* 1974, *8,* 583–614.

Manasse, G. Self-regard as a function of environmental demands in chronic schizophrenics. *Journal of Abnormal Psychology,* 1965, *70,* 210–213.

Maris, R. W. Deviance as therapy: The paradox of the self-destructive female. *Journal of Health and Social Behavior,* 1971, *12,* 113–124.

Marks, P. A., & Seeman, W. *The actuarial description of abnormal personality.* Baltimore: Williams & Wilkins, 1963.

Matteson, R. Adolescent self-esteem, family communication, and marital satisfaction. *Journal of Psychology,* 1974, *86,* 35–47.

McCandless, B. R., Bilous, C. B., & Bennett, H. L. Peer popularity and dependence on adults in pre-school age socialization. *Child Development,* 1961, *32,* 511–518.

McClelland, D. C. Examining the research basis for alternative explanations of alcoholism. In D. C. McClelland, W. N. Davis, R. Kalin, & E. Wanner (Eds.), *The drinking man.* New York: Free Press, 1972.

McCord, W., & McCord, J. *Origins of alcoholism.* Stanford, Calif.: Stanford University Press, 1960.

McGuire, W. J. Personality and susceptibility to social influence. In E. F. Borgatte & W. W. Lambert (Eds.), *Handbook of personality theory and research.* Chicago: Rand McNally, 1968.

Medinnus, G. R. Adolescents' self-acceptance and perceptions of their parents. *Journal of Consulting Psychology,* 1963, *29,* 150–154.

Melges, F. T., Anderson, R. E., Kraemer, H. C., Tinklenberg, J. R., & Weisz, A. E. The personal future and self-esteem. *Archives of General Psychiatry,* 1971, *25,* 494–497.

References

Miller, D. H. Suicidal careers. *Dissertation Abstracts,* 1968, *28A,* 4720.

Mindlin, D. F. Attitudes toward alcoholism and toward self: Differences between three alcoholic groups. *Quarterly Journal of Studies on Alcohol,* 1964, *25,* 136–141.

Mirels, H. L., & McPeek, R. W. Self-advocacy and self-esteem. *Journal of Consulting and Clinical Psychology,* 1977, *45*(6), 1132–1138.

Moore, S. G. Displaced aggression in relation to different frustrations. *Journal of Abnormal Psychology,* 1964, *68,* 200–204.

Moore, T., & Ucko, L. E. Four-to-six: Constructiveness and conflict in meeting doll play problems. *Journal of Child Psychology and Psychiatry and Allied Disciplines,* 1961, *2,* 21–47.

Morris, R. R. Female delinquency and relational problems. *Social Forces,* 1964, *43,* 82–89.

Mussen, P., Harris, S., Rutherford, E., & Keasey, C. B. Honesty and altruism among preadolescents. *Developmental Psychology,* 1970, *3,* 169–194.

Mussen, P. H., & Jones, M. C. Self-conceptions, motivations and interpersonal attitudes of late- and early-maturing boys. *Child Development,* 1957, *28,* 243–256.

Nickols, J. E., Jr. Changes in self-awareness during the high school years: A study of mental health using paper-and-pencil tests. *Journal of Educational Research,* 1963, *56,* 403–409.

Nisbett, R. E., & Gordon, A. Self-esteem and susceptibility to social influence. *Journal of Personality and Social Psychology,* 1967, *5,* 268–276.

Nocks, J. J., & Bradley, D. Self-esteem in an alcoholic population. *Diseases of the Nervous System,* 1969, *30,* 611–617.

Offer, D. *The psychological world of the teenager.* New York: Basic Books, 1969.

Pearlin, L. I., & Radabaugh, C. W. Economic strains and the coping functions of alcohol. *American Journal of Sociology,* 1976, *32,* 652–663.

Pepitone, A., & Wilpizeski, C. Some consequences of experimental rejection. *Journal of Abnormal and Social Psychology,* 1960, *60,* 359–364.

Petersen, A. C., & Kellam, S. G. Measurement of the psychological well-being of adolescents: The psychometric properties and assessment procedures of the how I feel. *Journal of Youth and Adolescence,* 1977, *6*(3), 229–247.

Powell, G. J., & Fuller, M. *School desegregation and self-concept.* Paper presented at the 47th annual meeting of the American Orthopsychiatric Association, San Francisco, 1970.

Purkey, W. W. *Self-concept and school achievement.* Englewood Cliffs, N.J.: Prentice-Hall, 1970.

Rasmussen, G., & Zander, A. Group membership and self-evaluation. *Human Relations,* 1954, *7,* 239–251.

Rathus, S. A., & Siegel, L. J. Delinquent attitudes and self-esteem. *Adolescence,* 1973, *8*(30), 265–276.

Rebelsky, F. G., Alinsmith, W., & Grinder, R. E. Resistance to temptation and sex differences in children's use of fantasy confession. *Child Development,* 1963, *34,* 955–962.

Reckless, W. *The crime problem* (4th ed.). New York: Appleton-Century-Crofts, 1967.

Reckless, W., Dinitz, S., & Murray, E. Self-concept as an insulator against delinquency. *American Sociological Review,* 1956, *21,* 744–746.

Reed, C. F., & Cuadra, C. A. The role-taking hypothesis in delinquency. *Journal of Consulting Psychology,* 1957, *21,* 386–390.

Rempel, H., & Signoi, E. I. Sex differences in self-rating of conscience as a determinant of behavior. *Psychological Reports,* 1964, *15,* 277–278.

Rogers, A. H. The self-concept in paranoid schizophrenia. *Journal of Clinical Psychology,* 1958, *14,* 365–366.

Rosen, G. M., & Ross, O. A. Relationship of body image to self-concept. *Journal of Consulting and Clinical Psychology,* 1968, *32,* 100.

Rosenberg, M. *Society and the adolescent self-image.* Princeton, N.J.: Princeton University Press, 1965.

References

Rosenberg, M. Which significant others? *American Behavioral Scientist*, 1973, *16*(6), 829–860.

Rosenberg, M. The dissonant context and the adolescent self-concept. In S. Dragastin & G. H. Elder (Eds.), *Adolescence in the life cycle: Psychological change and social context*. Washington, D.C.: Hemisphere, 1975. Pp. 97–116.

Rosenberg, M., & Simmons, R. G. Black and white self-esteem. In *The urban school child*. Washington, D.C.: American Sociological Association, 1972.

Rosenkrantz, R., Voge, S., Bee, H., Broverman, I., & Broverman, D. Sex-role stereotypes and self-conceptions in college students. *Journal of Consulting and Clinical Psychology*, 1968, *32*, 287–295.

Rothaus, P., & Worchel, P. Ego-support, communication, catharsis, and hostility. *Journal of Personality*, 1964, *32*, 296–312.

Salzman, L. Obsessions and phobias. *Contemporary Psychoanalysis*, 1965, *2*, 1–25.

Sappenfield, B. R., & Harris, C. L. Self-reported masculinity–feminity as related to self-esteem. *Psychological Reports*, 1975, *37*, 669–670.

Scarpitti, F. R. Delinquent and nondelinquent perceptions of self, values and opportunity. *Mental Hygiene*, 1965, *49*, 399–404.

Scheff, T. *Being mentally ill: A sociological theory*. Chicago: Aldine, 1966.

Schneider, D. J. Effects of dress on self-presentation. *Psychological Reports*, 1974, *35*, 167–170.

Schwartz, M., Fearn, G. F. N., & Stryker, S. A note on self-conception and the emotionally disturbed role. *Sociometry*, 1966, *29*, 300–305.

Schwartz, M., & Stryker, S. *Deviance, selves, and others*. Washington, D.C.: American Sociological Association, 1970.

Schwartz, M., & Tangri, S. S. A note on self-concept as an insulator against delinquency. *American Sociological Review*, 1965, *30*, 922–926.

Sears, R. R. Relation of early socialization experiences to aggression in middle childhood. *Journal of Abnormal and Social Psychology*, 1961, *63*, 466–492.

Sears, R. R. Relation of early socialization experiences to self-concepts and gender role in middle childhood. *Child Development*, 1970, *41*, 267–289.

Sears, R. R., Maccoby, E. E., & Levin, H. *Patterns of child rearing*. Evanston, Ill.: Row, Peterson, 1957.

Sears, R. R., Ray, L., & Alpert, R. *Identification and child rearing*. Stanford, Calif.: Stanford University Press, 1965.

Sharoff, R. L. Character problems and their relationship to drug abuse. *American Journal of Psychoanalysis*, 1969, *29*, 189–193.

Sherwood, J. J. Self-identity and referent others. *Sociometry*, 1965, *28*, 66–81.

Short, J. F., & Strodtbeck, F. L. *Group process and gang delinquency*. Chicago: University of Chicago Press, 1965.

Silber, E. & Tippett, J. Self-esteem: Clinical assessment and measurement validation. *Psychological Reports*, 1965, *16*, 1017–1071.

Silverman, J. The problems of attention in research and theory in schizophrenia. *Psychological Review*, 1964, *71*, 352–379.

Simmons, R. G., & Rosenberg, F. Sex, sex roles, and self-image. *Journal of Youth and Adolescence*, 1975, *4*(3), 229–258.

Simmons, R. G., Rosenberg, F., & Rosenberg, M. Disturbance in the self-image at adolescence. *American Sociological Review*, 1973, *38*, 553–568.

Slaughter, D. T. Relation of early parent–teacher socialization influences to achievement orientation and self-esteem in middle childhood among low-income black children. In J. C. Glidewell (Ed.), *The social context of learning and development*. New York: Gardner Press, 1977.

Smart, R. G., & Whitehead, P. C. The uses of an epidemiology of drug use: The Canadian scene. *International Journal of the Addictions*, 1974, *9*, 373–388.

References

Smith, W., & Lebo, D. Some changing aspects of the self-concept of pubescent males. *Journal of Genetic Psychology*, 1956, *88*, 61–75.

Spangler, D. P., & Thomas, C. W. The effects of age, sex, and physical disability upon manifest needs. *Journal of Counseling Psychology*, 1962, *9*, 313–319.

Stein, A. The effects of sex-role standards for achievement and sex-role preference on three determinants of achievement motivation. *Developmental Psychology*, 1971, *4*, 219–231.

Stotland, E., Thorley, S., Thomas, E., Cohen, A. R., & Zander, A. The effects of group expectations and self-esteem upon self-evaluation. *Journal of Abnormal and Social Psychology*, 1957, *54*, 55–63.

Sykes, G. M., & Matza, D. Techniques of neutralization: A theory of delinquency. *American Sociological Review*, 1957, *22*, 664–670.

Tanay, E. Psychiatric study of homicide. *American Journal of Psychology*, 1969, *125*, 1252–1258.

Taylor, R. Personality traits and discrepant achievement: A review. *Journal of Counseling Psychology*, 1964, *11*, 78–81.

Thomas, D. L., Gecas, V., Weigert, A., & Rooney, E. *Family socialization and the adolescent.* Toronto: Lexington Books, 1974.

Tippett, J. S., & Silber, E. Autonomy of self-esteem. *Archives of General Psychiatry*, 1966, *14*, 372–385.

Tittle, C. R., & Rowe, A. R. Moral appeal, sanction threat, and deviance: An experimental test. *Social Problems*, 1973, *20*, 488–498.

Trow, W. C., & Pu, A. S. T. Self-ratings of the Chinese. *School and Society*, 1927, *25*, 213–216.

Usdin, G. L. Civil disobedience and urban revolt. *American Journal of Psychiatry*, 1969, *125*, 91–97.

Vanderpool, J. A. Alcoholism and the self-concept. *Quarterly Journal of Studies on Alcohol*, 1969, *30*, 59–77.

Videbeck, R. Self-conception and the reactions of others. *Sociometry*, 1960, *23*, 351–359.

Voss, H. Differential association and containment theory: A theoretical convergence. *Social Forces*, 1969, *47*, 381–391.

Waldo, G. P., Chiricos, T. G., & Dobrin, L. E. Community contact and inmate attitudes, an experimental assessment of work release. *Criminology*, 1973, *11*, 345–381.

Washburn, W. C. Patterns of protective attitudes in relation to difference in self-evaluation and anxiety level among high school students. *California Journal of Education Research*, 1962, *13*(2), 84–94.

Washburn, W. C. The effects of sex differences on protective attitudes in delinquents and non-delinquents. *Exceptional Children*, 1963, *30*, 111–117.

Webster, M., Jr., & Sobieszek, B. *Sources of self-evaluation: A formal theory of significant others and social influence.* New York: Wiley, 1974.

Welch, B. L. The generalization of student's problems when several different population variances are involved. *Biometrika*, 1947, *34*, 28–35.

Wells, L. E. Theories of deviance and the self-concept. *Social Psychology*, 1978, *41*, 189–204.

White, W. F., & Gaier, E. L. Assessment of body image and self-concept among alcoholics with different intervals of sobriety. *Journal of Clinical Psychology*, 1965, *21*, 374.-377.

White, W. F., & Porter, T. L. Self-concept reports among hospitalized alcoholics during early periods of sobriety. *Journal of Counseling Psychology*, 1966, *13*, 352–355.

Williams, A. F. Self-concepts of college problem drinkers: (1) A comparison with alcoholics. *Quarterly Journal of Studies on Alcohol*, 1965, *26*, 589–594.

Wilson, L. T., Miskimins, R. W., Braucht, N., & Berry, K. L. The severe suicide attempter and self-concept. *Journal of Clinical Psychology*, 1971, *27*, 307–309.

Wood, A. L. A socio-structural analysis of murder, suicide, and economic crime in Ceylon. *American Sociological Review*, 1961, *26*, 744–753.

References

Wyer, R. S., Weatherley, D. A., & Terrell, G. Social role, aggression and academic achievement. *Journal of Personality and Social Psychology*, 1965, *1*, 645–649.

Wylie, R. C. *The self-concept*. Lincoln: University of Nebraska Press, 1961.

Yamamoto, K., Thomas, E. C., & Karns, E. A. School-related attitudes in middle school-age students. *American Educational Research Journal*, 1969, *6*, 191–206.

Ziller, R. C., & Golding, L. H. Political personality. *Proceedings of the 77th Annual Convention of the American Psychological Association*, 1969, *4*, 441–442.

Zucker, R. Sex-role identity patterns and drinking behavior among adolescents. *Quarterly Journal of Studies on Alcohol*, 1968, *22*, 868–884.

Author Index

Numbers in italics refer to the pages on which the complete references are listed.

A

Adams, J. E., 12, *232*
Adelson, J., 83, 102, *233*
Ageton, S. S., 185, *231*
Alinsmith, W., 190, *238*
Alpert, R., 190, *239*
Anderson, R. E., 156, *237*
Archer, D., 81, *231*
Arieti, S., 179, *231*
Aronson, E., 112, *231*

B

Bachman, J. G., 43, 82, 83, 84, 96, *231*
Baker, C. T., 190, *237*
Bankes, J., 117, *237*
Baron, P. H., 156, *231*
Becker, E., 180, *231*
Becker, H. S., 220, *231*
Bee, H., 83, *239*
Beller, E. K., 192, *231*
Bennett, E. M., 191, 205, *231*
Bennett, H. L., 191, *237*
Berg, N. L., 116, 171, *231*
Berkowitz, L., 172, *231*
Berry, K. L., 117, 120, *240*
Bilous, C. B., 191, *237*
Bloom, S. W., 184, *236*
Bogo, N., 192, *232*
Bohrnstedt, G. W., 51, *232*

C

Boyd, I., 184, *236*
Braaten, L. J., 119, *232*
Bradley, D., 183, *238*
Bradshaw, H. L., 49, *234*
Braucht, N., 117, 120, *240*
Brock, T. C., 192, *232*
Broverman, D., 83, *239*
Broverman, I., 83, *239*
Brownfain, J., 26, 140, *232*
Burgess, M., 172, *234*
Burke, E. L., 192, *232*

Cartwright, D. S., 130, *234*
Chamblis, W., 60, *232*
Chananie, J. D., 192, *237*
Chapman, I., 220, *232*
Chason, K. J., 82, 83, 84, *235*
Chiricos, T. G., 185, *240*
Clark, J. P., 28, 35, *232*
Clifford, E., 43, 45, 56, 140, *232*
Clifford, M., 43, 45, 56, 140, *232*
Coelho, G. V., 12, *232*
Coghlan, A. J., 179, *232*
Cohen, A. K., 219, 220, *232*
Cohen, A. R., 140, *240*
Cohen, F., 172, *234*
Cohen, L. R., 191, 205, *231*
Consentino, F., 192, *232*
Coopersmith, S., 12, 28, 96, *232*

Subject Index